Anthony Powell

Revised Edition

Twayne's English Authors Series

Kinley Roby, Editor

Northeastern University

TEAS 158

ANTHONY POWELL
Photo by Jerry Bauer

Anthony Powell

Revised Edition

Neil Brennan

Villanova University

Twayne Publishers
An Imprint of Simon & Schuster Macmillan
New York

Prentice Hall International
London   Mexico City   New Delhi   Singapore   Sydney   Toronto

Anthony Powell
Neil Brennan

Twayne Publishers
An Imprint of Simon & Schuster Macmillan
866 Third Avenue
New York, NY 10022

Library of Congress Cataloging-in-Publication Data
Brennan, Neil Francis
Anthony Powell / Neil Francis Brennan.
p.   cm.—(Twayne's English authors series; TEAS 158)
Includes bibliographical references and index.
ISBN 0-8057-4545-9
1. Powell, Anthony, 1905–   —Criticism and interpretation. 2. Autobiographical
fiction, English—History and criticism. 3. England—In literature. I. Title. II. Series.
PR6031.O74Z63 1995
823'.912—dc20
[B]   94-49326
                                                              CIP

The paper used in this publication meets the minimum requirements of American
National Standard for Information Sciences—Permanence of Paper for Printed Library
Materials, ANSI Z39.48-1984. ∞ ™

10 9 8 7 6 5 4 3 2 1

Printed in the United States of America.

For Maxine

Contents

Preface   *ix*

Chronology   *xi*

Chapter One
Background   1

Chapter Two
The Early Novels   29

Chapter Three
The Music of Time   67

Chapter Four
Later Works and Conclusion   136

Notes and References   *169*
Selected Bibliography   *177*
Index   *185*

Preface

Anthony Powell's stature among novelists has only increased in the 20 years since the first edition of *Anthony Powell* appeared. Anthony Powell has published eight books in the interim, and awe grows as the craftsmanship continues, the steadiness of the thought, the hardness of the wit. But the conclusion remains: two of Powell's early novels are among the hundred best novels of the century, and the vast sweep of The Music of Time makes it one of the artistic accomplishments of our era.

Yet Anthony Powell remains a problem. The first basis of literary understanding is sympathy, and it must be admitted that the cool, aesthetic, and aristocratic culture Powell represents has often been misrepresented in this century of the common man. For one thing, Powell's aesthetic takes for granted a love of beauty. When the party-going London of his first novel is invaded by an American publisher who repeats several times during the evening, "I can't get along without beauty," we may need an un-American viewpoint, perhaps, to see that he is merely claiming to be human. Because the publisher then passes out drunk in the middle of the party, readers have been known to conclude, not without disgust, that the only character in the novel who truly loves beauty is an American who is being satirized by Powell. Far from it. The tone Powell takes in *Afternoon Men* is one of detached amusement, not didactic moralizing. Both his culture and his aesthetic tradition oppose crude satire, whether of drunks, Americans, or people who think a love of beauty makes them somehow exceptional.

The appearance of four volumes of memoirs by Powell in the meantime has added to our understanding of the novels. By delineating the family from which his values emerged, the education and friendships that helped form his theories of art, and the political times that gave his wit its ironic edge, the memoirs clarify the real attitudes behind the art. The first chapter of this edition can only summarize the salient features.

Mention must be made again of friends who helped with the first edition of *Anthony Powell:* Gordon Ray, Arthur Mizener, Robert Slabey, George Murphy, Diane Eby, and Linda Morley. It is a pleasure to add to their names those of Professors Charles Cherry and John Fielder, who subsequently introduced me to word processing; Joan Lesovitz and Daniel McGee of the Computer Center at Villanova University, who led me to the wonders of electronic scanning and through the wiles of the Internet; and especially Dr. Jack Schwarz, without whose help with logistic and other matters this revision would not have been possible.

Others are not forgotten, though their names do not come as readily to mind. May they forgive me when we meet again.

Chronology

1814   Anthony Powell's maternal grandfather, Edmund Wells-Dymoke of Grebby Hall, Lincolnshire, born.

1847   Anthony Powell's paternal grandfather, Lionel Lewis Powell of The Elms, Melton Mowbray, born.

1864   Edmund Wells-Dymoke marries Laura de Blair Jefferson of London.

1878   Lionel Lewis Powell marries Jessie Kate Adcock of North Lodge, Melton Mowbray.

1882   Anthony Powell's father, Philip Lionel William Powell, born.

1897   Philip Powell becomes a military cadet at Sandhurst.

1901   Lt. P. L. W. Powell serves with the Welch Regiment in South Africa against the Boers.

1904   Capt. P. L.W. Powell marries Maud Mary Wells-Dymoke.

1905   Anthony Dymoke Powell born in London 21 December.

1908   Capt. P. L.W. Powell becomes adjutant of the 13th London Regiment, The Kensingtons.

1912   Violet Pakenham, third daughter of the fifth Earl of Longford, born.

1914   Outbreak of World War I. Powell's father goes with his regiment to France and Belgium. Powell enters preparatory school.

1915   Death in battle of the Earl of Longford.

1916   Maj. P. L.W. Powell awarded the Distinguished Service Order.

1918   Lt. Col. P. L. W. Powell made a Companion of the British Empire.

1919   Anthony Powell enters Eton.

1920   Becomes a member of the Eton Arts Society.

1923   Studies French near Tours in the summer. Matriculates at Balliol College, Oxford.

1924   Spends summer with his father in Finland.

1926   Down from Oxford, joins the book publishing firm of Duckworth.

1928   Visits Paris, Sylvia Beach's bookshop; meets Ford Madox Ford. Father resigns from the army for reasons of health. Duckworth's publishes Powell's first book, his edition of the Barnard Letters, in November.

1930   Powell's father becomes a barrister-at-law in the Inner Temple. Anthony vacations in Southern France, near Toulon; begins a novel.

1931   First novel, *Afternoon Men,* published by Duckworth's in May.

1932   Second novel, *Venusberg,* published in December.

1933   Third novel, *From a View to a Death,* published in October.

1934   Marries Lady Violet Pakenham 3 December. Honeymoon in Greece.

1935   Takes up residence at 47 Great Ormond Street, London. Works part-time as scriptwriter for Warner Bros. in England.

1936   Fourth novel, *Agents and Patients,* published in January. Travels to Russia. Leaves Duckworth's, becomes full-time scriptwriter for Warner Bros. outside of London.

1937   Moves to 1 Chester Gate, Regent's Park, London. Goes to Hollywood by way of the Panama Canal. Returns to London by way of New York in December.

1939   Fifth novel, *What's Become of Waring,* published in January. Outbreak of World War II, 3 September. Commissioned a lieutenant in the Welch Regiment in December; begins 18-month tour of duty in North Ireland.

1940   First son, Tristram Roger Dymoke, born in May.

1941   Attached to headquarters of the 53d Division, in command of the defense platoon. Becomes staff liaison officer with Army Intelligence at the War Office, Whitehall, in August.

1943   Promoted to major.

1944   Serves in France and Belgium; attached to 21st Army
       Group.

1945   Awarded the Order of the White Lion of Czecho-
       slovakia; Order of the Oaken Crown of Luxembourg;
       Croix de Guerre of Luxembourg; and the Order of
       Leopold II of Belgium. Demobilized in September.

1946   Second son, John Marmion Anthony, christened 22
       February. Does book reviews for the *Spectator* and occa-
       sional journalism.

1947   Joins the staff of the *Times Literary Supplement* under the
       editorship of Alan Pryce-Jones.

1948   Study of John Aubrey, *John Aubrey and His Friends,* pub-
       lished in December.

1949   Acquires a Regency house, The Chantry near Frome,
       Somerset.

1951   First volume of The Music of Time, *A Question of
       Upbringing,* published in January.

1952   Second volume of The Music of Time, *A Buyer's Market,*
       published in June.

1953   Joins the Punch Table under the editorship of Malcolm
       Muggeridge in March.

1954   Mother dies.

1955   Third volume of The Music of Time, *The Acceptance
       World,* published in May.

1956   Attends investiture at Buckingham Palace to receive
       order of Companion of the British Empire.

1957   Visits Austria in the summer. Fourth volume of The
       Music of Time, *At Lady Molly's,* published in October.

1958   Accepts invitation to Writers Conference in Venice,
       August. Travels to Italy with wife and son John. Eton
       College Film Unit produces short film "Manhunt,"
       with script by his son Tristram, "a very recent Old
       Etonian who has adapted an episode . . . in *A Question of
       Upbringing.*"

1959   Following Malcolm Muggeridge's resignation from *Punch,* becomes a book reviewer for the *Daily Telegraph.* Father dies.

1960   Fifth volume of The Music of Time, *Casanova's Chinese Restaurant,* published in June.

1961   Visits the United States, talking informally at Dartmouth, Amherst, and Cornell. Writes book reviews for the *New York Times.*

1962   Appointed trustee of the National Portrait Gallery, London. Sixth volume of The Music of Time, *The Kindly Ones,* published in June.

1963   A dramatization of *Afternoon Men* opens in London, 22 August. Departs for Venice to begin Hellenic cruise.

1964   Seventh volume of The Music of Time, *The Valley of Bones,* published in February. Invited to Japan for the 400th Shakespeare Anniversary Festival. Also visits Manila, Saigon, Bangkok. Serves on Duff Cooper Memorial Prize Committee.

1965   Visits the United States in May. Son John attends Cornell University.

1966   Guided tour of Pakistan and Northern India. Eighth volume of The Music of Time, *The Soldier's Art,* published in September.

1968   Son Tristram marries painter Virginia Lucas, granddaughter of Field Marshall Lord Grenfell. Ninth volume of The Music of Time, *The Military Philosophers,* published in October.

1969   Tour of Southern India and Ceylon.

1971   Tenth volume of The Music of Time, *Books Do Furnish a Room,* published in February. Two plays, with set designs by Osbert Lancaster, published together in August.

1972   Visits Mexico in the summer.

1973   Eleventh volume of The Music of Time, *Temporary Kings,* published in July.

1974   Contributes an essay on a former Oxford mentor to *Maurice Bowra: A Celebration.*

1975   Final volume of The Music of Time, *Hearing Secret Harmonies,* published in September.

1976   First volume of memoirs, *To Keep the Ball Rolling, Infants of the Spring.*

1978   Second volume of memoirs, *Messengers of Day.*

1979   Third volume of memoirs, *Faces in My Time.*

1982   Final volume of memoirs, *The Strangers All Are Gone.*

1983   Short novel, *O, How the Wheel Becomes It!* and *To Keep the Ball Rolling,* paperback abridgement of the four volumes of memoirs. *Invitation to the Dance,* hour-long tribute to Powell's masterpiece, The Music of Time, broadcast by BBC-TV, featuring Kingsley Amis, Clive James, Alison Lurie, and others.

1984   Contributes a "brief life" of his friend to *Oxford, China, and Italy: Writings in Honour of Sir Harold Acton.*

1986   Publishes major novel, *The Fisher King.*

1987   Wife Lady Violet Powell publishes *The Album of Anthony Powell's "Dance to the Music of Time."*

1990   Publishes a collection of essays and reviews, *Miscellaneous Verdicts: Writings on Writers 1946–1989.*

1991   Publishes second collection of reviews and essays, *Under Review: Further Writings on Writers, 1946–1989.*

1992   Publishes reviews in the *Spectator.*

1995   Publishes *Journal 1982–1986.*

Chapter One

Background

When Anthony Dymoke Powell was born in 1905 his career as a novelist was in part determined. His father, an officer in the British Army, was of Welsh descent, and the novels Powell was to write—works of art equal to any in our time—were to show an unusual sympathy with the army and a leaning toward things Welsh. Anthony Powell's mother also linked him prenatally to another tradition, for the Dymoke family enters history distinguished by the duty imposed on the eldest Dymoke to rise to the defense of each newly crowned British monarch. Recognition must have come to Anthony Powell long before he reached adulthood that he was a man of family and tradition, that duty had established certain parameters, that life was to do the rest.

The House of Powell

Anthony Powell's allegiance to things Welsh appears most clearly in his critical writings. In a review of *The Dictionary of Welsh Biography,* for instance, he questions the dictionary's principle of selection, its editor having omitted people, however famous, who were merely of Welsh descent. "In compiling a work of this kind stringent rules must be applied," Powell agrees. "All the same, the regulation inevitably leads to some anomalies." To illustrate his complaint Powell singles out the seventeenth-century school of poetry labeled "metaphysical" because of its religious bent: "George Herbert and Henry Vaughan are allowed [into the dictionary as Welsh]: John Donne and Thomas Traherne excluded: yet all these poets might reasonably be held to be linked together in their poetry and thought by their Welsh origins."[1]

The family of "Powell, formerly of the Travely and Landshipping House"—as Anthony Powell's branch of the family is referred to in *Burke's Landed Gentry*—is of Welsh origin and had "lived for at least three centuries within the adjacent parishes of Brilley, Herefordshire, and Llowes and Clyro, Radnorshire." The Travely was a house at Llowes just inside the border of Wales, which the family occupied "from a period prior to 1638 until the latter half of the nineteenth century."[2]

At the university Powell was to "read history"—he became what Americans would call a "history major"—but he was known to his friends even then as an expert in that branch of history known as genealogy. Tracing the roots of a family into the past had been a hobby of a Welshman three centuries before, a Welshman called John Aubrey, and in later life Powell was to devote years to the study of this Welsh scholar. The study was more a hobby than a vocation, but it led eventually to Powell's major scholarly work—the biography *John Aubrey and His Friends* published in 1948—and it was clearly a feeling of Welsh kinship that had led him to Aubrey. In the biography Powell notes that Aubrey's family was "not alone in having come out of Wales to settle in England: Vaughans, Powells, and Beavans had done so too."

Temperamental affinities also had drawn him to Aubrey. Aubrey had proved his otherworldliness in the seventeenth century by spending his life collecting biographical data—for biographies he could never get around to writing. Yet the quiet service that this gentle antiquarian and his notes rendered to British history, and to our knowledge of his era, is not easily calculated. His patience and tact, curiosity and good humor, devotion to what he thought his duty, and lack of ambition were qualities Powell admired, and considered typically Welsh.

The Welsh connection also leaves its mark on Powell's creative work, for when he came in the late 1940s to plan his great novel The Music of Time, he decided that novel needed a narrator like Aubrey, self-effacing and unambitious, a quiet, amused, observant, and contemplative recorder of life. Seeking a name for such a narrator, Powell chose a Welsh family name, one that figures often in the notes Aubrey left. Sir Leoline Jenkins, for one, was a Welsh knight, Aubrey tells us, who had a father who "was a good plaine countery-man," but with the generous spirit of the clan: "David Jenkins, that was prisoner in the Tower (maried [*sic*] a sister of Sir John Aubrey) was some remote kin to him; and looking on him as a boy towardly, diligent, and good, he contributed something towards his Education."[3] In the very name of his narrator Nicholas Jenkins, Powell thus projects the generous, curious spirit of Wales; and critics of The Music of Time who carp that Nick Jenkins tells us too little about himself might also note Powell's observation that, among all Celtic peoples, the Welsh are the least given to self-revelation.

Powell's Father

Philip Lionel William Powell entered the Army from Sandhurst (Britain's West Point) in 1901, and he "served when he was nineteen in the South African War as a Second Lieutenant, First Battalion, The Welch Regiment, receiving the Queen's Medal."[4] In 1904 he married; he became a father the following year; yet, like his own father, he was destined to have only one child.

Anthony Dymoke Powell, born late in 1905, spent the years of his childhood (those in theory at least the most formative) in a military environment. In 1909 his father was appointed adjutant to the 13th London Regiment, known as the Kensingtons; until the regiment went overseas at the outbreak of war in 1914, the boy saw army life from inside. What he saw impressed him, and that informed his novels.

Since the creation of the "very model of a modern Major-General" in Gilbert and Sullivan's comic opera *The Pirates of Penzance,* the army officer in literature has not often been treated sympathetically. Only a few novelists, like James Gould Cozzens in *Guard of Honor* (1948) and Ernest Hemingway in *Across the River and into the Trees* (1950), have regarded the problems of military command with sympathy.

Anthony Powell, in contrast, has created some of the most likable army officers in literature, from Captain Hudson, who writes biography with honesty and a clean style in *What's Become of Waring,* to Major General Aylmer Conyers, whose modesty and wisdom sound recurrent chords in The Music of Time. And the narrator Nicholas Jenkins (like the author) grows up in a military atmosphere.

The sixth volume of The Music of Time, for instance, takes us back to the beginnings of the narrator's social experience, to the household of Captain Jenkins near Aldershot, the British military base and training school, on the day in 1914 that the Great War begins. Within a few weeks Captain Jenkins has left his wife and son Nicholas for the battlefields of the continent.

Powell's own father was in Belgium with his regiment within 10 days of the outbreak of World War I. Captain Powell was later promoted to brigade major of the 95th Infantry Brigade, was mentioned (for heroism) in dispatches, and was in 1916 awarded the Distinguished Service Order, next to the Victoria Cross Britain's highest award for valor.

But young Powell saw more than empty honor in the professional army. In The Music of Time the children of seven military families receive private tutelage from Miss Orchard (6:51); six of their fathers are killed in the war (6:74); only Captain Jenkins survives.

After World War I, Powell's father was awarded a C.B.E., that is, made a Companion of the British Empire, and was appointed to the staff of the War Office. Although his son was away at school during much of the following period, vacations took him back into military society; and when his father was appointed attaché to the British Military Mission to Finland in 1924, he experienced embassy life abroad.

In Finland Anthony Powell was introduced to Marshall Mannerheim,[5] the savior of Finland, and it was no doubt during this period that his familiarity with the Baltic countries began, the familiarity that informs his second novel, *Venusberg.* On the other hand, there seems to be no indication that he accompanied his father to China in 1927, when his father's battalion was transferred to the Shanghai Defence Force. Unfortunately, in China Colonel Powell's health broke down. Invalided home, he retired from the army the following year. At least as late as 1936, however, Colonel Powell was still attending reunion dinners with former comrades of the Welch Regiment. There seems little doubt of his devotion to the service, a regard his son came to share.

And in the sixth volume of The Music of Time, when Nicholas Jenkins in 1939 is accepted into the army as an aged lieutenant, he asks for his father's old regiment and finds himself in Wales, where the men in his company sing Welsh hymns as they march off to chapel.

Aware that the larger world has illusions about life in the Army, Powell goes out of his way at times to enlighten it. A character points out in The Music of Time, for instance, that "It's a misapprehension to suppose, as most people do, that the army is inherently different from other communities. The hierarchy and discipline give an outward illusion of difference, but there are personalities of every sort . . . weak-willed generals and strong-willed privates" (7:108).

Few better introductions to "the idea of society" could have been devised, in fact, for the future creator of English literature's most complex society, that in The Music of Time. Even in the American army, "society" is more complex than the outsider may realize. A Captain George Patton may one year live next door to a Major Omar Bradley; and, while Patton as a millionaire may travel from post to post with a string of polo ponies, Bradley—his superior in rank but a man dependent on his salary—may count himself lucky to have a new Ford from time to time. And a year later both may meet with equal rank in a situation in which differences in wealth are irrelevant.

In the British army "society" is further complicated by the intrusion of family connection and title. The poor brother of an earl of ancient lineage may be the commanding officer of a regiment in which a rich beer magnate's son commands merely a platoon. From drill parade, where only rank would count, to leaves in Paris—where wealth would bed the lieutenant at the Ritz and, lack of it, the colonel in a dingy Hotel d'Angleterre—the network of relations between them would have almost infinite ramifications.

Another feature of society that young Powell noted more clearly in the army is the variability of status over time. Powell's novels often focus on the ironies attached to social escalations. With needs of its own, an army properly led always offers opportunity for change of status, and "it is not only in modern times, as is sometimes implied, that careers began to be forged by talent and industry."[6]

The "Establishment," as it is called—the power structure in Britain as seen from below, with church, militia, and civil service dominating the empire and in turn being dominated by an established upper class—was widely attacked in England after World War II. Angry Young Men stormed the "impermeable bastions of rank and privilege." But what Anthony Powell had observed in childhood was rather a permeable "establishment" in which the possibility of escalation in rank was a perennial factor sabotaging the idea of any simplistic societal hierarchy.

"If genealogy is anything else but simply and solely the truth about ancestors, it is worthless," Powell insists. Although the study of genealogy is "commonly thought of as a pursuit best adapted to keeping the various classes of society apart," it is a study that reveals instead "how extraordinarily close the classes are and have always been together." Powell traces the class system back to the military service of men who owed their lands to the king; heavy cavalrymen were expected to assemble for combat in person: the knights, as troopers; the barons, as officers. Yet even in those days in England there were no "legal and absolute class barriers."[7]

Any survey of Powell's attitude toward class must reach the conclusion that the only "establishment" Powell supports is a flexible one, in which transits take place both up and down. When Powell considers the French author Chateaubriand, he calls him the "younger son of an immensely ancient Breton family," a family having the "long pedigrees and short purses of Wales of the past, a less feudalised, but somewhat similar Celtic community where younger sons . . . might easily return to tilling the soil."[8]

Some of Powell's critics have failed to help readers in this matter. Even a critic born in England and writing in the *New Yorker* has pointed to The Music of Time as promulgating a view he identifies, oddly, as Powell's—a "view that the human race is divided into two sections—one that counts, consisting of Old Etonians, and one that doesn't, consisting of people who are either grubby or comic and who didn't attend the school."[9]

But even the first volume of The Music of Time makes it clear that four boys can graduate from the same English public school into four widely different and quickly shifting social positions, with only one of them (the character Stringham) being wholly "in" while being at the same time the one most on the way "out." Understanding of such complexity can come only after we admit that in Powell's view, society, although an ordered whole, is almost infinitely complex, with no simple key to its door, Etonian or other.

Powell's father conveyed to his son more than a set of social attitudes, of course. His interests in literature and painting aided Powell's development as an artist, for the arts were always part of his childhood. That his father was admitted as a barrister-at-law to the Inner Temple within a year or two after retiring from the army attests to more than ordinary verbal and analytic skills; and in remembering his father, Powell depicts him as being artistically inclined as well. "In contrast to what might be called my father's Sandhurst personality, he possessed . . . certain fin-de-siècle leanings. In one form, these were expressed by delight in the drawings of Aubrey Beardsley [and he] possessed a huge volume, the first reproductions in this country of Léon Bakst's Russian Ballet Designs."[10] Thus the home life of Anthony Powell as a child seems to have nurtured well a future novelist who would honor both the traditional virtues of his society and the classic disciplines of art.

Powell's Mother

Powell's name is to be found in Debrett's *Peerage,* and his tastes must be described as aristocratic; but he does not classify himself as an aristocrat. "On the whole aristocrats do not become novelists," he says in discussing Lampedusa's novel *The Leopard.* "I use the word 'aristocrats' here purely as a convenient term to describe persons who are the actual holders of comparatively ancient titles together with landed possessions of considerable extent and an ancestry connecting them closely with other families of the same sort."[11]

Powell implicitly defines his own position when he takes to task the biographer of the wife of American novelist Stephen Crane for making "great play with the grandeur" of her earlier marriage to a Captain Stewart of the Gordon Highlanders: "Captain Stewart was a younger son whose father had been made a baronet for military services in India. Stewart himself later received a K.C.M.G. for his work in what is now Kenya. To talk about the Stewart family opening 'charmed circles of London society' and Harrington Gardens being 'fashionable' is surely to lose sense of proportion." Powell describes the Stewart family instead as "a typically honourable, hard-working Services family. It seems worth making this point," he adds, "because in some ways the story would have been less extraordinary if the marriage had been more dazzlingly aristocratic and rackety."[12]

On the other hand, although Powell's family was also "a typically honourable, hard-working Services family," his father had married a woman whose ties to the English aristocracy were centuries old: "Maud Mary, daughter and eventual heir of Edmund Lionel Wells-Dymoke, formerly of Grebby Hall, Lincolnshire." Many may claim to have come to England with William the Conqueror, one historian of the Dymoke family observes, but "few indeed, even of our best families, can trace their lineage so far back and with such certainty as the Dymokes of Scrivelsby."[13] Robert Marmion, who married a niece of Baldwin II, King of Jerusalem, had received the Dymoke estate of Scrivelsby from Henry II's son Prince Henry around 1170. Nine generations later in the War of the Roses his descendant Sir Thomas Dymoke formed the Kingmaker's Plot with his brother-in-law Baron Willoughby d'Eresby and restored Henry VI briefly to the throne. And both Dymoke and d'Eresby were beheaded for treason in 1470.

Loyalty, or treason, of a different sort was displayed a century later when Sir Robert Dymoke was imprisoned in the Tower of London as a recusant (or Roman Catholic) and died there for his faith in 1580. The title by which he entered history has an oxymoronic irony of its own: he is known as "the Martyr Champion."

The Championship of the Kings of England had come down with the possession of Scrivelsby through the centuries. Each coronation time the head of the Dymoke family by tradition mounted the king's charger to enter Westminster Hall, where the coronation banquet was being held, to do his duty. Samuel Pepys describes the ceremony that marked the Restoration of the Stuarts, the coronation of Charles II in 1661. The sight of thousands of people lining the galleries excited Pepys:

But, above all, was these three Lords, Northumberland, and Suffolke, and
the Duke of Ormond, coming before the courses on horseback, and staying so all dinner-time, and at last bringing up the King's Champion, all
in armour on horseback, with his speare and targett [shield] carried
before him. And a Herald proclaims "That if any dare deny Charles
Stuart to be lawful King of England, here was a Champion that would
fight with him"; and with these words, the Champion flings down his
gauntlet [or steel glove], and all this he do three times in his going up
towards the King's table. To which, when he is come, the King drinks to
him, and then sends him the cup which is of gold, and he drinks it off,
and then rides back again with the cup in his hand.[14]

An old ballad celebrates the winning of the hand of Margaret de Ludlow,
the Marmion heiress, by Sir John Dymoke in the fourteenth century:

> And ever since, when England's Kings
> Are diadem'd—no matter where—
> The Champion Dymoke boldly flings
> His glove, should treason venture there.[15]

But as we have seen, not all the Dymokes were able to define "treason"
to their monarch's satisfaction.

Nor did all Champions add to family dignity. When the Champion of
James II in 1685 got off his horse to kiss the king's hand (according to
William Prynne's diary), he "fell down all his length in the hall . . .
whereupon the Queen sayd 'see you, love, what a weak Champion you
have.' To which the King sayd nothing, but laught, and the Champion
excused himself, pretending his armour was heavy, and he himself was
weak with sickness." Pretending? He died within the year.

Pomp and glamour mingled with the comic again at the coronation of
George IV in 1821. According to the London *Times,* "The knightly
appearance and gallant deportment of the Champion obviously gave
considerable pleasure to his Majesty, who, taking the goblet . . . drank to
the bold challenger, with a corresponding air of gaiety. The Champion,
on his part, having received the cup, drank to the King, but pronounced
the words 'Long live his Majesty King George IV' in somewhat of a
schoolboy tone." To nearly universal laughter.

On this occasion the "knight" was a young Mr. Dymoke in his teens
acting on behalf of his father, a clergyman for whom so martial a duty
might have been unseemly; what's more, riding steel-shod on the par-
quet between the Marquis of Anglesea and the Duke of Wellington, he

may have been understandably nervous. Yet in an age of steam engines, the picture of an armored knight riding into Westminster Hall to do battle was too quixotic to be missed by English wits; and satiric verse gave the coup de grace to the ceremony—at least for the rest of the century.[16] And by 1895, after scores of coronations, only seven of the jeweled gold cups remained at Scrivelsby; for the family had had its economic reverses.

Appropriately (for a future novelist), one reverse had a literary origin. A standard analysis has it that class is determined by difference in "rank, wealth and education"; and when we turn to the intellectual or cultural status of the Dymoke family, we also find some distinction. Dymokes figure modestly in the literary history of Shakespeare's time, for instance. Shakespeare's contemporary Samuel Daniel ("tipped by some as the Rival Poet" alluded to in Shakespeare's sonnets) dedicated his own sonnets in 1602 "to his patron, Sir Edward Dymoke," the son of "the Martyr Champion."[17]

About the same time, Sir Edward's younger brother Talboys Dymoke was writing a play that proved more expensive than patronage. Talboys' play satirized his tyrant uncle, the second Earl of Lincoln, was judged libelous, and resulted in a fine of £1,000. "The huge fine upon Sir Edward, representing at least ten or twelve thousand pounds according to present values," a scholar observed in 1934, "must have been an important cause in the financial decline of the family."[18] Although the family was further impoverished by its loyalty to Charles I at the time of the Puritan Revolution, literary creativity had exacted more than the usual price.

Schooling

About the time that World War I began, Powell was sent to a preparatory school in Kent that he later compared with the infamous private school in Charles Dickens's novel *Nicholas Nickleby*. It "reflected in some degree the atmosphere, if not the conditions, of Dotheboys Hall."[19]

But here Powell made his first friendship of importance and began to ponder the strangeness of coincidence, an interest that was to mark his later novels. On the day his father took him on a first visit to the school, a school that catered to the children of naval and military officers, the headmaster, to make a point about the student body, called out "Yorke!" and a boy stepped forward, a boy who had almost no military connections at all. Yorke was to become the first friend to share Powell's

interest in the arts and was to remain a lifelong friend. That the headmaster had singled out, on Powell's first visit, the young man Time was
also to single out was a coincidence the two of them mulled over often in
later years (*Infants,* 47–48). But even when Henry Yorke had become
celebrated in the literary world for the distinguished series of novels
written under the pseudonym of Henry Green, a sense of something
strange remained. And coincidence was to play an important role in The
Music of Time.

Eton College, when Powell arrived in 1914, was organized as a series
of some 25 houses, each quartering 40 or 50 boys ranging in age from
10 to 18. Powell had "the good fortune to be sent to a very 'bad' house,"
he says. He was amused by "the unusual personality" of the housemaster, A. M. Goodhart, who would come "bursting like a sea-lion into
boys' rooms when they least expected him, playing the Wall Game with
almost homicidal violence, giving imitations of Mr. Gladstone, perform-
ing on the harmonium at prayers in the evening while we sang All
Things Bright and Beautiful, or hurrying feverishly through the passages
with some huge volume illustrating the History of Footgear through the
ages" ("Glade," 151). We might note that in The Music of Time the
schoolmaster Le Bas is similarly regarded with amusement early on
(1:26–51) and later predominantly with detached affection (3:170–97).

It struck Powell as odd that men at Eton, who could have earned fortunes merely by walking across a music-hall stage, should teach unruly
boys the classics. "It is true that sometimes masters proved unequal to
the grueling course they had to run and left to be cabinet ministers or to
become political bosses in truculent Balkan kingdoms, spheres where the
maintenance of discipline came easily after what they had been
through." But Powell's appreciation of "peculiar mannerisms and eccentricities of appearance" seems to have begun at Eton; and again Powell,
as a future comic novelist, was lucky: "There was a long-standing tradition at Eton that masters should be a little odd . . . the school was on the
whole admirably staffed" ("Glade," 152–53).

A dozen of Powell's contemporaries at Eton were to become famous in
the arts and another dozen in the political world. Frank Pakenham, who
was to become Powell's brother-in-law and later First Lord of the
Admiralty; Harold Acton, novelist and art historian; Robert Byron, the
Byzantine critic and explorer; Cyril Connolly, most distinguished perhaps
as editor of the avant-garde periodical *Horizon;* and Henry Yorke were
merely those closest to Powell personally. All affected his art in one way
or another, but the ones to affect it most were those with a love of art.

In 1920 half a dozen students, repelled by Eton's singleminded exaltation of sports and abetted by the headmaster, decided to band together. "I fled the company of those in my house," Henry Green recalls in his autobiography, "to a set then beginning to form. They were to be known by the term, which at school spelt leprosy, of 'the aesthetes.' "[20]

The Society of Arts, as it was officially called, came into being as a club to hold weekly debates on topics related to art. But, according to Henry Green, debates were few and wild speeches many. Such feelings as have led other artists to pen manifestos of independence, these Etonians expressed in the pages of the *Eton Candle,* a magazine they founded and brought to national attention by soliciting contributions from Aldous Huxley, Osbert Sitwell, and Max Beerbohm. Here Powell's first publications appeared.

The *Eton Candle* was edited by Brian Howard, thought by most (but not Powell) to be a youth of great literary promise. His classmate Cyril Connolly recalls Howard as belonging "to a set of boys who were literary and artistic, but too lazy to gargle quotations and become inoculated with the virus of good taste latent in Eton teaching . . . and who gained much from Eton because of the little they gave. There was Harold Acton, a prince of courtesy, his brother William, Robert Byron . . . the two Messels, Anthony Powell . . . and Henry Green, who described them in his novel *Blindness.*" Connolly's cleverness had earned him a place in Eton's top club—and he snubbed Howard when invited to tea, perhaps wisely, since Howard's invitation was part of the plot of the Society of Arts to get one of its own elected to "Pop." The plot failed, but Connolly gave himself a failing mark in the affair. "They were the most vigorous group at Eton, yet my moral cowardice and academic outlook debarred me from making friends with them."[21]

The hostility of the school forced the members of the Society of Arts into yet closer association, and perhaps, by inducing them to cast about for some method of self-defense, it intensified their sense of the comic. Green's novel *Blindness* (1926) suggests as much: "It is 'the thing to do' now to throw stones at me as I sit at my window," the narrator of *Blindness* records in his diary, disgusted at the philistia of Noat ("Really, it might be Eton!") while he formulates outrageous but amusing epithets ("Milch cow!") with which to retaliate.[22]

In his autobiography, *Pack My Bag,* Green claims that the Eton Society of Arts was provocative by plan: "we hoped to arouse more than disdain, we were out to annoy by being what we called 'amusing.' . . . We took a fearful joy in making fun of all that we thought the school held sacred. . . . We tried to show that we were proud [that] we were no good at football or cricket" (Green 1940, 9, 170).

This aggressiveness was supported not only by shared tastes but by self-respect, several of the members being, even then, Green notes, "well on in their age in literature, in their knowledge of painting and most of all in the point of view. . . towards the life led about us. We were witty already even by the low standard which was set by wider circles afterwards and which we were to know when we said goodbye to Oxford" (Green 1940, 156). "We made humour one of our symbols," Harold Aeton recalls in his *Memoirs of an Aesthete,* and fought aesthetic crusades under the banner of the comic.[23]

The nostalgic essay on Eton that Anthony Powell contributed to *The Old School* suggests a more pacific attitude, but he laments that he "was not in the division that bribed a tramp to sit with them during a Greek lesson, nor . . . one of the three boys who went to see their tutor one Sunday morning and found a glass of milk and a slice of cake on a plate by his desk. One drank the milk, one ate the cake and the third broke the plate. Perhaps the story has no lesson to teach," Powell adds in the aesthetic tradition, "but for some reason it has always amused me. There is something stimulating about it" ("Glade," 159–60).

At Eton, the aesthetic, social, and political attitudes that were to characterize their art took form. The beautiful and the comic were co-determinants in their appreciation of the arts. In the aesthetic tradition of Oscar Wilde and Max Beerbohm, they tended to be dandies: "I have fallen hopelessly in love with the ties in Bartlett's window. I shall have to buy them all, even though they are quite outrageous" (Green 1928, 18). It became a mark of their identity to express themselves fearlessly, even with a sort of joyful insolence. Typical was the occasion when several, dressed as Etonian dandies, intervened in a political election: "We found all the Socialist working-men-God-bless-them drawn up in rows on either side of the street, so we three went down the rows haranguing. We each got into the centre of groups, and expected to be killed at any moment, for there is something about me that makes that type see red." In apprehension, the police forced their way in and "marched us off, I shaking every man's hand that I could see. So we returned shouting madly. It was too wonderful; never to be forgotten" (Green 1926, 23–25).[24]

When Powell left Eton in 1923, he bore away neither the grudge of Cyril Connolly, who expanded a theory later 'that the experience undergone by boys at the great public schools is so intense as to dominate their lives and to arrest their development," nor the disdain of Osbert Sitwell, who describes his education for *Who's Who* as having been acquired during vacations from Eton.

Powell claims to have been more fortunate: "The whole of my life at Eton was spent in well-deserved obscurity. I have no triumphs to look back on and I think myself lucky to have reached at last the House Library"—the senior group that "managed" Goodhart's house. "It was . . . possible for someone like myself, quite ludicrously bad at games and none too high up in the school, to achieve this distinction by intrigue on the part of friends" (*Infants,* 154). But in these words there is a pose of indolence.

Oxford

At Oxford, Powell matriculated at Balliol College. Today Balliol is still perhaps as well known as any college at Oxford, and Powell entered it only a year behind the novelist Graham Greene, but the Balliol Powell may have expected no longer existed. "The Balliol of Jowett, the Balliol of the victims of the Somme, the Balliol of Graham Greene are three quite different institutions worthy of a brief 'Decline and Fall,'" Cyril Connolly wrote later, and Powell agrees: "When I went up to Balliol in 1923, some vestige of the former greatness of the college remained, at least in the minds of those unconnected with the university."[25]

Benjamin Jowett as Master of Balliol around the turn of the century had educated great public leaders; after his death the sons of his pupils held their own until the Somme, that early battle of World War I that wiped them out as a group. After the war Balliol changed, and Powell refers to A. D. ("Sandy") Lindsay, Master of Balliol 1924–49, as a Balliol disaster. Lindsay had had a reputation even among the future "victims of the Somme" as a dull tutor; yet the parents of the "Anna" aristocrats induced him to accompany their sons on summer travels abroad. In this regard, he resembles the don Sillery in The Music of Time; and yet, also like Sillery, who is revealed to be a fellow traveler in the 1930s, Lindsay "was a thorough-going 'underdogger' all his life." As a Balliol student of more conservative bent, Powell's emotional conflict with "the Balliol of Graham Greene" was inevitable.

But Powell fell in love with Oxford itself. "It is right," Powell says, "that Aubrey's bones should lie at Oxford—the place that he used to long to see 'with the longing of a woman'" (*Aubrey,* 246). Yet unlike Evelyn Waugh, Powell was to write no novel about Oxford. Later

volumes of The Music of Time do allude to the aesthetic Oxford of the
1920s. The poet Mark Members, who was at the university then, is said
to have profited from the Aesthetes and to have moved on to psychoanalytic literature. More amusingly, we meet Hugo Tolland, the narrator's
youngest brother-in-law, who is an Oxford aesthete—one out of his time
in the 1930s:

> "Even Sillery says Hugo goes too far. . . . He drives all the other dons
> quite mad. . . . The other undergraduates are very disapproving too.
> Apart from anything else, aesthetes have gone completely out of fashion
> at both universities these days. I told Hugo when I saw him the other day
> that he was hopelessly out of date."
> "What did he say?"
> "'My dear, I love being dated. I hate all this bickering that goes on
> about politics. I wish I'd lived in the Twenties when people were amus-
> ing.'" (4:34)

The tone may be that of Anthony Blanche in *Brideshead Revisited,* but the
architecture is Powell's own.

Upon reaching Oxford in 1923, Harold Acton had founded a periodical, the *Oxford Broom,* with the financial aid of a young relative of Mrs.
Bernard Berenson—an "aesthetic" broom to sweep away what Acton
called "fin-de-siècle cobwebs." That autumn the London book publisher
Duckworth's brought out Acton's first book of verse, *Aquarium* (1923),
which had been solicited from him at Eton perhaps at the suggestion of
the Sitwells. As a poet who had been "published" and as the founder of
a new magazine, Acton was the outstanding man of his year at Oxford;
and chanting his poems through a megaphone from a Christ Church
College balcony to crowds passing below did nothing to diminish his
panache.

Collectively, the aesthetes "enveloped" the Hypocrites Club, recently
founded at Oxford in a comfortably seedy part of town but already
acquiring notoriety. Acton's *Memoirs of an Aesthete* gives a brilliant picture
of the club in the early 1920s, before it gained so much notoriety that it
was closed by the Proctors. The curious can find the club's story in many
other memoirs of the time, such as Claud Cockburn's *A Discord of
Trumpets* and Powell's own *Infants of the Spring.*

Not all of Powell's friends were club members: "The Hypocrites was
uncongenial to [Peter] Quennell, though he probably appeared at the
Club at one time or another: to Connolly The Hypocrites was not even
to be thought of." And "In due course I was to know [John] Heygate

well, but . . . He was not of The Hypocrites world" (*Infants,* 154, 161). But most of Powell's friends belonged, and the club seems to have carried on that mingling of the social, the comic, and the aesthetic begun by the Eton Society of Arts, though with a healthful, astringent admixture of new members such as Cockburn and Waugh and the perhaps pleasanter addition of women newly liberated by their Oxford colleges.

Even before his Balliol contemporary Graham Greene became editor of the *Oxford Outlook* in 1924, Powell was contributing artwork and critical essays to Oxford periodicals. And yet over the three years of his residency he seems to have drifted to the periphery, away from earlier friends, perhaps because more serious about his education. Evelyn Waugh includes Powell among his friends at Oxford, though he adds Powell to the list "not because of any intimacy I then enjoyed with him. . . . At Oxford we stood on friendly terms though barely in friendship."[26]

Scholarship may have played a role in this estrangement. Soldiers returning from the war in 1919–20 had brought to Oxford considerable "indifference to academic success," and the mood spread in the 1920s. "The result was that . . . there has [never] been a time in Oxford's history when its undergraduates were so wholly indifferent about their degrees," Christopher Hollis concludes. "I do not think that I exaggerate when I say that the greater number of undergraduates who have won intellectual success in afterlife—Evelyn Waugh, Alan Pryce-Jones, John Betjeman, Tony Bushell, and others—all went down without degrees."[27] In this respect, Anthony Powell was an exception. When he left Oxford in the summer of 1926, it was with degree in hand.

Perhaps Powell's more scholarly attitude may account for a cryptic entry in Evelyn Waugh's diary, where he records an evening of drinking, at a later stage of which "my recollections became blurred. I got a sword from somewhere and got into Balliol somehow and was let out of a window at sometime having mocked Tony Powell" (Waugh, 213).

And later years were to spread Powell and his friends spatially while reuniting them aesthetically, for Henry Green went to Yorkshire to work in a family factory, Waugh went to Wales to endure schoolmastering, Powell went down to London to make his way in publishing, and all turned to writing comic novels.

Bohemia

Henry Green's first novel, *Blindness,* deals with young men at a public school; Evelyn Waugh's first novel, *Decline and Fall,* begins with young

men at a university; but the first novel of Anthony Powell depicts another world altogether. In fact all five of Powell's early novels derive from
Bohemia, the London art world.

Powell's young men move out from London, it is true, to a seaside
cottage for a while in *Afternoon Men* (1931), to the grimmer world of a
Baltic capital in *Venusberg* (1932), to the fox-hunting country of the west
in *From a View to a Death* (1934), to the nightclubs of Paris and Berlin in
Agents and Patients (1936), and to the sunshine of the Riviera in *What's
Become of Waring* (1939). But in each case the painter, or film scenarist, or
publisher's reader, or fugitive plagiarist has been formed by the
Bohemian London that he leaves behind—and that draws him back.

When Anthony Powell "went down" from Oxford after the summer
term of 1926, he entered a London publisher's office "to learn the busi-
ness." The publishing firm of Duckworth's had been founded in 1898 by
Gerald Duckworth, a graduate of Eton and Cambridge, and by A. R.
Walter, who afterward became secretary to the Cambridge University
Press. As a younger brother of George Duckworth, Lord of the Manor of
Frome, Gerald Duckworth also had landed connections.

As the son of Julia Prinsep, Gerald Duckworth also had connections
with Bloomsbury. When he was eight, his widowed mother had married
Sir Leslie Stephen; a few years later she became the mother of Virginia
Woolf. On the other side, his elder brother George married Lady Margaret
Herbert, a daughter of the Earl of Carnarvan, and George Duckworth for
20 years was chairman of the wine committee in the Travellers' Club, the
first club of social importance to which Powell was elected.

But it was an army friend of Powell's father who steered him to
Duckworth's and opened the door. When his father had been ordered to
brigade headquarters in 1915 and needed to choose a staff captain to
assist him, he picked Thomas Balston of the Gloucesters, "who possessed
earlier Territorial experience with the lawyers' unit, the Inns of Court
Squadron. The Division moved very soon . . . to Yorkshire," where
Powell, for the summer holiday, joined his parents in a hotel requisitioned for the war. There he met Balston, who, he said, "was to play an
important part in my subsequent life." After the war, when Powell was
at Eton and Balston installed as a publisher in London, Powell's father
sent Balston a copy of the *Eton Candle* containing some of his son's work,
presumably with an eye toward his subsequent career. In his memoirs,
Powell speaks of Balston becoming "a director of the house of
Duckworth; in consequence of which, a dozen years after . . . I myself
was employed there."[28]

Much of Powell's work in the publishing office was dulling routine, but it widened his acquaintance with the arts. No family was more in England's literary eye in the 1930s than the Sitwells of Renishaw Hall, for instance; and all three Sitwells had transferred their publishing activities to Duckworth's about a year before Powell joined the staff. Osbert Sitwell had had contact with the Eton Aesthetes, and in the world of art his stature had grown. Indeed, it was said that "Osbert's epigrams echoed round the town . . . as Wilde's must have done, thirty years before."[29]

Edith Sitwell had come to Oxford in Powell's time to read her poem "Facade" through masks designed by Oliver Messel, to a jazz accompaniment, one of the major aesthetic "outrages" of the time. And Sacheverell, the youngest Sitwell, collaborated with Powell's friend Constant Lambert—the former writing the poetry, the latter the music for the symphony *Rio Grande* in 1931. The nature of the Sitwell-Powell relationship is further suggested by Evelyn Waugh's allusion to Powell as he records (as an instance of Sir Osbert Sitwell's generosity to the young) that he once offered a young man who worked for the publisher of his early books—"now a fine novelist"—his London house to give a party for his friends.[30]

What Powell admired in the Sitwells besides talent and humanity was what he found in T. E. Hulme: a "reaction from what might be called Bloomsbury and Bertrand Russell; an opposition with plenty of wit and energy, that was at the same time not itself philistine."[31] He protests one commentator's "describing Sir Osbert Sitwell as 'Bloomsbury,' even though Sir Osbert may have attended parties sometimes in that district. The Sitwells . . . surely represent, aesthetically speaking, something very different from the former Bloomsbury Group; if not, indeed, the precise converse."[32]

The Sitwells also provided a link socially to an era of the past that fascinated Powell, the period of Wilde and Beardsley. Ada Leverson, the friend whom Wilde had called both "the Sphinx" and "the wittiest woman in the world," in her old age was a favorite of the Sitwells, often taken under their wing socially. "I used myself to meet The Sphinx sometimes years ago," Powell recalls. "The vision of her remains as a little old lady, always in black, swathed in stoles and veils, picking her way, as she smiled gently to herself, through an infinitely rackety pack of persons most of whom were at least forty years younger."[33] A selection of correspondence, *Letters to the Sphinx from Oscar Wilde,* was published by Duckworth in 1930.

At Duckworth's, Powell was able to aid friends and no doubt the company as well. Waugh remembers that when he was, in 1927, "very hard up and seeking a commission to write a book, it was Tony who introduced me to my first publisher" (Waugh, 201). Waugh's biography of Dante Gabriel Rossetti was published by Duckworth's in May 1928. But when Waugh offered Duckworth's the manuscript of his now famous first novel, *Decline and Fall*, a few months later, it was declined. According to Harold Acton, "Duckworth's dare not publish *Decline and Fall* without copious bowdlerizations, and I am glad I persuaded Evelyn to stand firm. It is odd to look back on the spinster prudery of our publishers in the nineteen-twenties, reputed to be so naughty" (Acton, 202).

Embarrassing as this snarl must have been for Powell, he could do nothing about it at the time; only a decade later, with the appearance of his own fifth novel, *What's Become of Waring* (1939), did the frustration find an outlet in art. In Waugh's second novel, *Vile Bodies* (1930), reaction to Duckworth censorship found an earlier expression in his caricature of the publisher who takes it upon himself "to 'ginger up' the more reticent of the manuscripts submitted and 'tone down' the more 'outspoken' until he had reduced them all to the acceptable moral standard of his day."[34]

The world of London when Powell arrived in 1926 reflected what he calls "that odd sense of intellectual emancipation that belonged, or, at least, seemed . . . to belong, to the art of that epoch" (2:16). And it was but a short walk from Duckworth's on Henrietta Street to "the now legendary Bohemian world of Fitzroy Street, and writers as disparate as Edmund Gosse and Aleister Crowley, Norman Douglas and Stephen Gaselee."[35] Fitzroy Street was in part a Bloomsbury outpost, since Roger Fry and his Omega Workshops were located there; but it was also the locale of Walter Sickert and the Fitzroy Tavern; and around the area prowled eccentrics of a type Bloomsbury did not countenance.

As weird as any was Aleister Crowley, whose dark rituals at the Abbey of Thelema at Cefalu (in Sicily) had been broadcast to the world. In the Abbey of Thelema, so it was said, he had ritually murdered Raoul Loveday, the "Adonis of Cefalu," a former member of the Hypocrites Club. It was a rumor that Crowley did not discourage, and when Betty May, the Jacob Epstein model who had married Loveday, came in 1929 to publish her memoir, *Tiger Woman: My Story,* it was published by Duckworth's. As the publisher's representative, Powell met Crowley about this time, and Crowley treated him to luncheon in the Strand, exhibiting, for all his sinister qualities, "something ludicrous about him, especially his accent . . . probably derived . . . from . . . Nonconformist sects."[36] Crowley was fond of enigmatic, portentous formulas—"Love is the Law, Love under Will"—and he had already attracted the attention of Somerset Maugham, whose novel *The Magician* (1908) is perhaps as faithful a capturing of Crowley as his novel *The Moon and Sixpence* (1920) is of Gauguin. Crowley was to enter Powell's fiction most clearly as a major component of Dr. Trelawney in *The Kindly Ones.*[37]

If Powell's school friends did most to form his aesthetic creed, new friends and acquaintances, musicians and painters, did most to provide its materials. Perhaps the dispersal of Oxford friends to the antipodes helped effect Powell's entry. "The hiatus between coming down from the university and finding some place for myself in London had comprised," the narrator of The Music of Time recalls, "an eternity of boredom" (5:15). Whether or not that passage may be taken as reflecting Powell's experience, he soon came to know two musicians who were to be of creative importance, Constant Lambert and Philip Heseltine.

Constant Lambert is probably best known today as a music critic, though pieces of his music continue to be heard on American public radio. Powell has often referred to Lambert's critical book *Music Ho!* (1934) as "very brilliant," and years after Lambert's death Powell continued to quote his judgments—that the biographer Enid Starkie "tidies Baudelaire into a bore," for instance, or that the Joyce of *Finnegans Wake* is like a man who is "too shy to write a love letter except in the form of a crossword puzzle." Powell speaks of Lambert as "an old and close friend of mine . . . of tremendous brilliance,"[38] and others seem to have agreed about the brilliance. Wyndham Lewis in the 1930s formed "a congenial little group," the editor of his letters records; and Lewis, "far from monopolising the conversation, in a . . . civilised fashion kept it going from one to another, inciting Lambert in particular to sparkling brilliance of wit."[39]

Like the character Moreland in *Casanova's Chinese Restaurant* (1960)— and like Powell—Lambert was intrigued by the classic austerity of the new Russian ballet. "In 1926 Diaghilev chose [Lambert's] ballet, 'Romeo and Juliet,' as his first work by an Englishman and produced it at Monte Carlo." Lambert was then only 21, and in the following year he gained further accolades when Nijinsky danced in his *Pomona*. Even his art bears affinities with Powell's. The piece *Music for Orchestra,* which he at one time considered his best, might be thought to resemble The Music of Time in being "an extremely intellectual, almost wintry work, remarkable for its bold architecture." And in reporting that Lambert had been

taken up by "an advanced set," the suggestion was made, in 1931, that
Lambert's social success might be due to the fact that his music reflects
"the post-war generation . . . touching the surface of the emotions but
leaving the depths undisturbed," a description that would apply as well
to Powell's *Afternoon Men,* published the same year.[40]

But Lambert enters the world of Powell's fiction not simply *à clef* but
as a character in a net of personal relationships. And of course Powell's
greatness as a novelist lies less in creating isolated characters than in
tracing social patterns. Other novelists have become identified with one
social pattern or another—Dickens, with the orphan buffeted about in
an alien world until the adoptive guardian is found; Anthony Trollope,
with the clergyman stickily involved in the politics of the cathedral close;
Somerset Maugham, with the irrational but powerful attachment of one
person for another who has nothing to offer in return—but Powell has
made several other patterns his specialties, among them the hostile
friendship.

The hostile friendship may be described as the involvement of people
who on some grounds detest each another but are so drawn together on
other grounds that, despite the pain, they find it difficult to separate
permanently. Such was the relationship in the seventeenth century
between John Aubrey and his fellow antiquarian and cross-tempered
rival Anthony à Wood, linked by their selfless passion for knowledge,
and such is the relationship between Atwater, a museum official, and
Pringle, a painter, in Powell's first novel, *Afternoon Men:* "From the first
they had felt a certain mutual antipathy, but at the time they met in
Paris at the Coupole Bar, by contrast and comparison fellow-countrymen
had seemed more nearly tolerable. . . . For some reason the acquaintance
had persisted . . . long after the earlier reason for putting up with each
other's vagaries had been forgotten."[41]

More comic is Pringle's struggle with a fellow painter, Barlow, who
tries persistently to inflict his will upon Pringle: "Pringle had the best of it
in the end, because he used to lend Barlow money and ask for it back at
awkward times, but Barlow in periods of affluence publicly contradicted
everything that Pringle said and forced him to do things he disliked. His
greatest triumph had been to make Pringle buy an expensive saloon car,
but while he was away in Paris one Christmas Pringle had sold it" (6). In
The Music of Time such "illogical" but only too real human ties are traced
on a dozen planes, and Powell may have first become aware of the comic
possibilities during his early years in London as he observed not two
painters but two composers, Lambert and Philip Heseltine.

Heseltine, who came from a good family, was a composer and music critic by profession; yet his social reputation quickly grew seedy, and if he survives in the history of art it may well be in the history of the novel. D. H. Lawrence met him during World War I, Heseltine's biographer tells us, before he "translated himself into the hearty, bearded composer Peter Warlock; he was at this time an Eton-and-Oxford aesthete, with grandiose ideas, chewed nerves, and violent affections and antagonisms—the Halliday of *Women in Love*." Lawrence and Heseltine spent several months in Cornwall together, but within the year Heseltine had rejected Lawrence as a writer who had "no real sympathy" with other people and who sought only "converts to his own reactionary creed." He taunted Lawrence by sending him mock reviews of Lawrence's forthcoming novel and reported to the composer Frederick K. Delius that Lawrence was "quite comically perturbed."[42]

Heseltine reveled in pugnacity, and he especially enjoyed feuds with other musicians and critics: "I do not think there was a single one of eminence," his friend Cecil Gray reflects, "who was not at some time . . . the object of his aversion and the recipient of his insults and abuse" (Gray 1934, 250). In several memoirs of "the Heseltine circle," we see the homicidal violence that Huxley in *Antic Hay* relates to Rimbaud in glamorizing the character he modeled on Heseltine.[43] Powell relates it to Algernon Swinburne in disparaging him. "A comparatively small amount of drink overcame Swinburne," Powell notes, "whereupon there was an almost instantaneous change from lively conversation to utter intoxication. In this and certain other respects—the violently anti-Christian outbursts, the dancing, the scenes like Swinburne's kicking top hats about in the cloakroom of the Arts Club—one is reminded of the composer, Peter Warlock (Philip Heseltine), also a passionate student of the Elizabethan period. No doubt they belonged to a somewhat similar psychiatric type."[44]

Heseltine figures also in the origin of a character type Powell depicts brilliantly (and may have originated), one perhaps the converse of the lonely romantic artist struggling against a callous society to bring beauty to birth. The Tory in Powell could see that as often as society victimized the great artist, the second-rate artist victimized society. The professional artist in Powell's early novels is often a power-hungry predator, a devotee of Nietzsche.

Glancing around the studio of the painter Barlow in *Afternoon Men*, the visitor saw "some books. Not many. One of them . . . was *Thus Spake Zarathustra*" (49). Little is said about Zarathustra's connection with Barlow's unscrupulous, predatory conduct in regard to Pringle's girlfriend; but significantly Barlow brings Nietzsche to Pringle's cottage where, in Pringle's absence, he finds his girlfriend compliant. They are discovered together by Pringle. Later Barlow is sitting with his Nietzsche in a deckchair when he learns that Pringle has not, after all, committed suicide (198). The connection between the philosopher and the painter's conduct is only implicit, but it is hardly mistakable.

In Powell's third novel, *From a View to a Death,* he draws an even more detailed study of the artist-predator, the painter Zouch who considers himself, as a superman, above common morality. (In fact, fearing that Americans would not recognize the words of the traditional final dance song at English hunt-balls and would miss the ironic significance of the title *From a View to a Death,* the American publisher retitled that novel, a bit crassly perhaps, according to its theme, *Mr. Zouch, Superman.*)

In constructing this portrait of the Nietzschean "womanizer" Powell was no doubt to some extent using Heseltine as a model. Heseltine's early idol, Delius, was "the avowed disciple of Nietzsche, the champion of the manly, pagan virtues as opposed to those of Christianity," Cecil Gray tells us in *Musical Chairs*, recalling their "common admiration of Nietzsche. True we had . . . but a very patchy acquaintance with his works and had by no means understood all we had read, but we discerned in him—in *Zarathustra* especially—an attitude and opinions that appealed to us."[45] Powell's fiction was to have its fun with such Nietzschean devotees.

Although the title of Powell's great work The Music of Time suggests the world of music, it comes from the pictorial arts, from Nicolas Poussin's painting *A Dance to the Music of Time.* In his novels Powell also alludes more to paintings and painters than to operas or musicians, and as a novelist he views the world with a painter's eye. Jenkins's first view of his first girlfriend, for instance, is of an "arrangement of lines and planes: such as might be found in an Old Master drawing, Flemish or German perhaps, depicting some young and virginal saint" (1:74). And periodically in The Music of Time character groupings stand as if time-frozen in the way a painter might visualize a set piece.

At parties and at pubs in Bohemia, Powell gained a quite unsentimental appreciation of the painter's world, and consequently Rudyard Kipling's *The Light That Failed,* the sentimental story of a painter going blind but struggling on into the darkness, was not the kind of novel that he would write. "The art world is one of a toughness to make an Al Capone hesitate to join in its commercial transactions," Powell observes, "transactions to which piquancy is given by the fact that beauty and scholarship play a part. Finer feelings need not disturb the agents who put through a smart deal in steel or rubber."[46]

A painter sympathetic to Powell was Adrian Daintrey, dedicatee of Powell's novel *The Acceptance World* (1955) and a guest at Powell's wedding in 1934. Daintrey's autobiography, *I Must Say* (1963), paints in words one of the richest scenes of the epoch available outside of Powell's novels; and the scene links Maclean the Communist with Powell the Tory, Soho with Petworth.[47]

Another painter obviously liked by Powell was Nina Hamnett, who "brings with her wherever she goes," a friend remarked in later years, "a nostalgic breath of the old spirit of Montparnasse and Fitzroy Street in the 'twenties." The daughter of an army officer, she had, coincidentally enough, first received professional tutoring in painting from the father of Constant Lambert, Lambert's father having been during her teens an instructor at the London College of Art. Some of the raffish models and feminine painters of The Music of Time must owe something to her, as may the former artists' camp follower Betty Passenger, who neatly sees through Mr. Zouch in *From a View to a Death*.

Nina Hamnett was obviously fond of Powell: her second volume of memoirs contains her "Drawing of the Novelist, Anthony Powell, made in 1927," four years before his first novel was published.[48] That Powell was fond of her may be inferred. "What an unfailingly zestful individual she was," the *New Statesman* remarked in citing the passing of her as a "Bohemian landmark" in 1956: "You may say that her neglect of her talents—especially perhaps as a portrait painter—was tragic. Nevertheless, she had a time-defying capacity for living in the moment that amounted almost to a form of higher mysticism. She would preside—in a room much of which was taken up by a motorbicycle—from a bed made of orange boxes, over a tea party that included a Negro boxer, an Irish jockey and two poets." Wild as Nina Hamnett's conduct may have been, she had what Powell found in Constant Lambert and in Rosa Lewis of the Cavendish Hotel: Bohemian attitudes firmed by a conservative backbone. "A friend reveals encountering her in Charlotte Street late on the night of the abdication of Edward VIII. With her disregard of convention and her ready sympathy, he expected to find her defending the lovelorn [king]. Not she. 'He's let us all down, my dear,' she explained, tossing her head. There spoke the Colonel's daughter and former pupil of the Royal School, Bath."[49]

One observer recalled Nina Hamnett at the Fitzroy, singing a Cockney song about Madame Tussaud's waxworks and the bust of the singer's mother in the "Chamber of 'Orrers" there, the mother who "done in" her husband with a comical smile. The song "was sung to me

by the late Nina Hamnett, the talented artist who neglected her work in
order to pursue the role of Queen of Fitzrovia. . . . She was (a fact which
is not generally known) temporarily engaged to be married to Anthony
Powell . . . I can see her now sitting, one blue October Saturday afternoon, at a table in the Fitzroy Tavern. . . . And as Nina, getting . . . a little noisy, raps on the table with her pink gin glass, and trolls out her
'waxworks' song, half hoping her fiance might join in (which, of course,
he was far too diffident to do) a barrel-organ opens up its myxolidian
jangle."[50]

That was Bohemia.

Among the features of John Aubrey that attracted Powell was that he
had joined two worlds, each attractive, as he moved "familiarly through
the more or less Bohemian world of intellect and fashion [to] the out-
skirts of the court," from painters' studios in London to the great country houses (*Aubrey,* 100, 131).

High Bohemia where art and society come together, where Chelsea
and Mayfair overlap, provides the background for several other figures in
Powell's novels. Blore-Smith in *Agents and Patients,* lured to London by
the promise of "Life," is inveigled by some sharpsters into substituting
filmmaking for painting, the cinema being, they argue, "the art form of
tomorrow." Other wealthy or aristocratic men and women are lured
toward High Bohemia, notably Mary Passenger in *From a View to a
Death.* But the portraits of Eleanor Walpole-Wilson and Lady Norah
Tolland in The Music of Time are most detailed. The diplomat's daughter and the earl's daughter alike withdraw almost completely from high
society, without quite being able to join wholly into Bohemian society.

Family Life

The ties of Anthony Powell also overlapped. Family connections and
school friends drew him at least occasionally to the West End, to the
world of high society; and it was there that he was to marry and settle
down. With perhaps no direct autobiographical correspondence, Powell
has the narrator of The Music of Time move in a similar trajectory at
roughly the same period of history. Nick Jenkins falls in love with a
debutante, the sister of a youth he had known only slightly at school, as
he walks with her one afternoon in Kensington Gardens. He sees her
briefly when she comes in from the country that Christmas; and the following May, as the London Season begins, he comes to know her better:
"one afternoon, when I was correcting proofs in the office, Barbara rang

up and asked if I could dine at Eaton Square that evening for the Huntercombes' dance" (2:24).

The Season, or social season, stretching in London from late spring into early summer, is the time for coming-out parties; and in the late 1920s the guest lists at debutante balls, reported on the Court Page of the *Times,* often included the future wives of Henry Green and Evelyn Waugh, along with Nancy Mitford and Lady Mary Pakenham. Young men without title are not normally listed; yet one may presume that Powell was now and then among them.

The most eligible young men, heirs to titles and elder sons of bankers, were called at that time The White 400, as Lady Mary Pakenham notes in her memoir *Brought Up and Brought Out.* But these young men did not flock to the Pakenham townhouse until several years later, when her younger sister Violet at 18 "entered circulation."

Lady Violet Pakenham had pursued a course parallel to Powell's in her development. She too was the daughter of an officer in the Army and was familiar with the service's exacting requirements.[51] When she was three her father had been killed in action. A private school for girls on Harley Street gave her a preliminary education.[52] Declining her mother's offer of art school—an older sister Mary was already the family painter and another sister Pansy was married to the painter Henry Lamb; indeed it was while visiting Lamb's studio that she first read Powell's novels, some time before meeting the author—she instead entered the London School of Economics. Even before her debutante years, however, her great sense of fun attracted her to the world of London nightclubs and studios, and she obviously found Anthony Powell quite congenial.

The wedding of Anthony Powell and Lady Violet Pakenham took place early in December 1934, at All Saints' Church in Ennismore Gardens, London. It was not a large wedding as society weddings go, but the reception was held nearby at the Pakenham townhouse, at 12 Rutland Gate, and the modest guest list included Violet's uncles Lord Dunsany and Lord Dynevor, Violet's grandmother the Countess of Jersey, and artists and writers in abundance.[53] After a honeymoon in Greece, the Powells returned to take up residence on Great Ormond Street, London, and Powell cast about for a new profession.

Changes at Duckworth's were making his position there uncomfortable, and he was attracted by the chance to work, at first part time, as a scriptwriter. The change came in stages. He had done his first work for Warner Bros. Studios in England in 1934, and he left Duckworth's for good in 1936.

The new profession meant working in the suburbs on scripts for quota films. The movies he worked on were called quota films because of a law designed to protect the floundering British film industry from foreign encroachment by establishing a quota: so many films locally produced, so many Hollywood films imported. At least the work was different, if not totally agreeable. American studio executives compelled to produce "British" films imposed American working standards: Be at the studio at nine and write until six, etc. Such a regime, scarcely tolerable to any writer, was, even to a disciplined writer, depressing.[54]

The new profession did lead to Powell's first visit to the United States in 1937, a trip suggested by his agent in hopes that he might find work as a scriptwriter in Hollywood. Powell later described Hollywood as a "distressful place," but he met there one of the men he most admired in a literary way, F. Scott Fitzgerald, who at the time was "helping to make a film called *A Yank at Oxford*" and needed an authority on Oxford slang. Sheila Graham, the gossip columnist who was to become his mistress, "saw Fitzgerald for the first time on July 14, 1937," Powell notes, "and I met him a few days later at luncheon in the M.G.M. commissary and found him a most enjoyable contrast to Hollywood life. . . . He was charming, an amusing talker . . . He looked washed out but somehow gave the appearance of inner vitality against the zombies of the movieworld." But what Powell calls the "grimness of a script-writer's position"—of having to deal every day with tycoons who pursue "their passion for the obvious with a love greater even than the love of money"—led him, after a side trip to Mexico and a flight to New York, back to England (*Faces,* 61–67).

The film writer's life led to Powell's fourth novel, *Agents and Patients,* and also plays a part of some magnitude in *At Lady Molly's,* the fourth volume in The Music of Time. "I've got to get up early tomorrow and write filmscripts," Jenkins says at the end of a pub-crawl. "Good God," Ted Jeavons exclaims.

The introduction of Jenkins to Ted Jeavons had been effected at the beginning of *At Lady Molly's* by a fellow scriptwriter named Chips Lovell, who is courting a niece of Lady Molly. The nearest model for Lovell seems to be a fellow scriptwriter at Warner Bros. named Tommy Phipps. Though also a slave to the dulling studio, Phipps was from a family distinguished in polo circles on both sides of the Atlantic, and was a brother of Joyce Grenfell as well. Once, driving Powell from the studio back to London, Phipps found himself confronted suddenly by three cars racing nearly abreast toward them. Coolly braking the car and steering sharply, Phipps muttered, "This is just going to be a question of upbringing"—and not only saved them but gave Powell the opening title, *A Question of Upbringing,* for his major work (*Faces,* 38)

But the portrait of Chips Lovell and Powell's introduction to scriptwriting may owe more to an Eton-Balliol acquaintance who, after they met in London years later, had become a friend. John Heygate was later to inherit his uncle's baronetcy, but in the midst of the Depression he shared Powell's feeling of insecurity. A few years older than Powell, Heygate was also a novelist by inclination, and among the novels he published, *Decent Fellows* (1930) seems to reflect his experiences at Eton, while *Talking Picture* (1934) deals with experiences shooting a film on location in Germany.

But with Heygate, we see again in Powell's life not merely an individual but the individual as part of a pattern crisscrossing in society. Evelyn Waugh, on the strength of the publication of his first book by Duckworth's, had married in 1928 the Honorable Evelyn Gardner, who was then sharing a flat with Lady Mary Pakenham, later to be Powell's sister-in-law. The Waughs' marriage lasted less than two years, and in 1930 Waugh's former wife married John Heygate. In 1933 Powell dedicated *From a View to a Death* "For John and Evelyn." Their linkage in the dedication was not, as it turned out, an augury of permanence. In 1934 they attended Powell's wedding, even assisted in the arrangements for his honeymoon; but two years later they were divorced, and each remarried almost immediately. Nevertheless, the Honorable Mrs. Nightingale (as Evelyn Gardner was then called) became godmother to Powell's second son in 1946[55] and remained a friend until her death in 1994.

As a scriptwriter, Powell seems always to have worked in that limbo of collaboration that inhibits any ascription of credits. Looking back, the only work he could claim was the script for a documentary about the philanthropist Dr. Barnado that was never filmed (*Faces,* 40–43). That the scriptwriting affected his novel-writing style, as some critics have implied, is of course possible; but this theory needs questioning. Years before he became a scenarist, his first novel not only had as a subtitle "Montage" but used montage in its presentation of scenes (as certain novels had been doing for years). And in his second novel, *Venusberg,* we find the action ultimately reduced in the protagonist's mind to a reel of film[56]—and that before any behind-the-camera experience on the author's part.

Upon his return to England, with the doors to publishing and scriptwriting closed behind him, Powell became a book reviewer for the

Spectator. In the decades since, book reviewing has remained one of his principal sidelines. Having begun professionally in 1936 with reviews for the *Daily Telegraph,* he wrote for the *Spectator* until 1939 and revived that connection after the war. In 1946 he joined the staff of the *Times Literary Supplement,* where a number of his reviews appeared anonymously. In 1953 he switched to *Punch* (again with editorial duties as well), and in 1958 he returned to the *Daily Telegraph* as literary editor. Summing up this aspect of his career, Powell reviewed nearly a book a week for 30 years.

International events were closing in on all artists in the late 1930s, however. Powell completed his fifth novel as Neville Chamberlain returned from Munich waving his umbrella and announcing "Peace in our time!"—after an accord with Hitler that even then was being labeled "infamous." The first half of Powell's career had come to a close, and with it an era. London itself seemed gone, as The Music of Time records, with old friends out of town or in uniform. World War II settled in drearily. "In this atmosphere writing was more than ever out of the question," the narrator of The Music of Time recalls; "even reading could be attempted only at short stretches" (6:206). But Powell's five early novels would have secured a place for him in the history of the English novel even if he had written no more. His art had not been on a gigantic scale, but it had been well formed.

Chapter Two
The Early Novels

Critics differ as to the worth of Powell's early novels. Lifting an aged witticism (that the comic plays of Somerset Maugham are mere "Wilde and water"), one critic argues that "[t]he five amusing minor novels that he wrote before the war are Firbank and Waugh and water—or perhaps soda water. They do not bear comparison at all with the six volumes so far published in 'The Music of Time' series, upon which Firbank's influence is indiscernible." John Carter asked in reply if the reviewer had read the early novels recently. "Their elegant, wry flavour and the spare, detached style are individual to Mr. Powell; and . . . they travel, across the decades, remarkably well."[1] Certainly two of these novels, *Afternoon Men* (1931) and *From a View to a Death* (1933), demonstrate that John Carter is right. Although comparisons with Firbank and Waugh may be inevitable, they are also invidious. Powell experimented with the novel on his own—and both his failures and his accomplishments are unique.

Afternoon Men

The central character of *Afternoon Men,* Powell's first novel—its "hero," or antihero—is a young museum official named William Atwater; and the plot that involves him is not an intrigue to be eluded or a mystery to be solved. The plot is that of destiny, which is not so easily evaded; the mystery, that of life, which is not to be solved. Instead of being faced with a sequence of obstacles to be surmounted in the Victorian high-hurdle fashion, Powell's hero is drawn along by time to perceive submerged obstacles all the more formidable because they are buried in the currents of society and his own character. Little could seem more forbidding in its gloom than such a theme. In the hands of a romantic writer, a Gissing or an Orwell, the effect could be depressing; but amused stoicism renders the texture of *Afternoon Men* delightful page by page; and the overall effect is of a zany comic perspective on a wry, not unpleasant melancholy.

The novel opens with fewer "stage directions" than a play by Maugham or Wilde would provide:

"When do you take it?" said Atwater.

Pringle said: "You're supposed to take it after every meal, but I only take it after breakfast and dinner. I find that enough."

The two men are talking, we later discover, in the basement bar of a private club in central London. What "it" refers to—the "it" that Pringle takes—we never discover. The conversation drifts away from this vaguely medicinal area without another clue; on the first page of Powell's first novel, the reader's frustration may have begun. But a vital fact is clear: Pringle's disregard of sensible rules. And disregard of good sense is what the novel is about.

That the novels of Powell differ essentially from those of Waugh in being moved "by sense rather than by outraged sensibility," as one distinguished critic puts it, also seems clear from the beginning.[2] Since Pringle the painter continues to disregard "sensible" conventions throughout the novel, any precise definition of the introductory "it" would be superfluous anyway. And to define *it* would be, at least on a symbolic level, undesirable: the essence of Powell's meaning, in the novel as a whole, is the apparent lack of meaning in life, or, as rationally conceived, life's "non-sense." The conversation does not complete its "sense"; the random fragment of conversation is in turn a fragment of social life; and, with society being in turn a part of nature, the only "sense" one makes of nature is that man's lot is to remain ignorant.

Man does not live "by bread alone," nor does he act by sense alone. "The absurdity of supposing that exact reasons for marriage can ever be assigned had not then struck me," the narrator of The Music of Time later concludes (2:197); but in *Afternoon Men* the existential absurdity latent in all human behavior has to be conveyed by the structure, for this novel has no such *raisonneur* or, more exactly, no character groping for the meaning with enough success to have grown articulate about his lack of progress. As the Sisyphus myth represents man's eternal but absurd hope that he will eventually roll the boulder of truth to the top of the hill, or has "at last solved," or at least is "just about to solve," the mystery of existence, the structure of Powell's novel is circular. The end finds the two men, Atwater and Pringle, back in the bar, without love again and bored again with each other's company; but with another "gay party"—and with all that "gay party" connotes of man's futile hope of finding any lasting happiness, sensual or intellectual—looming suicidally ahead (221).

Atwater and Pringle, who are diverse in profession and personality, have the curious love-hate relationship that—absurdly—compels them to seek each other's company. Although the secret of this compulsive friendship is never made explicit, they do share a worldview that isolates them from most of the other characters: both are artists whose realizations have not matched their conceptions, and both are destined to wrestle throughout the novel with love for women who prove to be unattainable.

The two young ladies are unattainable not in a tragic way but in a comic way, for the girl worshipped by Pringle has a brief affair with Atwater, to whom she means little; the other woman, loved by Atwater, elopes to America with a cool realist to whom she means little. In both cases the nature of the ideal seems to render its realization impossible and thus to render the characters' condition "absurd."

The title *Afternoon Men,* which comes from Robert Burton's *Anatomy of Melancholy* (1621), seems to imply that Atwater and Pringle, far from being creatures of free will, exist as if under the spell of the "enchanted horn of Astolpho, that English duke in Ariosto, which never sounded but all his auditors were mad, and for fear ready to make away with themselves . . . they are a company of giddy-heads, afternoon men."

Atwater is "a weedy-looking young man with . . . rather long legs, who had failed twice for the Foreign Office. He sometimes wore tortoiseshell . . . spectacles to correct a slight squint, and through influence he had recently got a job in a museum." As a portrait, this is caustically antiromantic. Indeed, though Powell is being stringently detached, it may be that he detaches us too far. That a "hero" should be parasitic, lazy, and ambivalent about life itself tends to kill our sympathy; and, from bare tolerance of him, the novel twists us a bit uncomfortably as it unfolds item by item Atwater's negative virtues—his stoicism, dry wit, and patience. He gains our sympathy in the end, but the reader approaching *Afternoon Men* for the first time has some wrestling to do.

Atwater, sent to France years before to learn the language for the diplomatic career that his quiet parents hope for him, had met an English art student, Raymond Pringle, who "came of a go-ahead family. [Pringle's] father, a business man from Ulster, had bought a Cézanne in 1911. That had been the beginning. Then he had divorced his wife. Later he developed religious mania and jumped off a suspension bridge" (2–3).

In this contrast of families we see in embryo the relationship between Jenkins and Widmerpool in The Music of Time: Pringle, though a

painter, is a power seeker (like Widmerpool), one whose energy leads
him into absurdities. Atwater (like Jenkins) is quiescent, a man whose
apathy is in itself somewhat absurd.

Atwater's type could be observed widely in the 1920s, but no doubt
Powell puts something of himself into Atwater's portrait. At 20 Powell
reviewed a novel in which the hero, John Christian Harbottle, rocked by
misfortunes, sets out on a "pilgrimage in search of an answer to the rid-
dle of existence." "It may be that I am myself a Harbottle," Powell
added. "At least the Sin of Innate Inertia is not without its appeal to
me."[3] No greatness is prophesied for Atwater, but he has ambitions in
art and spends his spare hours at the museum trying to write a novel,
one he is happy to forget on evenings spent with Pringle.

Beauty is a term used in Powell's comic novels only in reference to
women.[4] The "sunset touches" that give us pause, as Browning's
"Bishop Blougram" would say, in Powell's work come almost exclusively
in glimpses of lovely girls; and one is sitting at the bar as the novel
opens. Harriet Twining "looked very dazzling" with "fair hair and a
darkish skin, so that men often went quite crazy when they saw her, and
offered to marry her almost at once" (4).

Harriet is with an American publisher named Scheigan ("His
Christian name is Marquis. Isn't that sweet?") discussing her own about-
to-be-published book ("He likes culture"). Others enter the bar, and she
takes them all, Atwater and Pringle included, in a pair of taxis to a party
given by a woman whose name they never learn. A second beauty—the
one who deflects the trajectory of Atwater's life as sharply as Harriet is
to deflect Pringle's—had been discussed, among fragments of gossip,
even before they left the bar:

> Harriet said: "Is it true that Undershaft is in America living with a
> High Yaller?"
> Brisket said: "That's one thing. The other is that Susan Nunnery has
> left Gilbert."
> "She's so lovely."
> "Very special."
> "She's sweet," said Harriet. "I adore her. Don't you think she's sweet,
> William?"
> Atwater said: "I've never met her."
> "You must have seen her."
> "No, I've never seen her."
> "You must have."
> "I haven't."

"I say," said Barlow's brother. "Do any of you ever go to the Forty-Three?"

"Aw," said Mr. Scheigan. "Don't gossip. Let's enjoy ourselves. Let's have a good time."

"Tell him about your museum," said Harriet. "He likes culture. We might be going to the party soon." (10–11)

At the party, chaos has already set in. A fat woman says to a man passing Atwater:

"You're host, aren't you? Two girls have fainted in the bathroom and can't get out."

"Nonsense. I don't believe it."

"They can't."

"There's no lock on the door," he said. "I took it off before the party started." (22)

The American publisher soon finds his "good time" and passes out:

"He ought to be moved a bit," said Pringle. "People are tripping over his head. He's becoming a nuisance."

Barlow said: "Nonsense. I like seeing him there. He gives the room a lived-in feeling."

"He lets down the tone of the party."

"Not so much as when he's awake." (25)

Through this alcoholic miasma drift the specters of cliché. A young naval officer on leave is asked four or five times if it isn't true that in the Navy he gets his drink cheap. And Atwater has to endure yet another repetitive discussion of Susan (28) before meeting her. Just as the response "You must have!" starts to become a comic refrain, Susan arrives.

When Atwater sees Susan, no comment is made by the author as to the state of his mind; but her entrance is engineered to produce, amid the babble of the party, a moment of silence. Hers, so to speak, is the hyacinth-girl effect of *The Waste Land.* Elsewhere, Powell speculates on the phenomenon of "love at first sight" as being the result of a perception mysteriously "projected out of Time" (2:215). The word too often profaned is not at the moment uttered; but Atwater's own refrain ("I'm a dying man") is stilled. Susan in the doorway looks amused, surprised, and disappointed, as if the party "had been just what she had expected and yet it had come as a shock to her when she saw what human beings were really like" (23).

Like Harriet physically attractive, Susan is more than that: her mind
is individual, fresh, free from cliché. Powell speaks elsewhere of Henry
James as "tortured by the very thought of cliché," and there is a passage
in a novel Powell praises, Wyndham Lewis' *Tarr* (1918), that is apropos
in that it illustrates the damaging effect of cliché on love, for the painter
Tarr grows disgusted with the cliché-ridden mind of his fiancée. In her
apartment "there was the plaster-cast of Beethoven (some people who
have frequented artistic circles get to dislike the face extremely) [and] a
photograph of *Mona Lisa* (Tarr could not look upon the *Mona Lisa* without a sinking feeling)" (40).

At the party yet another young woman, Lola, had spilled a drink on
Pringle—to his fury—and Atwater had met her. But like everyone else
who meets Atwater and learns he works in a museum, this young
woman says: "That must be very interesting work, isn't it?" Susan
responds on the other hand—and to Atwater's surprise unconventional-
ly—with a proposition: "May I visit you there?" Nowhere does Powell
comment on the relative intelligence of the two women, but the idea
that life with Lola would be dull, with Susan bright, is amply conveyed.
Moreover, as the *New Yorker* cliché expert Frank Sullivan demonstrated in
the 1930s, dull as cliché may be, the perception of cliché can be in itself
a source of comedy.

Lola, met before Susan arrives, has piquant incongruities: an "oafish"
expression and "the look of a gnome or prematurely vicious child. But
underneath the suggestion of peculiar knowingness an apparent and
immense credulity lurked." She has adopted the name Lola. Atwater
tells her his name is William: "I was christened it. I'm still called that."
Lola's "liberalism" extends to other "intellectual" areas:

> "When I feel hopeless," she said, "I read Bertrand Russell."
> "My dear."
> "You know, when he talks about mental adventure. Then I feel
> reinspired."
> "Reinspired to what?"
> "Just reinspired."
> "Do you feel hopeless now?" (21)

Atwater suggests a visit to his flat to talk about "inspiration, and so on"
and to take a look at his "interesting first editions." Lola is still wavering
when Susan first appears in the doorway; as Lola decides to accompany
him, the sight of Susan has changed his attitude. Yet later, when Susan

leaves the party with someone else, there is, ostensibly, no reason not to proceed with Lola.

In the taxi to his flat, Atwater hopes that Lola will not "begin on Bertrand Russell again"; and, when she asks about the first editions, he decides that he cannot "do all the stuff about the books" (31) that evening. Pleading fatigue, he rather ill-manneredly allows her to walk home alone (33).

Lola telephones him at work a few days later; with Susan being still unavailable, he proceeds to Lola's apartment and into one of the most amusing representations of boring talk in literature; talk that concludes on the central issue, with all its stale conventions:

> "When did you first notice me at that party?" she said.
> "Oh, as soon as you came in."
> "I think sometimes people do just feel that at once, don't you?"
> "I'm sure they do."
> "Are you always falling for people?"
> "Yes, always."
> "You brute."
> "I'm sure everybody falls for you," he said.
> "No, they don't."
> "I'm sure they do."
> In her serious voice she said: "Don't you think sexual selection is awfully important?"
> "Of course."
> "Don't," she said. "You're hurting. You mustn't do that."
> Slowly, but very deliberately, the brooding edifice of seduction, creaking and incongruous, came into being, a vast Heath Robinson mechanism, dually controlled by them and lumbering gloomily down vistas of triteness [to] the inevitable anti-climax. . . . Later they dined at a restaurant quite near the flat. (82–83)

It has been well said by Richard Vorhees that "no other novelist has made party-going seem so dreary, and not even Aldous Huxley has made promiscuity seem so depressing."[5]

Powell may have had Ernest Dowson's "Gone with the Wind" poem in mind in these scenes—certainly, he had some similar concept of unfaithful fidelity in mind, some separation of lust and love; for Atwater is faithful to his Cynara, but in his fashion. He succeeds finally in getting a date with Susan and takes her to a restaurant, where he hopes to be alone with her, but friends show up and steal his time with discussion of fashionable weight-reducing salons. No one being interested in anyone else, the conversation is a riot of non sequiturs:

> "There's a place one can go to just outside Munich. They say it's very good."
> "Didn't Mildred go there?"
> "It was Mildred's nerves."
> "Doesn't he do that too?"
> "Mildred went to the man at Versailles. He makes you scrub floors. Mildred said she felt quite different after it."
> "Then there are readings from Croce in the evening. It's terrible if you don't understand Italian. You're made to listen just the same." (93)

Only Chekhov and Firbank have done as much to make a comic art of the non sequitur, the zany colloquial irrelevance; and Powell, like Chekhov, uses the non sequitur not only as a means of showing the indifference of people to one another but also as a kind of structural symbol. Life itself may become a kind of non sequitur, as Atwater discovers when a neatly dressed man named Verelst, who "hardly looked like a Jew at all,"[6] is attracted to Susan's table. "His moustache was arranged so that it made him look as if he might be in the Brigade of Guards, but although it was plausible it was not really convincing" (93). Verelst outpoints Atwater in winemanship and insists on giving him "the address of a quite excellent hotel. . . . Of course the place is always full of international gourmets, if you can stand that." The only clue given to the state of Atwater's mind at this point is his hope "that lots more people would come and talk and drink and sit at the table and make assignations with Susan . . . because then it would become funny and he might feel less angry" (96).

Verelst is seen again as a respectable collector of art at Pringle's private showing. Then Susan telephones the bar where she was to meet Atwater for their second date to say, "So sorry I shan't be able to see you tonight. I'm in the country—" (117). An aging man with a well-displayed book called *L'Ersatz d'Amour* is trying to buy Atwater a drink, so he departs for a friend's, and, finding the friend on his way out, he drifts to Lola's, precipitating another comic "waste of shame":

> The divan creaked. Lola said:
> "No, dear, no."
> "Yes."
> "No, really, no."

"Yes."

"Draw the curtains, then."

As Atwater drew the curtains he noticed that it was spotting with rain outside and in one of the back rooms opposite a man wearing an overcoat was playing the piano. Lola said:

"In modern sculpture I think the influence of Archipenko is paramount." (122)

With this fragment of Archipenko pretentiousness, the curtain closes—and the chapter too.

Atwater's third date with Susan is designed to get them away from "arty" friends; he takes her to a second-rate boxing hall in the slums.[7] The boxing is reminiscent of the bullfighting in Ernest Hemingway's *The Sun also Rises* (1928), not only in its anti-intellectualist turn to violence but in its use of the combat within the arena to counterpoint the struggle going on among the characters. To Atwater, each of the fights seems symbolic. The first matches a Welshman and a Jew; and the former turns "pink in the face" with effort, while the latter's hair remains neat as he wins. Two fights later, a boxer named Ernie Hyams kisses a girl's coat and a brassiere before his bout:

"Is that his girl's too?"

"I don't know. Perhaps he's got two girls and one wears the coat and the other wears the whatnot."

"I think it's sweet."

"His having two girls?"

"I think it's sweet his kissing the things like that."

"Would you like me more if I did that sort of thing?"

"I like you all right," she said. "What I tell you is that it is no good either of us liking the other." (137)

Although Atwater predicts Hyams's defeat, his opponent, Gunner Haskins, hits him below the belt, admits his fault, and the fight goes to Hyams. Susan chooses the next break to refer to Lola, exhibiting an "illogical" hint of morality:

"Anyway, if you feel like that, what about your little friend who wears the funny clothes?"

"What about her?"

"Do you still see her?"

"Sometimes."

"Oh, God," she said. "I don't really care."

> "I know you don't."
> "I mean I understand about all that."
> "Yes?"
> "Yes," she said. "That's not why."
> "Why, then?"
> "I don't know. Just I feel like that, I suppose."
> "Yes, I see."
> She said: "You're rather sweet really."
> "Aren't I?"
> "Yes. But that's how I feel."
> "Anyway, I never see you, so it doesn't make any difference."
> "Well, if it doesn't make any difference?"
> "Exactly."
> "Don't be like that," she said. (138–39)

This dialogue is like the visible portion of Hemingway's iceberg: strong emotions are hidden below. Two bouts later a Welshman with a straight-forward, emotional style is outboxed by an "intellectual faced man from Battersea." There is no underlining of correspondences, but Atwater's defeat in love's arena by the coolly rational Verelst and his panoply of romanticism is foreshadowed, as we see clearly enough in retrospect. Susan is, like the English crowd, for the underdog; for the Jew who was hit below the belt:

> "I like Jews."
> "I'd noticed it."
> "They all behave like that," she said. "Kissing the coat and so on."
> (137)

As they are leaving the arena, Susan and Atwater encounter a homosexual acquaintance with his "very pale young man":

> "Why, fancy meeting you here, Walter."
> "Not at all, I made the place fashionable."
> Seeing there was no escape, Atwater said: "Are we all going in the same taxi?"

So his third date with Susan ends with their resubmergence in the sterile crowd.

Discretion, reserve, and failures of communication also mark the denouement. Susan is going away but refuses to tell Atwater where; he leaves the city on vacation and, when he returns toward the end of the novel to the apartment house where her pleasant, alcoholic father lives, he finds that Susan has gone to America with Verelst. Atwater controls his emotions carefully until he is back on the street; then he walks unseeing:

> They had written each other no letters, but he thought of the inflections of her voice on the telephone, so that all the things she had said lost with the different tones he gave them any meaning that they once had had. And so she was gone, ridiculous, lovely creature, absurdly hopeless and impossible love who was and had always been so far away. Absurdly love-ly, hopeless creature who was gone away so that he would never see her again and would only remember her as an absurdly hopeless love. . . . What a fool. And yet, as she had said, what would the good have been? (215)

Their friend Undershaft is said to have come back from America, to have taken up Lola, and to have relayed one comment of Lola's on Atwater's suspenders that provides a clue, an economic clue to the question that Susan would not answer as to why "it" would have been no good: "She told Undershaft she thought it so funny the way you mended your braces [suspenders] with wire" (220).

A powerful line in retrospect, so funny it makes you cry.

The weakest aspect of *Afternoon Men* as a work of art seems to arise from the plurality of its title, the structure-distorting necessity of seeing how the other "afternoon man," Pringle, is also brought by thwarted love to the verge of doing away with himself. Having accepted Henry James's aesthetic of the novel—the novelist's self-imposed limit to a sin-gle point of view—and having elected the viewpoint of Atwater, Powell must interrupt Atwater's story to bring the reader to where Atwater can observe the Pringle story. The Victorian novelist would merely have said, "Now we turn to see how our other afternoon man is faring in his rela-tions with the other young woman." Such a crude authorial intrusion was not one that Powell (or any contemporary novelist he respected) would have permitted himself.

Sticking to Atwater's point of view then, the reader has to see Pringle reach his "afternoon" in a manner consistent with both realism and aes-thetic integrity. For this Powell has to arrange an occasion, and he man-ufactures such an occasion by having Pringle invite Atwater to the cottage he has rented for August near the sea.

Atwater is aware that no sentiment is attached, that the invitation came to him only because "Apfelbaum, the picture man, has fallen through," but at the moment Susan has gone elsewhere for the weekend and he fears boredom. When he arrives at Pringle's cottage, he finds Harriet, who has become Pringle's mistress, although, as she says, "That always sounds such a pompous thing to be" (153). The painter Barlow is there with his bovine, kind, mistress-model Sophy; and so is the elderly art collector Naomi Race, who has been met before as a London hostess and as a candid, generous friend of Susan's.[8] Barlow, on the other hand, is a crass Nietzschean—his copy of *Thus Spake Zarathustra* is much battered (49, 198)—and he has become a comic bore because of his insistence on discussing potential marriage partners with friends, though none of the possibilities includes good old Sophy. Indeed, none of the women among whom the friends are asked to decide is known to them.

Late the second day Pringle takes a walk with Atwater to discuss his own plans to marry Harriet:

> "We like each other a great deal."
> Atwater said: "That always makes marriage more satisfactory. . . ."
> "I think she's lucky in a way." (172)

As they grope their way back to the house in the dark, Pringle is thus doubly outraged to discover Harriet rumpled on a sofa with Barlow. He calls Barlow a cad.

> "I know. We both are. You said so only yesterday. . . ."
> "You've been a bad influence on me ever since I met you. I've felt my painting getting worse and worse."
> "In what way?"
> "In every way."
> "I'm sure you're wrong." (174)

Pringle storms into the kitchen and, in a scene of hilarious farce, catches his coat on the levers of the water faucets above the sink. Atwater tugs and pulls in vain to release him. Pringle curses at the suggestion that they solicit Barlow's help:

> They pulled again a good deal. Then Barlow came in to see what was wrong and why Pringle was making so much noise. He said: "Can I help?"
> Atwater said: "Yes."
> Atwater and Barlow lifted Pringle bodily into the air to take the weight off his coat. By pulling again in this position they managed to get

it free, but it took several minutes to do. Then they lit the candles . . . and went to bed. Pringle was white in the face. No one said goodnight to anyone else. (177)

The next day Harriet asks Atwater to take a walk with her; and high on the cliffs above the sea, with the air "fresh, rather metallic and Scandinavian," they spot Pringle walking on the shore below. They see him stop, undress completely, scratch himself for some time, swim out to sea, and disappear in the glare.[9] Harriet and Atwater, walking on, each discover that the other is in love, Harriet with a man in Spain—"But I never see him," she says,

> "so what's the good? Do you think that one of these days everything will come out right?"
> "No."
> "Neither do I," she said. She laughed again. (182)

They move rather mechanically into what might be called a seduction; and, when reality again becomes "more contiguous," Harriet giggles, combs her hair, and they wander home in the cold darkening air amid the more insistent noise from the sea.

At the house, in expectation of Pringle, luncheon has been delayed. When hunger overwhelms them, they move to the sideboard and discover a farewell note from Pringle "on top of the beef." Depressed by the failure of his life, the note says, he wishes his money to be divided between his maid and his sister. Only Sophy cries. "Mrs. Race said: 'I refuse to believe that this is not one of his heavy jokes. If we have lunch, I have no doubt he will turn up'" (188). Though all feel sure the note is no joke, hunger has already been staved off. Naomi's rationalization is accepted and they eat in wildly comic solemnity. Later, observing Barlow rehearse his "guilt symptoms"—"But it's absurd that I should have been the cause of it. I mean he always seemed to like me"—while he speculates again about the best marriage partner for himself, Atwater "wanted . . . to leave at once before he followed Pringle into the sea" (194).

At this moment, Pringle turns up alive. After surreptitiously and vainly seeking his note on top of the beef, he says, "I decided against suicide on the whole."

When we next see Atwater and Pringle, they are in the London basement bar where we met them. Pringle and Atwater are again "alone," Harriet having picked up another stranger: "I don't know what his name is, but he says a friend of his is giving a party and we can all come." They are all deciding to go to the party as the novel ends—the wheel full circle, the stone of Sisyphus again at the bottom of the hill. We foresee another "Montage" (the subtitle given to the first part of the novel) as new faces sift into the social frame; another "Perihelion" (the title given to the central third of the novel) in which Atwater dates the girl he loves, high in orbit, warm, blinded by the sun, so that later he cannot even recall what she looked like or even what she sounded like; and a final "Palindrome" (the third section's subtitle, a reference to reduplicating verbal forms) in which things, absurdly, are seen to read the same backward as forward. The structure of the novel brilliantly illustrates the relevance of the "palindrome" to most of our lives.

One of Powell's most important and least understood technical innovations is his development of a character type that may be called the parody-*raisonneur*. Its function is to express the novel's point of view, but making it sound absurd so that we see why others do not express it. In *Afternoon Men* the character who articulates what Atwater feels about the world is a man named Fotheringham, who suffers from what might be called a noisy weltschmerz. The subeditor of a spiritualist paper, Fotheringham has tried to get Undershaft to write an article on occult music, although of all people Fotheringham has come to like spiritualists least. Dropping by Hector Barlow's studio he finds also Sophy and Atwater, and they go out to a neighborhood pub:

> "Now listen to me for a minute. I may not be as talented as you, Hector, or as beautiful as Sophy, but don't you agree that I'm wasted?"
> "No, I don't think you are in the least."
> Fotheringham laughed. He said: "Now you're joking. Be serious."
> "Not a bit. You're very lucky to have a job at all."
> "You don't mean it?"
> "I mean what I say."
> "No, that's absurd," said Fotheringham. "I don't believe you when you say things like that. . . . You're merely offensive, Hector."
> "I mean to be."
> "You know, you go too far. People who don't know you as well as I do would never guess that you were joking." (56–57)

To balance Fotheringham's inflated concept of his abilities, we have his deflated view of man's destiny, expressed in pure cliché:

"Where is it all going to lead? I ask you that, Atwater."

"I don't know."

"No. You don't know. I don't know. None of us know. We just go on and on and on and on and on."

"We do."

"We sit here when we might be doing great things, you and I."

"Might we?"

"Do you know what we are doing?"

"No."

"Shall I tell you?"

"Yes."

"We are wasting our youth."

"Do you think so?"

Fotheringham said: "Every minute the precious seconds flit by. The hour strikes. Every moment we get a little nearer to our appointed doom." (60)

Boring talk is conveyed with comedy that almost amounts to grandeur as Fotheringham traps Atwater and Barlow at the bar and grows maudlin on the subject of "friendship." The passage is typical of Powell's skill as a creator of a cosmos between the lines. It needs to be quoted at length:

"No, no. Don't repeat it."

"Yes," said Fotheringham. "I shall say it again, and more than once again, how fortunate I count myself to have such friends as I have; and whatever people may say about friendship, and no one knows better than I that it's a quality that in these days is often rated lower than those temporary emotional connections between this or that sex . . . yet it is eventually a thing, in fact it is the thing, that in the long run the happiness of men like you and me . . . depend on most of all in this struggle, this mad, chaotic armageddon, this febrile striving which we, you and I, know life to be; and when we come at last to those grey, eerie and terrible waste lands of hopeless despair, unendurable depression and complete absence of humour that drink and debt and women and too much smoking and not taking enough exercise . . . lead us to, when the vast and absolutely impenetrable mists of platitude or, in the case of some, dogma envelop us and cover us up entirely, when we have . . . sunk to those slimy horrible depths of degradation . . . that comes to those who would sell their name, their intellect, their mistress, their old school, their honour itself for the price of a bitter; when love has come to mean the most boring form of lust, when power means the most useless pots of money, when fame

means the vulgarest sort of publicity, when we feel ourselves exiled forever from . . . debonair insouciance (pardon the phrase), which is, I suppose, the one and really only possible mitigation . . . for the unbridled
incoherence of this existence of ours, it is then . . . that we shall realise in
its entirety, that we shall in short come to know with any degree of accu-
racy . . . What was I saying? I seem to have lost the thread."
    "Friendship."
    "That was it, of course. I'm sorry. That we shall realise what friendship
means to each one of us and all of us, and how it was that, and that only,
that made it all worth while."
    "Made what worth while?"
    "Everything," he said.
    "As, for instance?"
    "I'm not a religious chap. I don't know anything about that sort of
thing. But there must be something beyond all this sex business."
    "Yes."
    "You think so?"
    "Oh yes. Quite likely. Why not?" [Atwater says] "But what?"
    "I can't help."
    "You can't."
    Atwater said: "But what has made you so depressed?"
    "Depressed?"
    "Yes, depressed."
    Fotheringham finished his drink at a gulp. He said:
    "I suppose I must have sounded rather depressed. You see I had rather
a heavy lunch." (61–63)

Here is the worldview of Atwater and Pringle, Susan and Harriet,
articulated at last—but in caricature. From "A million barmaids all
saying the same thing" and from "Drink . . . so nasty one can hardly
get it down," there seems to Fotheringham, in his optimism, one
escape: "'Ah,' said Fotheringham, 'America. But the date isn't actually
fixed yet'" (60). Susan, too, leaves for America, but the structure of the
novel denies Atwater that last exit. For America's gaiety is represented
by Scheigan, the drunken publisher, and America's love by the girl
whom Undershaft has left; and Undershaft, the pioneer of their circle,
has come full circle back from New York to London and is sleeping
with Lola as the novel ends. The year has come full circle, as Atwater
enters the club where we first met him, where another party is beginning its cycle and an effeminate stranger is to have the last, acidic
word on Susan: "She's very attractive in her way. . . . But too individual to be chic really" (221).

Venusberg

Anthony Powell's second novel *Venusberg* (1932) is both the most satiric of the early novels and the least successful. Most of the action takes place in an unidentified Baltic capital that resembles Riga (especially in the German *ritter,* or Tannhäuser, tradition that helps give the novel its title); but in its homogeneity the country is Ruritanian; and Ruritania (any imaginary European state where a romance may be staged), when it came to novel writing, was young Oxford's worst addiction. Graham Greene's second novel, *The Name of Action* (1931), similarly loses power as it moves "abroad" to an area that is unidentifiable, however much the French occupied Moselle-Trier region in the 1920s may have been in the back of Greene's mind. When the cable is cut, as Henry James observed, the balloon has a tendency to drift from reality; and Powell's "reality" would have been worth keeping in range.

The satiric object of *Venusberg* is "modernism," but its structure is conventionally triangular and thus seems at first a bit old-fashioned. In London we find a young journalist (Lushington) in love with a divorcée (Lucy) who in turn is hopelessly in love with the journalist's friend (Da Costa). Da Costa is so shy that to escape Lucy he has fallen back on family connections to secure a post as attaché at a Baltic capital. As the novel opens, Lushington, "who believed implicitly in eventual progress on a scientific basis," is being dispatched to the same Baltic capital by a press lord who shares his faith in progress. Foreign correspondents, the editor proclaims, have "taken the place of the old diplomat. Better educated. Better informed. Better paid. And of course, more reliable. But they carry on the same fine tradition" (1).

The actual structure of the novel, not the conventional triangle, is foreshadowed when Lushington meets an aging German baroness aboard the ship from Copenhagen who tells not only Lushington's fortune but that of a professor's wife and that of a Russian count whom he has met aboard. Count Scherbatcheff interrupts the fortune-telling on seeing the ace of spades: "Ah, yes, I see. You need not explain it. The card of death. My poor grandmother. I knew that it must come sooner or later. But . . . In spite of her obstinacy I am quite attached to her" (15). The count is a comic characterization of some merit (100), but there is perhaps too distinct a touch of Waugh's character Little Lord Tangent as we intermittently follow his growing illness (129) to the ironically powerful scene in which his grandmother walks through the slush to the cemetery to bury him (140).

The Baltic capital seems a cross between the world of Beerbohm's *Zuleika Dobson* and of Eliot's *The Waste Land,* an "unreal city" with a sky-line as illusive as "the dreaming spires of Oxford" (82), but the vista changes into that of abandoned apartment houses with rusting cranes still perched on their steel skeletons and dreary wastes of petrol cans between them. "The new railway station," a symbol of national pride, is "designed on a substratum of modernismus, with pylons and tumid, angular caryatids . . . in red stone . . . and it stood out uncompromising-ly against the sky" (42).

As uncompromisingly modern is the professor of psychology whose "spruce animal" of a wife Lushington had taken to bed on the boat. Professor Panteleimon Marvin is delighted to demonstrate his advanced views when a stranger later asks his wife to tango. "Woman has become her own master," he says (to his wife's lover). "And," Lushington replies, "very often someone else's mistress." The professor, delighted, copies down the wit that, at convocation, will "no doubt add in some measure to my popularity" (145). He later comes (in Restoration comedy fashion) to his wife's lover for counsel on love. That encounter ends when the Professor egoistically struggles to estab-lish his theory that his wife must be in love with Da Costa and is thus flirting with Lushington because she subconsciously suspects some sex-ual attachment between the two Englishmen and is jealously trying to break them up. Although the Professor has "always been a steadfast upholder of advanced thought," as he explains, the intricacies of life occasionally force him to be, in this fashion, unorthodox. He interprets Lushington's stunned reaction to a naive Englishman's shock that a married woman could love someone other than her husband, the English being by national reputation naïve. In Restoration mood again, the lover shortly thereafter orders his mistress to show more respect for her husband.

Lushington is a journalist, and Powell's novel could have antici-pated Waugh's *Scoop* (1938) in raking journalism over the satiric coals; and there are a few bits in *Venusberg* about Lushington as for-eign correspondent sending "long expensive cables to the paper which subsequently appeared in two lines." But the satiric eye focus-es instead on the diplomatic world of Da Costa. The French ambas-sador's corpulent wife derives her only fun in life from being rude to the German minister.

The American minister is seen at a nightclub "energetically lower-ing his country's prestige": "The tongue of Shakespeare and *The*

Saturday Evening Post is good enough for us and you can take it from me, Colonel—and you, Viscount, you bear this in mind too—if people are worth talking to they talk English" (155). The American minister has a Texan mannerism of pointing his finger at people and of saying Bang! or Pop!—habits that embarrass the southern gentleman who assists him.

Curtis Cortney, this quiet American, comes "from the New World, where we still try to retain our homely code of morals." But, like Fotheringham in *Afternoon Men,* Cortney is the parody-*raisonneur* and does a clearer job of caricaturing the traditional values upon which the novel rests than Lushington does of rediscovering them: "Now in America, I hope not too late, we are realising what a sacred institution the home is and how it is threatened by the stress of modern life" (64). Typically, he is the only character in the novel to use the word *aristocrat;* and each time he confounds the real aristocrat with the bogus. But he remains a stock figure, much like his own concept of the English gentleman. "How will it feel when the Recording Angel calls your bluff for the last time?" may be American idiom, but it is not that of a southern gentleman, however fatuous (177).

That the knight Tannhäuser was once held in thrall by Venus the novel's epigraph from Baedeker reminds us; and the climax of the novel comes on the night of the annual ball at the House of the Knights. All the diplomatic and social world is assembled, all but Professor Panteleimon, who is said to be at home with a migraine. Breaking out of enthrallment—but for no very satisfactory reason on the literal level— Lushington sends the professor's wife home with Da Costa as escort, at about the time General Kuno, the power behind the president of the country and a very unpopular man, leaves the ball. Apparently mistaking the drosky of Da Costa for that of General Kuno, "assailants" open fire and kill Da Costa (as the baroness had foretold). The assassins also kill the professor's wife. Lushington at last gets his "scoop" and returns victorious to London.

But whether the professor was actually at home, or whether, among the "many unprogressive prejudices" he confesses to having retained in spite of reason, revenge for cuckoldry is one—and has made Da Costa the stand-in for Lushington instead of for General Kuno (as Lushington reports to the world)—the novel does not make clear. A suspicion is aroused, without being laid to rest. Untidy.

We last see Lushington back in London with Lucy looking over the foggy Thames. The doorman at the News Palace has been eyeing Lucy,

she notices: "I expect he thinks I'm a tart," she says. And the novel closes with Lushington's acidic reply: "I was just wondering."

In view of Lushington's conduct, his last remark seems more prig-
gish than "disenthralled." The novel had begun by quoting Baedeker
on the Venusberg: "Here according to popular tradition, is the grotto
of Venus, into which she enticed the knight Tannhäuser; fine view from
the top." We end the novel *Venusberg* feeling that we have indeed
toured a Venusberg, but have not in the end been given a "fine view
from the top."

From a View to a Death

Anthony Powell's third novel, *From a View to a Death* (1933), draws its
title from the words to the song "John Peel," the music of which is the
traditional signal at hunt balls that the last dance is about to begin.
Although the title may seem to freight the novel with nostalgia, the
periphery of the novel turns toughly contrapuntal when the epigraph
quotes two lines from the song about the fox hunter's pursuit of the fox:
"From a find to a check, from a check to a view / From a view to a death
in the morning." Nowhere in the novel are the human correspondences
made overt. But the roles of hunter and hunted in the sporting world
can be superimposed with multiple ironies on the "views" and "checks"
of Powell's protagonists in the social world.

From a View to a Death opens, like Aldous Huxley's *Crome Yellow*
(1921), with the arrival of a young man at an English country house.
The young man (the fox, so to speak) is an artist named Arthur Zouch,
bearded and dressed in the hippie style of the day with "conventional
unconventionality." "He was ambitious, naturally, and painted bright,
lifeless portraits that would have been hung in the Academy if he had
sent them there but which he preferred to show in smaller galleries having the reputation for being modern." As a painter, he is second rate:
"He had some skill in catching a likeness, and this, combined with a
simple colour formula and an instinct for saying the sort of thing that
sitters expected of a painter, caused him to be spoken of as promising."[10]
What singles out Zouch from the run of mediocre artists is his recent
conception of himself as a Nietzschean Ubermensch, or Superman.

With this novel Powell modifies his technique. The point of view is
not that of a single character, as in earlier novels, but is authorial. That
is, evaluations of characters are made, not merely left to be inferred,
from the author's point of view, and the author's values are expressed

with clarity, however dryly. The evaluations of Zouch already quoted might have been made by the character of Betty Passenger—the elder, tougher sister of Mary Passenger, whom Zouch is pursuing—for she has to some degree Powell's own terse and unsentimental wit, but as the novel develops only the omniscient eye of an author could keep us apprised of the values underlying all the situations. Later in The Music of Time Powell was to solve the problem of combining depth with objectivity by creating as narrator Nicholas Jenkins, a man of keen percipience and tireless patience in matters of speculation and introspection.

One of the last scenes in *Venusberg* had shown Lushington, as a captive audience on the ship back to Copenhagen, listening to a bogus Russian count's solution to the "Woman Problem":

> "A good friend of mine, a Brazilian, once told me that the rich men in his country, when they smoke a cigar, take only the first two or three puffs. Then they throw the cigar away. Those puffs are the best and when they want more they can buy another cigar. Sometimes I think that it is good to be with girls as my friend was with his cigars. It is the sentimental who do most harm in this world of ours. You are no doubt familiar with the works of Nietzsche?" (183)

That Zouch conceives of himself as a superman ready to use women a few times and then throw them away is so far known only to a few women in his life. Others "would learn all in good time; and to their cost. Meanwhile he went on his way, taking but not giving, treating life as a sort of quick-lunch counter where you helped yourself and all the snacks are free" (12). At the moment he is congratulating himself for having looked ahead and charmed a country-house invitation from a young lady he met at the house of a London patron.

Mary Passenger, the young lady (or chicken number one), had made her debut some years before; but dancing and hunting have palled, and she has taken, with some unfortunate Madame Bovary side effects, to art. She likes Zouch "because he talked to her about persons who earned their living by writing or painting, and in this way he represented to her a world with which she had no first-hand contacts. She was not really interested in these subjects, but then for that matter neither was Zouch, and it made a nice change for her." Zouch has accepted her invitation for the "weekend" with the picaresque intention of extending his stay, by dint of charm, through the dull London summer, and he finds Passenger Court, at the end of a drive lined by gaunt lime trees, lovely. He finds Mary on the croquet lawn above the lake.

The Passengers are better fixed socially than financially. The family money came from Georgian successes, and *"mariages de convenance* of an earlier generation had left them related, even if distantly, to almost everyone of any importance in the world in which they lived" (43). A grandfather had served in Gladstone's cabinet and had turned down a peerage. But "for several generations none of them had had any clear idea of how to manage their business affairs and the family had become accustomed to having less and less money as the years went on" (13). Their townhouse near Belgrave Square (good) is "barely habitable on account of its draughts" (bad). On the other hand, their country house Passenger Court is comfortably graced with good food, but is "of no architectural interest" (14). And at Passenger Court is played out the classic comedy of the pretender hoist with his own petard.

When Zouch meets his host Mr. Passenger (the fox hunter, as it turns out) he recognizes at once another "superman," despite the fact that history recorded only the melancholy fact that Mr. Passenger had hitherto been consistently a failure:

> As a young man he had become tired of London society and had gone out to the Boer war as a volunteer, but a few days after his arrival in South Africa he had nearly died of measles. When he came back to England and before he had fully recovered his health he began to edit the works of a seventeenth-century minor poet. But his convalescence had allowed him little time for research and the edition was found on publication to contain so many errors that he withdrew the whole of it at his own expense. This incident had given him a distaste for the life of the mind from which he had never wholly recovered.

Having felt pro-German sympathies at the beginning of World War I, "it was no wonder that he was often morose" (30).

The belligerent Passenger is most happy when he can spend an afternoon "pottering round the town and aggravating some of his bêtes noires among the local tradesmen." Conflict with his guest Zouch, obviously a Bohemian artist, is almost automatic and is conducted by the rules of oneupmanship: "Mr. Passenger took every possible advantage that accrued to him on account of his age, position, and the fact that he was host, while in return Zouch presumed on his own standing as a guest, allowed himself considerable latitude of behaviour on account of his profession, and extracted the utmost from his status as Young Man" (42). Mr. Passenger, as a descendant of Whigs, is a bit given to self-pity.

"Mentally he compares himself to King Lear. A Lear without a Cordelia" (178). His elder daughter, Betty, has made a disastrous marriage to an Italian duke—Umberto, Duca di Civitacampomoreno—who abandoned her on learning she was not wealthy, possibly for "the lads at the Boeuf," and Passenger's younger daughter, Mary, has taken to art and invited a bearded painter into his home.

It is in the 1930s, and Zouch is beginning to sense that his beard is growing dated "and that with a newly acquired social consciousness he would soon do better with bare cheeks." To "do better" is what Zouch wants: power, not integrity. What intellectual curiosity he has stems from the aphorism that knowledge is power (95); and he dislikes the elder Passengers "with their eccentricities and prejudices about ambition, which he himself had always imagined to be a virtue" (131). He even has faith—among this fox-hunting crowd, a fatal trust—that "The will to power should teach him how to ride" (142). But he is essentially more philistine than his hosts. Betty Passenger's Bohemian language outrages him, for she is of the upper class yet speaks like "any little model of his acquaintance" (36).

Betty is among those who are at home where Mayfair and Bohemia overlap. Partaking of both Mary and Zouch, she quickly realizes their incongruity. "You're more like one of my friends," she remarks to Zouch. "I thought Mary only liked young men in the Foreign Service or the Brigade. She's always been terribly shocked by the people I know." She makes a joke of Zouch instead of opposing him, as her father does, with dreams of violence. Her sense of humor, as a matter of fact, is the keenest in the novel; and, despite the strict objectivity of Powell's technique, the author clearly finds her most sympathetic. Stranded with her daughter Bianca under the somewhat hostile wing of her father, she occupies a middle ground between her egoistic elders and her idealistic juniors.

When Zouch mentions her father's kindness in furnishing him with a "mount" for the fox hunt to come, Betty replies with frank good humor:

> "Oh, it isn't kindness with father, it's cruelty. Absolutely pathological, I can assure you."
>
> Zouch laughed heartily, thinking that what Betty said was all too true.
>
> "I haven't been on a horse for eighteen months," he said conversationally, and without any reference to actual fact.
>
> Betty said: "I haven't for eighteen years and it will be eighteen centuries before I do again."

"But, dear," said Mrs. Passenger mildly, "you used to like your pony so much when you were a child."

"I know," said Betty, "I know. But look how I've ended up. I'm a warning to all girls who like animals." (170)

The big event of Zouch's visit, as it lengthens into the summer, is a pageant held in commemoration of King Charles II's visit to the town 150 years before: the "Restoration Restored." Betty appropriately is to play Nell Gwyn. Big-hearted, she invites Joanna Brandon, the daughter of a relatively poor neighbor, to stay at Passenger Court for the festival.

Joanna Brandon (chicken number two) is toward the lower end of the social pecking order—the Passengers have a butler, chauffeur, gardener, maids; the Brandons have only a woman of all work—but Joanna is in society, local society; and Zouch has already spotted her at church. When Betty notices his roving eye and he protests that the girl's physical beauty means nothing to him except as a subject for his art, Betty laughs: "Well, you must be different from all the other painters I've ever met" (78).

Although Joanna has been courted by the local golfer, she dreams of escaping from her "provincial" mother to the art world of London. The widow of a naval officer, Mrs. Brandon has withdrawn from life and spends her days reclining on a sofa, "wearing a negligee of yellow material edged with fur," rereading "her favourite book, *The Story of San Michele*," and wondering why all books are not beautiful:

"Why don't writers only write about the beautiful things of life? You know, Joanna, there is so much beauty all round us."

"What's happened to the dogs? Why aren't they here?"

"Poor Spot has been sick."

"Again?"

"It was the mutton. . . . It was too stringy."

"I'll take him to the vet on Monday."

"Poor Spot must go see doctor. Give him nasty physic. Hand mother a cigarette, darling."

"I saw the young man staying with the Passengers. He has got a beard. It looks funny. But he seems rather nice."

"When I first met your father . . . he wore a beard . . . . He looked like a Greek god. I remember once saying that to Vernon Passenger and him saying, 'And he used to behave like one too.' Wasn't that a tribute? From someone as critical as Vernon Passenger, too." (54–55)

On his exploratory visit to the Brandon home Zouch leads Joanna to the garden house while her mother lies asleep: but he is rejected. Some instinctual mechanism in Joanna operates, but its operation later seems irrational to her: "Her conduct had been of the very kind which in theory she most despised. She thought of her favourite heroine, Marie Bashkirtseff, and also about Madame Bovary. . . . And then there was the whole of D. H. Lawrence's works. Besides she now knew that she was in love with Zouch" (123). Accordingly, she writes him a letter to apologize for her prudish conduct.

Betty Passenger's invitation to Joanna to stay with the Passengers during the Restoration pageant opens the free-lunch counter, and Joanna that night welcomes Zouch to her bed.

The next day, Mary Passenger, convinced that her "unreal" dream "about a tall husband with a country house" has been adequately replaced with a realistic concept of herself as "a fashionable painter's wife," presses Zouch into proposing to her. Consequently, when Joanna learns after her return home of Zouch's engagement to Mary, she wonders "whether this was called having your heart broken." She mounts to her room and cries. Later she remembers that "it was early closing day so that she had to go out and do the shopping after all" (155).

The Restoration pageant at which Zouch seduces Joanna enlists a third neighboring family, the Fosdicks—defined socially as having both a cook and a handyman—and introduces us to the second of the three social events around which the novel is organized: a cocktail party at the local pub, the Fox and Hounds, given by Torquil Fosdick. Torquil has been sent down from Oxford for a term, having failed an examination; but he had gained a reputation at his small college, someone having entered his room and smelled incense. "Torquil will be a great success in life," his mother says to Zouch. "We thought he would probably do well in the Diplomatic. . . . and then they say that they are getting a very nice type of young man in the B.B.C. now, and besides there's no examination for that" (132). Torquil enjoys knowing Betty is a duchess, "even though it might be only a Neapolitan one," and her talk baffles and excites him, while his bungling ineptitude brings out her maternal streak:

> "Oh, but, Betty, you can't say that. You've lived. You've had adventures. Known famous people! I'm still at Oxford."
> "That doesn't matter," Betty said. "It doesn't depend on what you've done. Look at Mary. She's never had any experience but she knows how to look after herself far better than I do. Look at Jasper. He's had plenty of experience and look what he is, even though he is your brother, my pet."

Torquil felt that he was getting into deep water. He said: "Anyway, I want to live too."

"You shall," said Betty. "One of these days I'll take you out and show you people and then you'll be able to judge for yourself. You can choose what you like from the whole cockeyed world."

This sort of talk made Torquil quite breathless. (62)

When later Betty proposes to Torquil "to cheer him up," she does so with no conviction that matrimony will ensue.

Their fathers hold a long-standing grudge. It began when Major Fosdick secured a lease on the North Copse of the Passenger estate, and since then Vernon Passenger has been convinced the major is ruining the area:

"He shoots all my game, his wife is for ever bothering me about the thousand and one committees that she sits on, his eldest son does nothing but ride on my hounds, and as for that boy Torquil—"

Mr. Passenger stopped . . . trying to find words strong enough. . . .

Mrs. Passenger folded up the piece of work she had in her hand and looked across, a little hopelessly, at her husband. . . . Betty said:

"Now, father, you mustn't say anything against Torquil. I like him very much."

"You like him?"

"Of course I do."

Mr. Passenger said: "He's the worst of the lot." (171)

When Betty blurts out that she is engaged to Torquil, "Even Zouch was outraged." In a splendidly comic bit of slow motion, Mr. Passenger shakes out his newspaper, folds it up carefully, tucks it with controlled fury under his arm, and walks out, pausing only long enough to say: "It is unbelievable" (172).

The articulation of the novel is subtle. Passenger has been annoyed for years by the very appearance of Torquil's father Major Fosdick, who has "the air of a legendary creature of the woods, Herne the Hunter almost, with a touch of the romantic gamekeeper, some Lady Chatterley's super-annuated lover, and yet at the same time he looked more of a country gentleman than perhaps any country gentleman could ever hope to look" (15). Passenger drives in a fury to Fosdick's to demand that the major assist him in breaking off the engagement; and, as he waits for the door to be opened, he conjures up a vision of the major in jodhpurs, carrying a crop, "dressed like the Old Squire in a melodrama" (177).

At the pageant Major Fosdick had stuffily objected to any changing of dress in public, even to have him portray the puritan General Monk: "It's absurd at my age. Dressing me up like this. I feel a regular figure of fun" (135). He is truculent about the North Copse largely because of class pride: "Just because they happen to have made a few good business deals in land at the time of George III I don't see why I should kowtow to them" (51).

But the major treads the hairline of sanity: he exists for the afternoons he can lock himself in his room and compose himself for writing poetry by donning a sequined dress and "singing and muttering a little to himself. Lately he had become very careless about the rest of his household finding out about his eccentricities" (155). At times he worries about this carelessness: "The more disciplined side of his nature told him that he would soon be going too far but there was also something in him which made him enjoy these risks of discovery" (156).

Alone in the house on the day Mr. Passenger learns of the engagement of his daughter to the major's son, the major had felt cold in his thin dress. Wrapping "round his shoulders the antimacassar from the top of one of the drawing room chairs," he had begun to write verse in an exercise book. He has stopped to seek a book on the breeding of retrievers from the downstairs hallway when Mr. Passenger impatiently opens the door (174).

Passenger had called the major insane for some years, yet he is surprised at discovering him in feminine attire. With dignity, as they face each other, the major opens talk by mentioning the North Copse: "I have been thinking it over, Passenger, and I have decided that you have a just cause of complaint about North Copse." They complete the transaction like gentlemen, but Passenger leaves "overcome by a sense of failure. He had not risen to the situation. As a superman he had let himself down. In this moment of emergency he had been thrown back on the old props of tradition and education and when he might have enjoyed a substantial revenge he had behaved with all the restraint in the world." He drives home slowly. "It had been a bad day" (181). The next we hear of Major Fosdick he has been taken to a sanitarium; Passenger's involuntary, "gentlemanly reprieve" has been to no avail.

Mary has hopes that a return to Passenger Court in the autumn accompanied by Zouch, now clean-shaven and pink-coated for the fox hunts, will change her father's attitude toward their engagement. As destiny has it, she comes down with a cold the week of the hunts. Zouch repeatedly postpones riding in hopes of making his debut backed up by

Mary, but he is "aware that every time he refused, it scored a point to
Mr. Passenger's hand"; and he finally agrees to ride. The following day,
stoked with whiskey to steady his nerves, he mounts Creditor. "Ah, 'e's a
playful little rogue, 'e is," the diabolical-looking groom says. The cold air
makes Zouch "feel all at once a little muzzy." The "leathers look to me a
trifle short for you," Mr. Passenger says to give him fair warning. The
road has a coating of light frost; and a large bus comes suddenly out of
the haze:

> "These things are the curse of the roads," said Mr. Passenger.
> "There seem to be a great many of them round here."
> "Far too many. Keep an eye on Creditor. He hates buses."
> They drew in a little to the side of the road, Zouch in front.
> The bus came rolling past. A cluster of putty-coloured faces looked
> out at them from behind glass. Zouch felt Creditor quivering under his
> weight. He tightened his hold on the reins. Creditor gave several quiet
> snorts. The bus passed on and Zouch relaxed his hold again. They walked
> on along the road. And then, quite suddenly, without any warning,
> Creditor was off. (195)

Passenger has shown up Zouch's pretensions to horsemanship, but all
might yet have gone well had the horse not slipped on the frost: "Zouch
came off, landing on his head."

At the beginning of the next chapter, the crowd at the Fox and
Hounds is discussing the death of Zouch—"one of those shapeless enti-
ties torn out of the abyss of time" (196).

At the Brandons', meanwhile, Joanna's mother is lamenting, as usual,
the state of her health, blaming inconsiderate doctors who tell her that
except for her heart trouble, there is nothing wrong with her; complaints
the maid, Mrs. Dadds, has heard before:

> "To-day I feel very weak. I shan't last much longer. I shall be gone
> soon. I don't expect I shall see another summer."
> Mrs. Dadds said: "We're none of us getting any younger. What's
> more there's a great deal of sickness about . . . and there's Miss Joanna
> looking as white as chalk . . . and my pains have been something terrible.
> . . . I've had to stop sometimes and sit down in a chair." (201)

The maid-of-all-work keeps talking for a while, wandering on to the
subject of her own husband, in her opinion a "sex-maniac," and his
funeral: "'Day of Wrath! 0 day of mourning! See fulfilled the prophet's

warning!' They played that and I shan't forget it if I live to be a thousand. I thought, You're getting your deserts by now, my man." After some time she starts to get back to her work:

> She was an unobservant woman and did not notice that her mistress was dead. She made a few more remarks about human nature, illustrating them from incidents from her late husband's career, and, as these called forth no response from Mrs. Brandon, she concluded that . . . Mrs. Brandon preferred sleep that afternoon to conversation. . . . Talking to someone who was asleep . . . cheapened her. She went back to the kitchen in a rebellious mood. (203)

At Passenger Court Betty's father is expressing relief at getting control of North Copse again:

> "It was annoying to have old Fosdick shooting at my birds. It was more than annoying. It was maddening."
> "It drove him mad anyway," Betty said.
> "You should not joke about that sort of thing, Betty. That is one of the sides of you which I can never understand. You never seem to be serious." (206)

More evidence that her father disapproves of her continued sojourn at Passenger comes after he leaves the room. Asked by Betty why the cigarette box is empty, the butler replies that her father has given orders that no more cigarettes are to be put out. Before the butler withdraws, she recalls a last relic of Zouch and asks him to "take the picture of Miss Mary off the easel in the old school room and hide it somewhere. I see that Miss Bianca has painted a moustache on the face." The novel ends as Betty, left alone, goes "to her father's desk to look for the cigar-box."

Comic to the end, pure in tone, beautifully written, acute in its depiction of society, and wise in its understanding of human nature, *From a View to a Death* is a small masterpiece.

Agents and Patients

T. S. Eliot argues in his essay "Tradition and the Individual Talent" that since "no poet, no artist of any art, has his complete meaning alone," the historical sense is "nearly indispensable to any one who would continue to be a poet beyond his twenty-fifth year." In Powell's fourth novel, *Agents and Patients* (1936), he seems to be taking Eliot's advice and to be looking back into history for "private admirations" to bring freshness of form to his materials. The branch of the English comic tradition next essayed at any rate is the one enriched by Ben Jonson in Shakespeare's time, the tradition of coney-catching comedy.

Coney-catching comedy goes back to Roman times. The fun of such drama derives from seeing a naïve young man (or a self-important old man) being (or about to be) fleeced by sharpsters. The comic tension is that between cat and mouse: the country bumpkin or rube comes wide-eyed into the city and is offered an opportunity to buy the Tower of London or the Brooklyn Bridge. Of course it would not be a comedy if the sharpsters were not overconfident and the "victim" not shrewd or lucky enough in the end to turn the tables and escape.

In Elizabethan drama, the potential victim came to be called the bunny-rabbit (or coney), and the would-be predator the coney-catcher. The pleasure seems to derive from the game, or the potential of reversal as the bunny seems to be blundering into danger.

To the Roman tradition Ben Jonson added a new ruse, the "latest science," alchemy, to bamboozle the innocent. The city slicker proffers the art of changing brick to gold, and the coney is asked to part with his money in exchange for the secret of the art. In the 1930s the "latest science" was psychiatry, so the coney has to be persuaded that he is in need of (expensive) psychiatric guidance. The latest art was no longer mere photography but the documentary film, which the rich gull can be shamed into supporting for the glory of art. In the widely acclaimed documentary *Nanook of the North* (1922), for instance, Robert Flaherty had visited an Eskimo village and with "great realism" had let the cameras roll as the Eskimos went about their daily lives, fishing, eating, and sleeping. An art form? The debate was in progress.

But that both the new science and the new art might support quacks or imposters was obvious enough, and Powell supplies us with an unlicensed "psychiatrist" and a would-be documentary filmmaker, both hungry and both unscrupulous about using the prestige of Science and Art to ease their way through the world. The action begins when a rich and innocent victim who honors Science and Art comes onto the scene, the point of contact being "modern," too, as the pedestrian is struck by a motorcar.

Powell has always had a weakness for dividing the population of the world into those who act and those who are acted upon; and he finds in John Wesley's sermons an operative line to serve as the novel's epigraph: "So in every possible case; He that is not free is not an Agent, but a

Patient." At first glance, the coney, or chief "patient" seems to be a young man just down from Oxford named Blore-Smith.

But from the first, Blore-Smith is not a "patient" simple enough to reduce the plot to farce. He has dignity; caution is mingled with his impulses toward rash action; and, like the character Erridge later in The Music of Time, he is aware of his gullibility in a general way and, like an educated bunny, tries to avoid coney-catchers. He has started "reading for the Bar, but he was not much interested in law and did it to have something to tell people when they questioned him about himself" (6). He has taken rooms in Ebury Street—a section of Belgravia steeped in art tradition; he has mounted his Medici prints and a reproduction of Van Gogh's *Sunflower;* and he spends "enjoyable" evenings there reading Roger Fry's *Vision and Design.* But he feels constricted by life and longs for "freedom."

The novel opens with the coffee-house talk of the coney-catchers (the "agents" of the title), picaros of some education and social standing in the modern manner; and the novel closes with a poker player's demand to see the winner's openers. Thereupon, one of them—with at least a touch of symbolism—flicks two knaves [Jacks] across the table. Oliver Chipchase, knave number one, is a bachelor engaged nocturnally (as his surname suggests) in the pursuit of low women; he is engaged by day as an art critic and amateur psychiatrist. He has even "published a short book on psychoanalysis in relation to automatic writing, but its sales had not been large."[11]

Knave number two, Peter Maltravers, has also dabbled in journalism—it "left both of them with its attendant paranoiac leanings"—but at present he is a scenarist for an English film company with a contract to work in Berlin, an intrigue to get himself to Hollywood, and a scheme to produce a revolutionary documentary film of his own. The documentary trend is the latest in the cinema world, he explains to Chipchase: "Russian peasants acting Russian peasants. Chinese looking oriental. . . . My extension of it is to collect a cast of . . . intellectuals . . . and watch them behave intellectually. All I need is a little backing" (3–4).

The three young men—Blore-Smith, Chipchase, and Maltravers—meet after Chipchase wheels his car around a corner and knocks Blore-Smith down. Finding Blore-Smith uninjured, Chipchase takes him along to a picture gallery and discovers that Blore-Smith is wealthy when he nervously blurts out acceptance of the first price asked for a painting. Encouraged by Chipchase, Blore-Smith reveals his secret desires:

> "London is such a disappointment," Blore-Smith said. . . . "One doesn't seem to get any of the things one expected."
> "What sort of things?"
> "Well, I mean life and so on."
> "But you seem to get plenty of excitement. For instance, I've just knocked you down in my car."
> "Oh, I don't mean things like that," Blore-Smith said. He hesitated. "Women," he said, and then he felt that he had gone too far. (32)

With this clue, Maltravers takes Blore-Smith to a flower shop called la cattleya (in the Firbank-Proustian vein), managed by "the most beautiful woman you have ever seen."[12] The beautiful Mrs. Mendoza, however, is threatening to move to Basra: "I shouldn't have everybody nagging at me there, living on my vitality, telling me all about themselves and their beastly affairs, and . . . never giving me a moment's peace. Nor should I have to look after this wretched shop. . . . Why, Peter, she said, how are you, darling? I heard the bell and thought it must be a customer" (35).

Mrs. Mendoza's backer in the flower business has begun to tire her, a Commodore Hugo Venables; he is portly and cheerful but exasperatingly unable to pick out a cigarette lighter of modern design. Like Susan Nunnery, Mrs. Mendoza is attractive mentally as well as physically. "You always want everybody's individuality taken away from them," she says to Chipchase. But Chipchase recognizes trouble in her fatigue and spirits Blore-Smith away to Maltravers's flat.

Maltravers's wife is out with a racing motorist named Nipper, with her husband's tacit consent, theirs being a "modern" menage; but Maltravers, to make room for Blore-Smith, reveals his irritation by throwing the manuscript of a novel she is writing on the floor. Blore-Smith is entranced upon meeting Sarah. When she later visits his flat and sighs, "Isn't life awful," he blurts out a proposition: "Will you be my mistress?" (115). Sarah laughs and reports the proposal to her husband and Chipchase.

> "But, I say," said Chipchase. "What frightful cheek! Did he really now?"
> "I believe you put him up to it," Sarah said.
> "My dear, don't be so absurd. . . . He must have gone off his head."
> "What do you mean?" said Maltravers. "I hope you aren't trying to suggest that Sarah isn't attractive."

"This isn't a moment for your habitual bad taste," Chipchase said. "It's a preposterous thing to have happened."

"But I like my wife to have successes. It gives me confidence in myself."

"Is that really all you have to say?" Sarah said.

"What else do you expect me to say, darling? What did you do anyway?"

"I didn't do anything. I was laughing too much."

"There you are. You treat the thing as a joke yourself and then expect me to be furious." (118–19)

This is not a comedy about marital infidelity, as the Noel Coward tone here might suggest, but a comedy about the absurd discrepancy between the characters' feelings and their principles, their "primitive" instincts and their "up-to-date" rationalisms. In the course of a minute, the values have been reversed. Maltravers grows indignant at the thought of Blore-Smith's income and his wife's callous neglect: "You only laughed at him! You stand there discussing a man who is admittedly such a mass of nerves that he had to get Oliver here to put him right psychologically and . . . you only laughed at him. . . . You've probably done irreparable damage" (120).

Chipchase induces Blore-Smith to be his "patient" by alluding to ominous symptoms and allowing time to prey upon his worries. The psychoanalysis stays on the surface of Blore-Smith's mind, so far as the novel is concerned, with couch sessions beginning as chapters end ("Have you had any more dreams about the Prime Minister . . . ?"). Persuading Blore-Smith that he needs "psychic release," Chipchase gets him to underwrite an expedition to Paris, where Chipchase hopes to regain a lost girlfriend.

American artists discussing their conquests loudly at the Dome, drunken Continental aristocrats *A la Vache enragé,* frescoes "conceived in a spirit of complete moral detachment" Chez Zouzou, various homosexuals, and a girl named Yoyo lead Blore-Smith into the life that Torquil Fosdick had longed for in *From a View to a Death.*[13] That Yoyo makes off with Blore-Smith's wallet can be chalked up to "buying experience," Chipchase assures him as they return to London with a new secretary (the girl Chipchase sought) who has been hired to take notes on Blore-Smith's "case."

Maltravers, on the other hand, begins his assault on Blore-Smith's money by maneuvering him into admitting that he believes the cinema to be "the most living of the arts":

"Once decided you will not be able to turn back," Maltravers said. "Think it over. Do you want to spend your money in the cause of Beauty? Wouldn't you rather invest in something more gilt-edged?"

Blore-Smith made an effort to control himself. He muttered: "Is there anything more gilt-edged?"

Maltravers banged on the table so that the group of waiters posed near him all jumped at the same time like a perfectly trained corps de ballet.

"Excellent," Maltravers said. "Excellent."

Blore-Smith knew that for once he had said something worth saying. For perhaps the first time in his life he had come up to scratch. (50–51)

Berlin in the 1930s was the center of cinema considered as an art form, and second only to Hollywood in the number of films produced. The group, after leaving Paris, travels to the cinematic Berlin of Christopher Isherwood, but Powell's Berlin is seen through a different lens.[14] From the name of their hotel, the Sans Souci Palast, to the mostly transvestite clientele at the Eden Bar, an ironic eye surveys the Germany of the early 1930s—where, as Stephen Spender said urging a friend to join him there, "youth has started to live again, free of the shackles of the past and ossifying bourgeois conventions" (Lehmann, 176).

At the Eden Bar the beautiful Mrs. Mendoza overtakes Chipchase and Maltravers and charms Blore-Smith away from the epicene crowd. On a café terrace in the heart of this city of ultimate pagan "freedom," they sit together "for some time in silence watching a child prostitute with a face like a white mask, passing and repassing along the pavement below them":

"Do you know . . . why I should most like to have been born a man? . . . I could have learned Greek," Mrs. Mendoza said.

Blore-Smith caught his breath with surprise. . . .

"Is it too late to take lessons?" he said.

"Don't be absurd," Mrs. Mendoza said, so crossly that in order to cover his mistake as quickly as possible Blore-Smith added:

"Some of Herodotus was very amusing, I remember."

But Mrs. Mendoza was not listening.

"The Greeks knew how to live," she said. "If they heard music they danced; if they saw a stretch of golden sand they raced along it. . . . They were natural, beautiful, free. They didn't live horrible constricted fussy little lives like us."

Mrs. Mendoza clenched together her hands and held out her arms stiffly on either side of her, looking, Blore-Smith thought, like Artemis carved on the prow of a ship.

"Don't you like Berlin, then?" he said.
"Like it? I hate it. Every minute I stay here is sheer hell." (144–45)

The final action takes place at Broadacres, an English country house where Maltravers is about to shoot his film. The estate is owned by an art collector who hopes to keep a French aristocrat Gaston, Marquis de la Tour d'Espagne, amused with filmmaking while he dickers with him for the sale of his chateau full of ancestral art treasures. Maltravers has arranged "pictorially" a sizable number of intellectuals on the lawn of the estate with camera poised waiting for something "psychological" to develop—in order to begin his documentary film on the intellectuals—when a hoodless two-seater grumbles up the long curved drive.

Commodore Venables, abandoned by Mrs. Mendoza, drunk on the champagne he has brought to her cottage as a peace offering, and accompanied by the dismal medical student she had left to watch her cottage for days with nothing to eat but caviar—comes stumbling angrily across the field toward Mrs. Mendoza and the intellectuals just as an airplane swoops down to land in the polo field. The plane contains the agent of a rival art collector who persuades the French aristocrat to sell his ancestral art treasures to him. Gaston in turn quickly persuades Mrs. Mendoza to elope, and wheels to meet the pursuing Venables, charges like a goat to butt him in the stomach, and takes off with Mrs. Mendoza in the chauffeured airplane for Paris. "Cut!" shouts Maltravers to Chipchase, who has been working the camera.

The intellectuals have behaved like—intellectuals, or human beings at least; and Blore-Smith has disappeared. In the first unscrupulous act of his life, he commandeers a chauffeured car and is driven back to his rooms in Ebury Street. When Chipchase and Maltravers call on him later with their final bills, for the film production and for their psychiatric service, they assure him that he has had his money's worth: "You don't suggest . . . you would have had the courage to talk to me like this when we first met?" (212).

But though the novel ends with this cool detachment, the French aristocrat has stolen its emotional focus with his recitation of a poem[15]; the attractive Sarah Maltravers as a character has been lost to view; and the symbol of the chains Blore-Smith set out to break is lost. And classic aloofness is lost by Powell in what seems to be a catering to public taste. When Sarah (in her job as motoring correspondent for *Mode*) says, "I'm writing an article on French bodies," the author informs us that "Blore-Smith could hardly believe his ears" (112–13). Such underlined humor is at some remove from that which depends on recognition of clichés. Descents in style and structuring run counter to what now seems to be Powell's natural development; and *Agents and Patients* remains an interesting exhibit, but not a fine work of art.

What's Become of Waring

Three years elapsed before Anthony Powell's next novel appeared, and *What's Become of Waring* (1939) broke step with his aesthetic past in more radical ways than had *Agents and Patients*. And is a better novel for it. Two differences are fundamental: it has the comic incidents of the earlier novels but not the comic tone; the ironic denouements of a comic novel, but not the structure. As the title suggests, the novel, built on a question, is structured like a detective story to answer that question. A better analogue perhaps is A. J. A. Symons's book *The Quest for Corvo,* the fascination of which grows on the reader as Symons interviews people who knew the mysterious Baron Corvo, reads his letters, visits the scenes of his activity, and tries to fit the pieces together, only to unveil new puzzles.

The central figure of *What's Become of Waring* so far as the theme is concerned is a writer who appears in only one brief scene and then is revealed to have half-a-dozen aliases. But the central figure structurally is the narrator, a publisher's reader who manages, somehow gracefully, to exist throughout the novel without a name. Were any of the characters to address him by name, they might call him Jenkins; for *What's Become of Waring* is technically, as well as thematically, a precursor of The Music of Time. The theme of the tentative nature of most of what passes for human "knowledge" is here, though not yet generalized; and the mode is conversational and social.

As the narrator picks up bits of fact and pseudofact, he reveals only enough about himself to become a plausible character: he has moved from the advertising to the publishing business in order to have more time to work on his literary study, *Stendhal: And Some Thoughts on Violence* ("After three years the second chapter, 'Laughter Is Power,' remained uncompleted" [141]). Two brothers head the publishing firm, and the narrator is the "hired [manuscript] assassin" for the younger, Hugh Judkins, a man of Nonconformist background who is absurdly torn between the two alien strains of that tradition: the fundamentalist and the rationalist. Hugh seeks out spiritualists, for instance, and then tries to "expose" them (96, 224). His favorite author is a writer of inspirational travel books named T. T. Waring, whose style has the "woolly" quality "that appeals irresistibly to uncritical palates . . . tinny echoes of a biblical style" (27).

The novel opens when Hugh takes the narrator to a séance during which a medium called "Mimi" ("Don't forget that Mimi is George Eliot. We only call her Mimi because she asked us to" [24]) seems uncooperative. Mimi says only "tee-tee" during the course of the whole evening—but prophetically, it appears, when news headlines announce the death abroad of T. T. Waring.

As publishers of T. T. Waring's books, the brothers Judkins must decide who shall write his biography, and the narrator breaks their stalemate by introducing an admirer of the life of action Waring apparently has led, a Captain Hudson, who is writing his regiment's history in a cliché-free style. Captain Hudson's motive in undertaking the biography is financial and amatory: to speed his marriage to his fiancée, Beryl Pimley.

There is a skeleton in the Pimley family closet—Beryl's vanished brother, Alec. Alec had been a remittance man whose escapades annoyed his father, Major-General Pimley, Retired, and delighted his grandfather, Captain Pimley, Retired, who, outranked at home by his own son, supports underdogs wherever they can be found.

Hudson's first discovery is that his idol T. T. Waring has cleverly plagiarized much of his material from books "unlikely to be translated." When he makes this report to the narrator at a café in Southern France, the arm of coincidence (that later is a hallmark of The Music of Time) begins to arrange events. In a neighboring harbor town, Hudson and the narrator discover the missing brother, Alec Pimley. Under the name of Mason, he has married a rich American widow and is living on her yacht. As he attempts to conceal that change of identity, he reveals that he is also T. T. Waring, alias Robinson; and to escape his creditors he has announced his "death" as an author (after marrying the rich widow) by sending a cable to a New York newspaper.

Although Waring (or Robinson) promises to pay a minor debt the next day, when Captain Hudson and the narrator look back on the road to Toulon, they see his yacht moving out to sea.[16] Additional revelations come when we learn, after the death of Alec Pimley's grandfather, that the grandfather has all along concealed with delight the first act of plagiarism—Waring's purloining of Captain Pimley's own *Memoirs of Ceylon*—and with it the identity of T. T. Waring, his grandson Alec.

The novel ends with further comic twists. The younger publisher, Hugh Judkin, in a rationalist mood takes a young lady on a Scandinavian cruise and, when she holds him at bay, reverts to his fundamentalism and orders that the plates for a "hopelessly sprawling" American novel called *Lot's Hometown* be destroyed on the grounds that it is "muck." The yacht bearing Pimley-alias-Waring sinks in a storm, sending Waring to his death, whereby he not only "gives the world the slip" but also confirms the New York newspaper report that he drowned.

But *What's Become of Waring* as a whole lacks the humorous ambiance of the earlier novels. Powell at this point in his career seemed in danger of following Aldous Huxley from the comic into comic theory, from amusing the reader into patronizing the reader with descriptions of situations or people alleged to be amusing. He describes Hudson in Toulon, for instance, as looking "like an Englishman in a French caricature." Captain Hudson brings comic joy to the reader only structurally, when he departs at the end for "a camel" in Iraq and the life of action—action in the tradition of Richard Burton and Charles Doughty—that he and his "idol" T. T. Waring had lived only vicariously.

In *Afternoon Men* the Nietzschean painter Barlow enjoys manipulating Pringle; and the Nietzschean painter Zouch pursues his hopes of power through matrimony to the grave in *From a View to a Death*. But at the end of Powell's interwar novels, the narrator converts the question of what's become of Waring to the question of whether everyone seeks power, as he drifts off to sleep, a question that also points ahead to The Music of Time: "His schooldays. The masters had been a funny crowd. French. . . . It was power Hugh wanted too. Everybody wanted power. Bernard . . . Roberta. . . . It was an interesting question. . . . Was money power? . . . But . . . T. T. Waring wanted power more than any of them. . . . The milk arrived in the street, making a great clatter. . . . Sleep, like a long drink, came at last" (235–36).

Chapter Three
The Music of Time

A decade was to pass before Powell returned to creative writing. As the threat of war darkened over Europe, Powell tried to activate his reserve officer's commission and looked about for some form of writing that might still be done, if piecemeal, in possible interludes.

The Welsh antiquarian John Aubrey came to mind, a man who had much to give the world but whom the world had neglected. "Possibly even as far back as undergraduate days I had been interested in John Aubrey (1626–1697), antiquarian, biographer, folklorist, above all a writer in whom a new sort of sensibility is apparent, the appreciation of the oddness of the individual human being" (*Faces,* 88). No adequate biography of Aubrey had been written, and to write one in the midst of war seemed a task not only possible but congenial and worthy.

As early as February 1939 Powell began "preparations for war." Biography may not need sustained creativity, but it does need research. With his wife he made a motor-tour of the Aubrey country in northern Wiltshire, "looking at the place of his birth, the villages and country from which he drew so many examples in his writings" (*Faces,* 89). He also wrote letters asking the readers of the *Spectator,* among others, for aid in locating Aubrey documents. When Hitler invaded Poland at the end of the summer, Powell had in hand a project that should see him through.

For the next six years Powell felt, like his narrator Nicholas Jenkins, "incapable of writing a line of a novel . . . however long released from duty" (7:113). His memoirs speak of boring stretches when he tried to utilize what time he had to further Aubrey's biography, but working on any book was not easy for an officer in the Army. Indeed, the Aubrey biography was to suffer errors in the first edition, Powell admitted, owing to forced composition far from his notes.

Stationed in London during the last part of the war Powell also found less quiet and more distraction than he had anticipated, certainly less and more than if stationed in the highlands. But even during the Blitz he could read, and among other things he reread Proust. He grew dissatisfied with his prewar novels. Their virtues he was not too modest to deny, but their limitations were painful. Much that he wanted to say about life had been left unsaid. Indeed, were he to write 5 or even 10 more comic novels after the war, important things would still be left unsaid. Walking through the blackout, he pondered what he would do afterward, if he survived.

The war ended in August 1945, and Powell returned to civilian life in September. Another letter in the *Spectator* early the next year asked readers for help in locating certain lost Aubrey manuscripts—and indicated to friends that a more concentrated effort was under way.[1] *John Aubrey and His Friends* was finished a few months later.

Delays followed. The manuscript was first sent to the Oxford University Press, but "[t]he suggested advance not being very exciting," Powell wrote in his memoir, "I took Muggeridge's advice, and gave the biography to Graham Greene to read." After the war Greene had become a director of the publishing firm of Eyre and Spottiswoode and, the terms they offered being acceptable, "a contract was signed in May, 1946, undertaking that the book would appear within nine months" (*Faces,* 200).

Paper shortages made some delay understandable, but when 1948 came and the book still had not appeared, Powell lunched with Muggeridge and Greene and asked Greene for help. Apparently Greene saw the justice of his complaint, but the director of Eyre and Spottiswoode insisted that the contract be honored. There followed an office "row about the firm's treatment of myself . . . No doubt there were many other reasons why Greene no longer wished to remain a publisher; my own case, at least to some extent, seems to have provided a *causa belli* for [his] resignation from the Eyre & Spottiswoode board"(*Faces,* 202). But Eyre and Spottiswoode honored the contract finally and published *John Aubrey and His Friends* late in 1948.

There is an art to biography, and Powell is certainly at least half-right in complaining about "the appalling, genial verbosity of American scholars who write of great men as if writing the script of a Hollywood film."[2] But *John Aubrey* as a biography may suffer from the opposite fault, an overscrupulous avoidance of the dramatic. No doubt dry bones are better than romantic flab, and Aubrey's life had not been outwardly exciting, but the dryness makes *John Aubrey and His Friends* easy to lay down. Even Greene, who wanted to publish it, had in a moment of exasperation called *John Aubrey* "a bloody boring book" (*Faces,* 201), perhaps because the chairman of his firm was arguing that it would never become a best-seller. It did not. Still, *John Aubrey* is a work of interest, scholarly and useful.

After the war another friend of Powell had "become literary advisor to The Cresset Press." Learning of Powell's biography, John Hayward asked Powell to contribute (to a new series of classics his firm was putting out) a volume "to be called something like *Brief Lives: And Other Selected Writings by John Aubrey,* the title which was eventually used." Powell had edited books before—his edition of the Barnard Letters in 1928 was in fact his first book publication, and his first book publication after the war was *Novels of High Society* (1947), a collection of three Victorian novels apparently read or reread during the war—but to edit Aubrey's unpolished "brief lives" was a daunting task. "Aubrey's manuscripts and letters are beyond words chaotic" (*Faces,* 203). Powell persisted, worked on dusty manuscripts in the Bodleian Library in Oxford, finished the editing, and again met a disappointment. Some 75 pages of his work had to be cut to meet the requirements of the series.

During the war something more important had been going on in the back of Powell's mind. Biography was a sideline, useful but not a life work, and the creative work he had done before the war seemed at an end. Things he felt about human existence had been left unsaid, and to return to writing novels like *Afternoon Men* was not enough. What he felt he needed to resume his creativity and make the last half of his life useful were three things: a new method of narration, a new, more commodious structure, and a new style.

Needed first was a new method of storytelling, some narrator within the novel close to himself but not himself, who could evaluate, speculate, see the world as he did, complex and beautiful, horrifying and mysterious. At the end of the 1930s Powell had experimented with a faceless narrator in *What's Become of Waring.* But the "observer" there could have been a fly on the wall; the objectivity of this nameless recorder makes him seem inhuman. He makes no judgments, overtly anyway, and the reader tends to forget his existence. What Powell needed now was a narrator almost as faceless, perhaps, but with a stronger point of view, and the character of John Aubrey suggested a model. Aubrey's own character, modest yet shrewd, observant and reserved, seemed just about right for the sweeping novel he had in mind. Curiosity had led Aubrey to peer into the lives of contemporaries and predecessors, but humility led him to record conflicting anecdotes about them without attempting to force a reconciliation by means of theory or rationalization. Ego did not

obtrude. Aubrey's mindset was close to what Powell needed for his narrator to be, and Powell's thumbnail analysis of Aubrey (in 1948) fits
Nicholas Jenkins ("born" in 1951) well: either is a man who goes quietly through life marked by an "easy-going laziness, an inquisitive interest
in people, blending . . . unaccountably an unworldliness with a deep
appreciation of the world's ways" (115).

But to carry a long novel Jenkins needed a dimension Aubrey either
did not have or did not reveal. Aubrey remains objective, but Jenkins is
more like Proust's Marcel. His memories occasionally explode with emotion, "like wounds, unknown and quiescent, that suddenly break out to
give pain, or at least irritation, at a later season" (2:143).

What Powell needed too was a new form. At night, unable to write,
he reread Proust and ideas of form came to him. What one critic calls
"the mnemonic episodes" in *A la Recherche du temps perdu* and what
another terms "discontinuous memories . . . in homogeneous blocks" are
akin to the unit mode of structuring that Powell fashioned for The Music
of Time. Opening a volume almost at random we can see the new structuring as, for instance, an almost forgotten popular song, "Pale Hands I
Loved beside the Shalimar," brings into focus by way of the memory the
sequence of five distinct but related episodes in *Casanova's Chinese
Restaurant*.

The influence of Proust on Powell can be exaggerated, and usually is.
Whereas Proust emphasizes the exquisite, emotional pleasure that
springs from "remembrance of things past," Powell emphasizes the drier,
intellectual pleasure that comes to the understanding as memory suddenly throws into juxtaposition two areas of time, either of which may in
itself be only painful. The critic has two intellectual tools, T. S. Eliot
once remarked, analysis and comparison; and what may be called the
"Proustian memory" is used by Powell in The Music of Time as a double
agent in the criticism of life. As in *Casanova's Chinese Restaurant,* it is the
ugly sight of a bombed-out pub that evokes the lovely song "Pale
Hands" that in turn evokes the pleasurable agony of life in the 1920s.

And Powell also felt he needed a new style for the anticipated work.
The clipped staccato style of the early novels, derived perhaps from
Firbank and Hemingway, Wyndham Lewis and e. e. cummings, had
been excellent. It conveyed the staccato air of the 1920s, the elliptic
speech fashionable in the interwar years, the surface of things; but it had
its limitations. For one thing, it was unfit to cope with quiet analysis and
synthesis, the tasks Powell had in mind for Jenkins. Decades of change

cannot be correlated with an aphorism, or subtleties of motive conveyed with a wisecrack.

The narrator of The Music of Time drops a clue as to how a novelist might decide to refashion his style. Jenkins (who had published novels in the 1930s) begins during the war "to brood on the complexity of writing a novel about English life." Presenting the English in fiction is "a subject difficult enough to handle with authenticity even of a crudely naturalistic sort, even more to convey the inner truth of the things observed." A novelist, especially, is forced to regret that "[i]ntricacies of social life make English habits unyielding to simplification, while understatement and irony—in which all classes of this island converse—upset the normal emphasis of reported speech" (3:32). Given the almost infinite complexity of life (2:159), and the desire to give a major dimension to the scope of that complexity, the brisk dialogue style of the early novels seemed an inadequate instrument.

As truth comes only by surprise to the relaxed will, so the *Journal Intime* of Henri Frédéric Amiel came to Powell. Having long been what he calls a "memoir addict," even before the war Powell had specialized in reviewing memoirs and autobiographies for the *Spectator* (as he had specialized in reviewing novels for the *Daily Telegraph*). But during the war a fellow officer in Whitehall—Alexander Dru, brother-in-law of Evelyn Waugh, who became to Powell a figure as fascinating as Constant Lambert—drew his attention to Amiel's *Journal Intime*.

Amiel (1821–81) had been a professor of philosophy in Geneva, and Dru ranked him as a precursor of Freud and Proust in the shrewdness of his observations about human character. In his *Journal,* for one thing, Amiel was especially candid about his own lack of enterprise, treating it with "deprecatory humour" (*Faces,* 186–87). Published posthumously, the earliest fragment of Amiel's journal appeared in English translation only in 1885. But it was in reading Amiel that Powell realized new possibilities of conveying subtlety and indecision, the qualities of style he needed for the work to come.[3]

The new style, slow, sweeping, and judicious, is apt for conveying the process by which we actually arrive at resolutions and for conveying uncertainty of judgment as well. That "pressure from above" may have caused one diplomat's resignation is "a point upon which opinion varied" (2:19), and opinion varies about every character in The Music of Time. Perhaps opinion varies with all characters in all our lives; other novels had said as much, but no novel had dramatized this blanket tentativeness before. At moments in The Music of Time the very theme seems to be our ignorance of others—"how inadequate, as a rule, is one's own grasp of another's assessment of his particular role in life" (2:78); and the narrator—almost as if he personified the history of modern science, with mind and ears open to a fault, with a curiosity that is never tempered by boredom—is forever, like science itself, groping for a theory that will explain things, discovering errors of assessment, supplanting one assessment with another more tenable, and having to supplant that. Moving, perhaps, toward the truth?

"Who can be said to know. All men are mysteries," says Dr. Trelawney (6:191); and Dr. Trelawney might be called a keynote speaker of the series were he not in his dogmatic simplicity a parody-*raisonneur*, like Fotheringham and Cortney in the earlier novels. To raise the idea of complexity that Dr. Trelawney expresses above the level of platitude, Powell gives us intellectual characters such as General Conyers and Moreland, who, in addition to the narrator, wonder even about close friends: "One passes through the world knowing few, if any, of the important things about even the people with whom one has been from time to time in the closest intimacy" (6:217).

But as *raisonneur*, Moreland provides aphorisms rather than speculations and in a terse, 1920s, metaphoric style: "Valéry asks why one has been summoned to this carnival," Moreland says of life, "but it's more like blind man's bluff. One reels through the carnival in question, blundering into persons one can't see, and, without much success, trying to keep hold of a few of them" (6:217). Similarly, one reels through Moreland's aperçus finding them witty, entertaining, and in the end insubstantial. It is Jenkins the narrator who, without flash, illuminates the music in the end, and Jenkins in his ruminative mood owes much to Amiel.

The new style was to have its detractors. "Powell's method of getting on with the story," one complained, "must be the most ponderously inefficient of all time."[4] But since Powell's earlier style was brisk to the point of losing readers in the opposite direction, with too much needing to be read between the lines, it seems obvious that Powell made himself anew in middle age because he had something he wanted to do besides "getting on with the story." The new style is an admirable vehicle for conveying complexity and uncertainty, and it was forged by Powell, as consciously as the novel's structure, to convey what he had to say.

The major work of Powell's life began to appear with *A Question of Upbringing* in 1951, and the next volume, *A Buyer's Market,* followed rapidly in 1952. Subsequent volumes appeared at a more leisurely pace: *The Acceptance World* (1955), *At Lady Molly's* (1957), *Casanova's Chinese Restaurant* (1960), *The Kindly Ones* (1962), *The Valley of Bones* (1964), *The Soldier's Art* (1966), *The Military Philosophers* (1968), *Books Do Furnish a Room* (1971), *Temporary Kings* (1973), and *Hearing Secret Harmonies* (1975). Twenty-five years to write a novel—12 volumes emerging with a rhythm of their own—the work of a lifetime.

A Question of Upbringing

The first volume of The Music of Time introduces four boys at an English public school in the early 1920s. The narrator, Nicholas Jenkins, is having tea in the room of his aristocratic friend Charles Stringham when Peter Templer, the son of a rich but middle-class businessman, returns from a dental appointment. Together from a window the three observe a fourth boy, Kenneth Widmerpool, running doggedly and alone.

These are the players (or dancers) caught in the rhythm of time, caught initially by the arrival of the narrator's Uncle Giles, ending, for that day, their observation of Widmerpool. With the arrival of a relative the group of boys dissolves—but will form again. An inherited family pattern (in the person of Uncle Giles) flows into an improvised social pattern and the form of The Music of Time has been defined.

After leaving school, the four youths find that their paths (as subsequent chapters reveal) continue to interweave in both routine and mysterious ways. Jenkins visits Templer's home and is intrigued by his sister, Jean, who is to play a large role in his life. Sent to France to stay with a French family to improve his language skills before entering the university, he finds Widmerpool the runner staying with the same family.

Finally, an episode at Oxford in the mid-1920s brings the three friends together again and introduces a new set of characters, an Oxford don and his literary and political protégés.

But we must examine the opening image of The Music of Time again, for it is complex. Before turning to his friends, the narrator finds that his memory has brought an image of chilled British workmen outdoors near a fire, and that this image in turn summons another memory, of a painting in which four dancers move to the unheard music of a lyre. Almost totally dissimilar, the workmen and the dancers have important things in common, somehow, and the mind of Jenkins is forced to seek some connection.

But however involuntarily these images come into the mind of Nicholas Jenkins, the complex images came to Powell deliberately, for the opening image had to strike the keynote for the whole, it had to represent in miniature the massive work to follow; it had to serve as an objective correlative of a complex central theme. Probably Powell brooded about the opening image for years before beginning to write, though perhaps it came to him one day in a flash as he stood in London's Wallace Gallery. Modern novelists (Joyce, Woolf, Proust), more than their Victorian ancestors, seem to work as do composers: typically revealing in some manner the central theme of the work in a "prelude" and then beginning the elaboration. Powell's opening image is in this "musical" tradition.

Red lanterns locate men working on a foggy street. The narrator, Nick Jenkins, watches the men move "with large, pantomimic gestures: like comedians giving formal expression to the concept of extreme cold." Suddenly life breaks into the scene when one workman, "with a jocular demeanor and long, pointed nose like that of a Shakespearean clown," throws something, perhaps the remains of some kippers, onto the coals of the fire. The narrator remains forever uncertain about that part of the mechanism; but as flames shoot up from some impact, the scene revolves in an instant from romantic to classic, from freedom and chaos to order: "the physical attitudes of the men . . . as they turned from the fire, suddenly suggested Poussin's scene in which the Seasons, hand in hand. . . . tread in rhythm to the notes of the lyre that the . . . naked graybeard plays."

Poussin's painting *A Dance to the Music of Time* (which Powell had seen often in the Wallace Gallery, and which is reproduced well in Violet Powell's *Album*), although it dates from the eighteenth century, captures one essence of modern life; it captures the power with which music controls the pattern of the dance. Music itself is a correlative for a hidden power, something we all experience in the subconscious tapping of a foot to the tune from a radio rooms away, the seizure of the spirit by a Pied Piper, a couple moving, part consciously and part unconsciously, to the rhythm of an orchestra. But music is also a correlative for time—without time there would be no music, or as Yeats put it, without the flow of time how would we tell the dancer from the dance?—and the passage of people through life can be seen as a dance with its willed variations and unwilled and unpredictable variables. Without the flow of time there is no death, but also no art, no beauty.

Music is thus a key to Nicholas Jenkins and to the movement of his memory through the novel: "The image of Time brought thoughts of mortality: of human beings facing outward like the Seasons, moving hand in hand in intricate measure" (1.2).

If life is a dance like a quadrille (or like a barn dance without a "caller"), certain patterns are predictable: "certain people . . . seem inextricably linked . . . so that meeting one acquaintance in the street means that a letter, without fail, will arrive in a day or two from an associate involuntarily harnessed to him, or her, in time." The formal movements of this dance are jarred by awkward movements of one partner and, temporarily, by "seemingly meaningless gyrations" of another, although the reappearance of "partners," as in a quadrille, restores, fortuitously for the mind, "pattern to the spectacle" (1:225).

Insofar as the dancers are unable to control the tempo or the melody, they are subject to chance and verge on being creatures of a Bergsonian machine, comic in that they seem deprived of free will—"unable, perhaps, to control the steps of the dance" (1:225). Instances of human inflexibility—the man in the top hat approaching the banana peel and not perceiving it—often lead to laughter. But as the activities of human life return to some control of the will, they lead to other comic discrepancies in which even the narrator shares—discrepancies in form that lead to absurd efforts to adjust the will to the form in some cases; in others, to ridiculous failures of the will to change the form.

The first violation of good form evoked by the fire image is that of a public-school boy named Widmerpool who is trotting through the fog to discipline himself, by pure effort of the will, to an athletic eminence he is destined never to achieve. Widmerpool is seen from a warm room where his antics are being mimicked by the narrator's friend Stringham. At opposite poles socially, Widmerpool and Stringham are both within the social limits of a rich school; but Widmerpool bears with him (like Margot Asquith) the threatening onus of his father's reputation as a manufacturer of artificial manure; Stringham is the heir of that social group which looked with condescension on the low buffooneries of the Hanoverian Court and its "Royal" Family. Stringham's mimicry of Widmerpool thus seems to represent, on a symbolic level, the residual supremacy in the early 1920s of the British aristocracy; and it leads forward, on the plane of immediate action, to the first comic episode.

Practical jokes are perhaps akin to the juvenile mind and the first comic event involves one, beginning one afternoon a short time later when Jenkins, Stringham, and Templer leave the school grounds for a walk. Stringham reverts to his mimicry of Widmerpool's grotesque trot as they saunter along. They notice a wanted poster: the police are seeking an embezzler named Braddock-alias-Thorne, who on the poster looks like Woodrow Wilson or, Stringham suggests, like their housemaster, Le Bas. They later jump impetuously over a bank and nearly land on Le Bas, who is lying on the grass reading classical verse.

Moments later Stringham conceives a joke that he implements by telephoning the police, mimicking the voice of Le Bas, to report the presence of Braddock-alias-Thorne in the field where they have left Le Bas. Of the four students mentioned, only Widmerpool actually witnesses the arrest of Le Bas, and only Widmerpool is unaware of the joke. The narrator's attitude toward him, and toward Stringham and Templer, crystallizes around this first "comic" event.

The Music of Time is to a large degree structured on such comic events, each making a plateau of a separate day in a separate chapter, with reminiscences and speculations to bridge the chasms of time. *A Question of Upbringing,* the first volume, erects four such episodes. The second episode might be called the Stripling-Farebrother Chamberpot Reversal. Spending part of his vacation at Templer's home, "an enormously swollen villa, red and gabled, facing the sea," the narrator sees another side of the adult world in the struggle between Templer's brother-in-law, Stripling, a racing motorist noted for his horseplay and practical jokes ("none of which, in retrospect, sounded strikingly amusing" [1:93]), and Sunny Farebrother, a business associate of Templer's father. Stripling becomes the comic figure when his jokes on Farebrother embarrass him more than they do Farebrother. Farebrother's absurd "collar-turner" ruins his shirts, and Farebrother's innocent appearance in the hall as Stripling is about to substitute in his hatbox a chamberpot for Farebrother's top hat, deflates him further (1:98). The next day Farebrother steps out of Jenkins' life "for twenty years."

The third episode concerns the first major coincidence in the novel, as Widmerpool and the narrator, having gone their separate ways after school, become boarders with the same French family in Touraine. Farce dominates the action as Widmerpool, with his usual egocentric oblivion, intrudes on Jenkins' first love scene. Finding Jenkins with a French girl named Suzette in the summerhouse, Widmerpool "sat down between us and began to talk of *Les Miserables*" (1:151), thus ending Jenkins' first "absurdly romantic" moment.

The final episode brings the first volume full circle with the imbroglio of an auto accident outside Oxford. The accident leads to the estrangement of two of the three friends—Templer and Stringham. Their car ditched in the rain, and the absurd consequences, did not make Stringham dislike Templer for having gotten them into it: "On the contrary, he used to refer to Peter as frequently as he had done in the past; and the story of the drive . . . was embroidered by him until it became an epic of discomfort and embarrassment; and at the same time, something immensely funny" (1:200). Nonetheless, intimacy between them was over. A pattern, the opening pattern, is broken as the novel ends.

Each of the four scenes, as we see, embodies one of the great clichés of comedy. At the root of each scene, giving it form, is some familiar pattern of slapstick, farce, or burlesque. Although Powell had achieved in earlier novels more originality than most, in individual scene management in The Music of Time, he seems to eschew novelty deliberately and to stick firmly to the traditional. Here Powell is constructing a classical comedy by employing only time-honored comic myths.

Farce has patterns that do recur in life. The grotesque and the absurd are parts of the human condition, and "Even in the quietest forms of life," as the narrator observes, "the untoward is rarely far from the surface" (2:114). To employ hoary comic situations in this context is to follow tradition back to its roots in the primary comic symbols of the race and to treat them as if the function of the comic were to reconcile human beings to the absurd elements of their condition.

Even the most hackneyed sequences are treated with such care and precision that they are rejuvenated. For instance, in the narrator's account of the train ride that links his visit with Templer and his stay in France, we note the slow, almost pedantic accumulation of detail, every item in itself realistic, until by surprise we are sent skating down the edge of laughter. The young narrator has returned from the dining car to find his seat taken by a Frenchman:

> I decided that it would be less trouble, and perhaps cooler to stand for a time in the corridor. . . . After a while the corridor became fuller than might have been thought possible. I was gradually forced away from the door of the compartment, and found myself unstrategically placed with a leg on either side of a wicker trunk, secured by a strap, the buckle of which ran into my ankle, as the tram jolted its way along the line. All around were an immense number of old women in black, one of whom was carrying a feather mattress as part of her luggage.

At first the wine had a stimulating effect; but this sense of exhilaration began to change. . . . At last the throbbings in my head became so intense that I made up my mind to eject the man with the beard. After a short preliminary argument in which I pointed out that the seat was a reserved one, and, in general, put my case as well as circumstances and my command of the language, would allow, he said briefly: "Monsieur, vous avez gagné," and accepted dislodgment with resignation and some dignity. In the corridor, he moved skillfully past the priest and his boys; and, with uncommon agility for his age and size, climbed onto the wicker trunk, which he reduced almost immediately to a state of complete dissolution: squatting on its ruins reading *Le Figaro*. He seemed to know the girl, perhaps his daughter, because once he leaned across and pinched the back of her leg and made some remark to her; but she continued to gaze irritably out at the passing landscape, amongst the trees of which an occasional white chateau stood glittering like a huge birthday cake left out in the woods after a picnic. (1:107–8)

The situation is hackneyed; the style is the preservative.

Waiting for Jenkins at the station in France is a time-worn taxi out of opéra bouffe, driven by an ancient chauffeur whose mustache and peaked cap give him the air of a Napoleonic grenadier: "Even when stationary, his taxi was afflicted with a kind of vehicular counterpart of St. Vitus's dance, and its quaverings and seismic disturbances must have threatened nausea to its occupants at the best of times" (1:109).

Ancient joke though the collapsing taxi is, it is not more antique than the story of the narrator's repeated attempts to declare his romantic attachment to the French girl Suzette. The last of these involves the classic mistaken-identity routine, which begins when Jenkins finds the girl's sunbonnet missing from the hat rack and presumes she will be in the garden. In the summerhouse he sees the sunbonnet above a chair, seizes the hand of the woman wearing it as he approaches her from behind, begins to declare his affection, discovers he is addressing a middle-aged woman, and blunders on, using up the platonic "phrases that I had rehearsed so often for Suzette." There is probably no older joke in the history of romantic comedy, and yet, somehow, by virtue of the style, the incident is made amusing.

In a similar fashion, many of the characters in the classic mode represent banal types who nonetheless have unique identities. In Jenkins' own family we find a descendant of T. T. Waring, the remittance man, long a feature of English comedy, in the person of his Uncle Giles. He first appears as a seedy relative to embarrass the schoolboy among his friends, and to spark the housemaster's anger when he detects the lingering odor of tobacco in Stringham's room, and thus to set off Stringham's practical joke on Le Bas. Uncle Giles

> had been relegated by most of the people who knew him at all well to that limbo where nothing is expected of a person, and where more than usually outrageous actions are approached, at least conversationally, as if they constituted a series of practical jokes, more or less enjoyable, according to where responsibility for clearing up matters might fall. The curious thing about persons regarding whom society has taken this largely self-defensive measure is that the existence of the individual himself reaches a pitch when nothing he does can ever be accepted as serious. If he commits suicide, or murder, only the grotesque aspects of the event dominate the circumstances. (1:16)

And with a typical Uncle Giles joke, a quiet one, the first volume ends. Uncle Giles, who has mailed his nephew Nick Jenkins an invitation to dine with him, blandly assumes a student at Oxford will find dining in London no difficulty. As it happens, Stringham has invited Jenkins to London, only to drop him for a more attractive social engagement. Jenkins recalls the first invitation almost with surprise and decides to drop by the restaurant. "You're a bit late," Uncle Giles said. "So I started" (1:230).

Yet the most original of Powell's creations in *A Question of Upbringing* is the character of Widmerpool. At the same time, Widmerpool can be seen as belonging to a rather hackneyed type. On the literary side he descends from the fussy tutors Thwackem and Square in Henry Fielding's novel *Tom Jones* (1749) or the greedy schoolmaster in Washington Irving's "The Legend of Sleepy Hollow" (1820)—all of whom have, like Widmerpool, a yearning for power coupled with physical qualities so grotesque that the eye and the imagination are captured involuntarily. And Widmerpool is seen as a type. Even as a schoolboy he is noted for an overcoat so odd that schoolboys recognize it "immediately as a traditionally ludicrous aspect of everyday life" (1:16). Yet Powell adds freshness to the type by means of meticulous observation.

A Buyer's Market

In the second volume of The Music of Time, *A Buyer's Market,* the scene is London in the spring of 1928 and the contemporaries of Nick Jenkins are, so to speak, in the marketplace, or on the auction block.

Unfortunately for them it is not a seller's market. As the novel begins, none is doing well. Nick Jenkins works for a publisher of art books, and Stringham has gone to work for an industrialist named Sir Magnus Donners, CEO of the firm Donners-Brebner. Widmerpool also joins the staff; and despite his lowly status during their school life together, Widmerpool is the success in the end as he ousts the "coming young man" who had brought Stringham into the firm. And the power of love proves as pervasive as that of business: Stringham is being pursued by a socialite some years his senior; Jenkins finds himself oddly attracted by the same debutante who has attracted Widmerpool; and in the end the girlfriend of a leftist painter named Mr. Deacon euchres Widmerpool into paying for her abortion.

Stringham and Widmerpool together work in what is called by Londoners "the City." The term conveys roughly what New Yorkers mean by "the Street," taking Wall Street to be the symbol of the universe of banks and bonds. That part of London within the old Roman walls had developed over the centuries into the financial bastion of the empire, and in *A Buyer's Market* and *The Acceptance World* Powell skirts the area as he begins the general study of power hinted at on the last page of *What's Become of Waring*.

The City has rarely been described in print, Powell remarks in a review: "some literary critics seem to have no idea that, for the last fifty years at least, to 'go in to the City'—and work very hard there—has been a characteristic 'upper-class' vocation."[5] He cites as an example Lord Salisbury; but he might have cited as well his wife's uncle Arthur Child-Villiers, son of the Earl of Jersey, who became a director of Baring Brothers bank.

A City marriage that sheds light on Powell's conception of his fictional magnate Sir Magnus Donners may be seen in the 1963 wedding of Angus Ogilvy, a son of the Earl of Airlie, to Princess Alexandra of Kent. Along with a photograph of the prewedding ball at Windsor Castle, the *Times* headlined the story "Mr. Ogilvy's Chief Tells How Angus Made the Grade." The princess is to enter the "robust new world of big business" and "tycoon-studded parties," the interviewer assumes, for "Mr. Ogilvy is a protégé of Mr. Harold Drayton, the City magnate, who tells me that he is hoping that Ogilvy will not feel inhibited by his new social position. 'Damn it. I've trained him.'" Though Drayton himself had started as a cigar-counter clerk at a few shillings a week, he started Ogilvy at £600 a year "and told him he had two years to make good. With Angus the bell rang straight away and he remained." Asked how many companies he was now directing, Drayton replied he did not know: "There are so many new ones, y'see. Angus and the other little devils are always up to something."[6] It is this drive that Sir Magnus Donners looks for in his bright young men, half a dozen of whom figure in The Music of Time.

Sir Magnus Donners dominates what in the City in the early 1930s is a "buyer's market" in men, that is, he can pretty well hire whom he pleases. His firms deal vaguely in metals, possibly with munitions as well in the manner of Sir Basil Zaharoff, though Powell rightly leaves the "field" vague to retain about Donners an inky octopal atmosphere. The portrait of Sir Magnus may owe something to such press barons as Lord Beaverbrook, too, but his significance is more universal. Financially, Sir Magnus's power is international; but we suspect that behind his parade of "kept women" and the wildly conflicting rumors about his odd sexual predilections is impotence, that the beautiful women are bric-a-brac around his castle, or "conversation pieces" to conceal his area of failure. For Powell's thesis is already clear: as power corrupts, the absolute pursuit of power corrupts the sensual life absolutely. As Powell says of Sillery, the don who manipulates Stringham out of the university (without a degree) into the Donners-Brebner power structure, "Like many persons more interested in power than sensual enjoyment, Sillery touched no strong drink" (1:212).

Power is seen in *A Buyer's Market* in a multitude of facets. There is the familiar physical power as Widmerpool wrestles Stringham, the military power that stands in opposition to the artistic life, and unexpected varieties of power, some of them reminding us of the narrator of *What's Become of Waring* and of the chapter he is unable to complete on Stendhal, "Laughter Is Power." The legendary Lord Vowchurch—who got power in Edwardian days by way of his practical jokes (such as clockwork mice and monkeys released at a ball (4:4; 6:10)—may be seen as a variant of the least power hungry of them all, Nicholas Jenkins, whose social power seems to come from his skill in telling comic anecdotes.

In earlier volumes we learned that Stringham's greatest pleasure is the enjoyment of private jokes (2:202); and, perhaps significantly, in *A Buyer's Market,* when he no longer needs the audience Jenkins provided at school, they see less of each other. Jenkins still prepares "ribald jokes about Widmerpool's honeymoon for friends who knew him" (4:65), but his normally analytical eye apparently glances past the motives that connect the comic with the quest for popularity or peer approval. An eye for the comic in life, such as Jenkins has, gives the observant a share of power in the social sphere.

Structurally, *A Buyer's Market* is quite similar to *A Question of Upbringing* in focusing on four time-worn but exquisitely rendered comic moments. The first occurs at a society ball that we view in slow motion as Powell perfects a technique that seems almost to freeze the comic action into symbol. To Jenkins' shock, he has found Widmerpool attracted to the same debutante who has attracted him, and the three are together at the buffet table when Widmerpool attempts to restrain the girl from joining a third man across the room. Widmerpool's pressure on her wrist is only momentary, but she turns to snap, "You need some sweetening."

The passage that follows, describing the lifting of the sugar bowl, the tilting of it over Widmerpool's head, the sticking lid, the total inversion of the bowl, the lid suddenly giving, the sugar cascading over Widmerpool, bears requoting:

> More from surprise than because she wished additionally to torment him, Barbara did not remove her hand before the whole contents of the vessel . . . had descended. . . . Widmerpool's rather sparse hair had been liberally greased with a dressing—the sweetish smell of which I remembered as somewhat disagreeable when applied in France—this lubricant retaining the grains of sugar, which, as they adhered thickly to his skull, gave him the appearance of having turned white from shock at a single stroke. . . . He had writhed sideways to avoid the downpour, and a cataract of sugar had entered the space between neck and collar; yet another jet streaming between eyes and spectacles. (2:70–71)

The episode is not farce for farce's sake. The detailed registry of the horror brings a revelation about the character of the girl, which ends the narrator's infatuation.

The second episode, which has similar qualities of slapstick and dignity, takes place near dawn the next morning and involves a painter named Mr. Deacon. First seen in Paris in 1919 when Jenkins' father at Versailles was working in vain for a just peace with Germany, Mr. Deacon in the cocoon of his art and ego had been indifferent to the fate of the world. When the paths of Deacon and Nick Jenkins cross again at a Hyde Park coffee stall in the early 1930s, when a time for militant toughness might be thought to have come, Deacon is passionately distributing pacifist leaflets. At this moment of intersection Stringham also appears and invites them to a party given by Mrs. Andriadis, the woman who has been pursuing him. At the party a quarrel breaks out between Deacon, who has his own sexual peculiarities, and a Noel Coward-like pianist, Max Pilgrim, who loves to sing his own songs. Powell composes an appropriate song for the occasion:

> Even the fairies
> Say how sweet my hair is;
> They mess my mascara and pinch the peroxide.
> I know a coward
> Would be overpowered,
> When they all offer to be orthodox, I'd
> Like to be kind, but say: "Some other day, dears;
> Pansies for thoughts remains the best way, dears." (2:118)

Outraged at the flagrantly homosexual implications of the song, Deacon furiously opens battle: "There are always leering eyes on the lookout. Besides, your song puts a weapon in the hands of the puritans." Eventually Deacon storms away, pausing in the foyer below to gather up his bundle of peace pamphlets. Mrs. Andriadis, in pursuit of Stringham, who has left unexpectedly, reaches the door at the moment Deacon—still furiously bellicose, peace pamphlets crammed under one arm—is trying to break the jammed catch:

> All at once there was a sound as of the rending of silk, and the papers, like a waterfall, began to tumble, one after another, to the ground from under Mr. Deacon's arm. He made a violent effort to check their descent, contriving only to increase the area over which they were freely shed; an unexpected current of air blowing through the open door . . . helped to scatter sheets of *War Never Pays!* far and wide . . . even up to the threshold of the room beyond. (2:150)

The clash of personal wills, like the clash of national wills, leads to tragicomic consequences.

The third episode, equally farcical and symbolic, involves Widmerpool again. In the courtyard of the restored castle of Sir Magnus Donners, the industrialist he is trying to impress, Widmerpool concludes his business in apparent triumph but in departing starts his car in reverse gear, so that it shoots backward and knocks a tremendous urn into a sunken garden (2:217–23).

With the fourth section the focus returns to the painter Mr. Deacon as his birthday party adjourns to a nightclub. Offended by the odors in the men's room, Mr. Deacon dies for his ideals, protesting the inexorable nature of things. He is climbing the rickety stairs to the manager's office to complain about the odor when his fatal slip occurs (2:229).

This section has two epilogues, however, that diffuse this tragicomic effect: one deals with Deacon's slatternly pacifist girl-companion, the other with the home life of Widmerpool, who met the girl at Deacon's party. Jenkins in the meantime has been amazed to learn that Widmerpool had succeeded in his attempt to impress Donners and has ousted Stringham's champion from the firm. The terminal joke involves Widmerpool when he, without having had any carnal relations with Deacon's companion, Gypsy Jones, is pressured by her into paying for her abortion (2:232). The failures of Widmerpool's sexual life have begun—as he triumphs in the buyer's market.

Mr. Deacon was in part modeled after the London bookseller and bibliographer Christopher Millard, a "grey-haired, disreputable, handsome . . . bibliophile."[7] Perhaps such an identification is oversimple. The "wheeler-dealer in the antique world" aspect of him seems to derive from another bibliophile, T. J. Wise, exposed (in 1934) as a creator of faked first editions. "Pushing and vain"—so Powell describes Wise—"he ingratiated himself with most of the prominent men of letters of his period; and, to be just to him, his qualities as a collector, bibliographer and editor were very high. There is a particular kind of unctuousness and pretension to modesty in some of his letters . . . which must have put shrewd people on their guard. Even so, it would hardly have prepared them for the truth."[8] But less in accord with Millard or Wise is the early Mr. Deacon. When we first meet him in The Music of Time he is touring the Louvre and is still active as a painter of gigantic canvases; and a candidate for this aspect of his character has yet to suggest itself. Not that the history of Victorian art does not furnish candidates enough, Alma-Tadema for one.

The Acceptance World

Groans were heard when *The Acceptance World* appeared in 1955. Some reviewers were led by it to doubt Powell's ability to sustain the literary edifice the first volumes had projected. The title suggests that the volume will continue the investigation of power in the City, and it must be admitted that it does not, though in these early years of the Depression (1930–34) a further look at the community of business and finance might seem apropos. Moreover, initially only one new character is introduced: a fortune-teller named Mrs. Erdleigh who does not make a strong impression even upon the narrator. Most troublesome at first reading, *The Acceptance World* seems vagrant. We wander from one episode to another, as if no one were at the wheel, or we seem to; and this episodic effect tends to cast doubt on the promise of order given by Powell's aesthetic.

In actuality the title acts as a bridge between the business community of *A Buyer's Market* and the wider cultural and political community; it links the part of the financial world that deals in futures with the rest of the world, equally anxious about the future. It links Widmerpool and the seekers of power for self with Mrs. Erdleigh, who "tells fortunes" for others. Who will be the future secretary of the novelist St. John Clarke is of concern to two of Oxford don Sillery's young men, Mark Members and J. G. Quiggin, and what the future will hold for love becomes Jenkins' concern as he begins an affair with Peter Templer's sister. Further changes of partner occur when the painter Barnby loses his girlfriend to Dicky Umfraville, and Quiggin, having ousted Members as Clarke's secretary, is ousted in turn.[9]

Perhaps Powell makes a tactical error in allowing the title to focus imaginative attention on Widmerpool, now a financier, who is less central here. This focus comes when Jenkins meets Templer and passes on news of old acquaintants. One item of news is that Widmerpool is now in the City with Donners-Brebner. Jenkins's news is out of date, Templer suggests: "Widmerpool is joining the Acceptance World." Templer explains that Widmerpool is going to become a bill-broker and engage in the financial activity that in America is called "dealing in futures"—in this case, making present payment on expectation of future delivery. "If you have goods you want to sell a firm in Bolivia," Templer says—as an insider explaining to Jenkins "the nefarious ways of the City"— "you probably do not touch your money in the ordinary way until the stuff arrives there. Certain houses, therefore, are prepared to 'accept' the debt. They will advance you the money on the strength of your reputation" (3:45). This is the "world" Widmerpool is joining, but we see almost nothing of Widmerpool until the last chapter (3:178).

Indeed, we see less of big business itself in *The Acceptance World* than we did in *A Buyer's Market,* and only toward the end does the relevance of the title become thematic. At this point, Jenkins admits that he had been struck by the phrase:

Even as a technical definition, it seemed to suggest what we are all doing; not only in business, but in love, art, religion, philosophy, politics, in fact all human activities. The Acceptance World was the world in which the essential element—happiness, for example—is drawn, as it were, from an engagement to meet a bill. Sometimes the goods are delivered . . . sometimes . . . not . . . and disaster follows; sometimes the goods are delivered, but the value of the currency [has] changed. Besides, in another sense, the whole world is the Acceptance World as one approaches thirty; at least some illusions discarded. The mere fact of still existing as a human being proved that. (3:170)

The primary extension of the term is from the business community to the world of love, and it is here that *The Acceptance World* receives its focus. The first scene introduces us to Mrs. Erdleigh under the wing of Uncle Giles, who renders even this relatively sober scene comic. Mrs. Erdleigh, we might say, "deals in futures." She retails the "commonplaces of fortune telling," dealing cards for Nick Jenkins: "You live between two worlds. . . . You are thought cold, but possess deep affections, sometimes for people worthless in themselves. . . . You must make a greater effort in life." She refers to love, both past and future, Jenkins recalls: "a fair woman was not very pleased with me; and a dark one almost equally vexed!" (3:14–15). Suzette and Barbara? Jenkins finds the general applicability of the analysis too facile to take seriously, discounts Mrs. Erdleigh's "futures," and the chapter ends with the painter Barnby, always the *raissoneur* in the field of love, wondering why literary artists never portray woman as she really is, while ignoring the suggestion of Jenkins that painters had not done much better. Both conversations have arisen so casually the novel itself seems to have grown lackadaisical. But in retrospect we see that the ground work for *The Acceptance World* has been soundly laid.

Barnby on the train has met a new woman. "Like Valmont in *Les Liaisons Dangereuses* he set store 'upon what terms' he possessed a woman, seeking a relationship in which sensuality merged with power, rather than engaging in their habitual conflict" (3:24). The mystery woman has posed for Barnby but refused to reveal her identity; and Jenkins is able to assist Barnby's "futures" by providing her name.

For Jenkins, Mrs. Erdleigh has indicated three "futures"; and Barnby in turn supplies a clue that could have aided Jenkins in the resolution of one of them, the business "inconvenience" that "has to do with an elderly man—and two young ones connected with him" (3:16). The major problem facing Jenkins in the publishing business is getting St. John

Clarke to supply an introduction to the works of his friend Isbister. Supposing that Clarke's secretary Mark Members is the only young man who could be involved, Jenkins dismisses Mrs. Erdleigh as having simply reversed the proportion of young men and old. In this he errs. Clarke "fell in love with himself at first sight and it is a passion to which he has always remained faithful," Barnby says, but now he is even less likely to supply an introduction to the work of a dated painter because he is being converted to "Modernism."

The next chapters "take place" on successive days a year later. As one by one all three of Mrs. Erdleigh's predictions begin to come true, the very structure of *The Acceptance World* turns out to be pivoted upon "futures." First, the death of Isbister renders Clarke's continued failure to supply an introduction to his works even more "inconvenient." At the same time, its being written at all becomes less likely with the arrival of the predicted second young man in Clarke's life.

The second young man, the rival secretary, is J. G. Quiggin, whose hostile friendship with Mark Members had been noted in *A Question of Upbringing*. His Communist party line proves to be more fashionable in 1931 than the psychiatric jargon of Members. "When I first came to [Clarke] he thought Matisse was a *plage* [a beach]—no, I mean it," Members says. "Then one morning at breakfast he said Cézanne was 'bourgeois'" (3:123–26). "Bourgeois" as a Marxist pejorative is Members' first clue that Quiggin has begun to supplant him as Clarke's secretary.

As Jenkins awaits Members in the lobby of the Ritz, however, his dance in time again intersects that of Peter Templer, and another of Mrs. Erdleigh's predictions begins to resolve itself. Templer had been the authority at school in matters of the opposite sex and had bragged of picking up a woman of the streets while in London to visit his dentist (1:33). Moreover, at the very time Jenkins desired Templer's sister Jean and found himself to his chagrin too shy to break through the veil of her aloofness, he was forced to see that Templer had spent the night with a visiting divorcée (1:100). Further proof of the ineptitude of Jenkins in love came with the farce of his courtship of Suzette in France; and, in *A Buyer's Market,* the "dark woman," the debutante Barbara Goring, had been courted only platonically. Now the suppressed theme of love becomes dominant, as, under Templer's aegis, *The Acceptance World* centers on the first of Mrs. Erdleigh's predictions, that of "a much more important lady . . . and I think you have run across her once or twice before, though not recently. But there seems to be another man interested, too. He might even be a husband. . . . In business. Often goes abroad" (3:15).

Peter Templer is at the Ritz to meet his wife and his sister Jean, currently estranged from her husband, a businessman who is at the moment abroad. The occasion is Templer's first wedding anniversary, and he invites Jenkins to join them: "Afterwards, that dinner in the Grill seemed to partake of the nature of . . . a rite from which the four of us emerged to take up new positions in the formal dance with which human life is concerned. . . . But in a sense, nothing in life is planned—or everything is—because in the dance every step is ultimately the corollary of the step before; the consequence of being the kind of person one chances to be" (3:63). Jenkins had planned to dine with Members (in connection with the Isbister introduction), but the "well-known critic" J. G. Quiggin shows up instead. Amid the opulent decor of the Ritz, Quiggin's red tie and his black-leather coat make his reluctance to explain his presence both ominous and ludicrous, but Templer's ridicule of him later: "Is he one of those fascinating people you sometimes tell me about, who wear beards and sandals and have such curious sexual habits?" infuriates Templer's wife. In Quiggin, Mona glimpses the Bohemia she thought she had left behind without regret as her modeling career took off and her face began to appear on toothpaste billboards. Her interest in Quiggin sends Templer's marriage toward the rocks.

As in a quadrille, the severing of one couple is usually accompanied by the joining of another. That evening, in the back of the car as they drive through the snow to Templer's country house, Jenkins embraces Jean; and love comes to him for the first time in a plurality of senses: "her body felt at the same time hard and yielding, giving a kind of glow as if live current issued from it. I used to wonder afterwards whether, in the last resort, of all the time we spent together, however ecstatic, the first moments on the Great West Road were not the best" (3:65). That night (repeating the pattern Peter Templer had initiated with the divorcée a decade before) Jenkins visits Jean's room; and his affair is begun in a house where "Isbister's huge portrait of Mr. Templer still hung in the hall, a reminder of everyday life and unsolved business problems" (3:66).

The conduct of Jenkins and Jean is as discreet as Powell's handling of the details; though the affair lasts into the spring, Jean's brother, Peter, remains unaware of it—partly because of the breakup of his own marriage. Bored by the business world, Mona had insisted the day after the dinner that Templer invite J. G. Quiggin to the country. "To regard Quiggin as a competitor with Templer for a woman—far less his own wife—was ludicrous even to consider," Jenkins thinks (3:133). When Quiggin's arrival is followed by the startling arrival of Mrs. Erdleigh, and when the revelations she makes with a planchette board so prey on the nerves of Quiggin that he flees back to London in fear of losing his job as Clarke's secretary, we would suppose that Templer remained in control, matrimonially. But Quiggin's departure is interpreted by Mona as indifference to her flirtation, and she is intrigued; one of the laws of love has operated. Impossible as it seems, in the end the suave stockbroker loses the beauty on whom he dotes to an uncouth leftist critic.

Though life with Jean brings to an end Jenkins' inexperience, it does not end the mystery of love. Shock number one comes when Jean remarks almost casually that she has had an affair with her former brother-in-law, the stolid unappetizing type who had brought Mrs. Erdleigh to Templer's house. Her revelation is a flick of verbal sadism, and Jenkins is left to ponder the ways of love. But there are shocks to come in successive volumes, and pondering about the mystery of love is to grow more profound.

Mrs. Erdleigh's third prediction had been that she would see Jenkins again, but not before a year had passed; and she has. But her supervision of the planchette board is even more eerie. "Force is the midwife," the board writes, and Quiggin testily identifies the source as Marx. "I suspect it was Nick," he adds angrily, "as he is the only one who knows I'm a practising Marxist—and he persuaded me to come here." Quiggin refuses to accept Jenkins' denial of any such knowledge; but, when the planchette board suggests that St. John Clarke is ill in "The House of Books," Quiggin proves superstitious enough to rush back to allay his doubts.

Clarke is indeed ill and, in the absence of Quiggin, has called in the "psychoanalytic" or rival poet Mark Members. Quiggin returns just in time to prevent his own displacement. Yet in the fourth chapter we discover that Quiggin has in turn been displaced by one yet more "modern," the Trotskyite Werner Guggenbühl.

The central event in the chapter is a multiple meeting at Foppa's Restaurant, where Jenkins and Jean meet Barnby and his new "discovery," Lady Anne Stepney. There they all encounter a stray personification of the spirit of the 1920s, Dicky Umfraville, who has just arrived from Kenya. The time is the 1930s, and Umfraville is shocked to find most of his old friends have "become so damned serious, what?" He still feels sure of one old friend, Milly Andriadis—although, as he confesses later in the lift to her flat, their telephone contact has not been sentimental:

"She said, 'Oh, God, you again, Dicky. Somebody told me you had died of drink in 1929.' I said, 'Milly, I'm coming straight round with a few friends to give you that kiss I forgot when we were in Havana together.' She said, 'Well, I hope you'll bring along that pony you owe me, too, which you forgot at the same time.' So saying, she snapped the receiver down" (3:161).

But Milly Andriadis, too, has lost her frivolity; she has metamorphosed backward from butterfly to serious grub, or is trying to. She has picked up a new set of attitudes for the 1930s and a smattering of dialectic from Guggenbühl, St. John Clarke's new secretary. "I can't think why we don't have a revolution here," she says. To pile coincidence on coincidence, Guggenbühl arrives a bit later that evening. He is a German dramatist of the new school:

> "I think it would not interest you," he said. "We have done with old theatre of bourgeoisie and capitalists. Here is Volksbuhnen for actor that is worker like industrial worker—actor that is machine of machines."
>
> "Isn't it too thrilling?" said Mrs. Andriadis. "You know the October revolution was the real turning point in the history of the Theatre." (3:166)

The episode furthers the dialogue on love, for it leads to Barnby's loss of Lady Anne Stepney to the courteous father-figure Umfraville; and, by the end of *The Acceptance World,* both of the men whom Jenkins has looked upon as experts in love have lost the women they desire.

Umfraville has suggested to Jenkins that they attend an Old Boys dinner at the Ritz in honor of Le Bas, and Jenkins is surprised to find Templer there, too. "I've really come here tonight to see Widmerpool," Templer says, and refers to his sister Jean's husband, ignorant of the fact that Jean and Jenkins are having an affair: "Bob Duport is in England again. . . . I am rather hopeful things will be patched up with Jean, if Bob's business gets into running order again. . . . The whole family can't be in a permanent state of being deserted by their husbands and wives" (3:176). Jenkins sees an ironic layer of Jean's life below that seen by her brother—Jean's current involvement with himself—and yet he fails for the time being to see a layer below that.

In this final chapter, the comic focus is on Widmerpool, who gives a speech of such deadly tedium, it is implied, that Le Bas has a mild stroke. The sight of Widmerpool, oblivious to the stricken Le Bas, droning on with his speech so infuriates Stringham that he consumes a greater quantity of champagne than even his lush quota permits; and the evening ends with Widmerpool's marshaling a taxi to take him home. At home, Stringham recovers consciousness in horror. Widmerpool, with his usual cliché, insists they are putting him to bed "for his own good":

> "I haven't got my own good at heart."
> "We will get you anything you want."
> "Curse your charity." Once more Stringham attempted to get out of the bed. Widmerpool threw himself on top of him. . . .
> "So these are the famous Widmerpool good manners, are they?" Stringham shouted. "This is the celebrated Widmerpool courtesy. . . . Here is the man who posed as another Lord Chesterfield. Let me go, you whited sepulchre. . . ."
> The scene was so grotesque that I began to laugh. . . . He must have been quite powerful, for Stringham was struggling like a maniac. . . . And then, quite suddenly, Stringham began laughing too. He laughed and laughed, until he could struggle no more. (3:208)

The new order has conquered the old; and Widmerpool, who is to be the agent who effects the separation of Jean from Jenkins, emerges again in apparent triumph.

At Lady Molly's

Newcomers to Powell were troubled by *At Lady Molly's.* The novel so overwhelmed them with new characters and with allusions to old ones that cries for an index were heard, and more than one British weekly obliged.[10] But those who had freshly read the early volumes were delighted, for *At Lady Molly's,* unlike *The Acceptance World,* is from the opening lines tremendously entertaining.

The year is 1935, and Jenkins is working on a scenario for a movie when he is taken by a fellow scriptwriter to Lady Molly's house. There he begins meeting Lady Molly's nieces and nephews; by the end of the volume he has met all 10 of them, from Erridge, the Earl of Warminster, the eldest and most radical son, to Lady Isobel, with whom he falls in love and whom he is later to marry. In *A Buyer's Market* Widmerpool had surprised Jenkins by being attracted to the same girl; now he surprises Jenkins by contemplating marriage to a raffish aristocrat some years his senior. Life grows more serious for them both.

Among the dozen new characters, Lady Molly Jeavons and her husband, Ted, are two of the most attractive. Lady Molly is a true aristocrat, so confident of her position that she does unconventional things without a second thought; she is like an amalgam of Rosa Lewis of the Cavendish Hotel, famous for her love of dukes and Americans, and Lady Ottoline Morrell of Garsington, hostess to Britain's literati, though Powell had models closer to his own family tree, if less widely known.

Lady Molly's house is a shelter for all, irrespective of class, as long as they display good manners. When, for instance, "Lord Amesbury looked in on his way to a Court ball . . . she was giving the vet a meal she had cooked herself." But the title *At Lady Molly's* refers to two domiciles; before her unconventional marriage to a car salesman, Lady Molly had been the wife of the Earl of Sleaford and mistress of one of England's great houses, Dogdene.

Ugly and meaningless as the word Dogdene is—in the way of the names of great English houses—it connotes, to those in the know, centuries of cultivated taste, luxury, and art. When St. John Clarke in self-pity catalogues the real accomplishments of his career, he recalls bitterly as its zenith "One week-end at Dogdene twenty years ago" (5:191).

The network of associations of Dogdene with England goes back into history; Henry James had spent a weekend there[11] and Powell has fun contriving a bit of what might be called "pseudo-Pepys," since that seventeenth-century diarist recorded many a flirtation in more than one great country house. Powell invents a visit to Dogdene, where Pepys meets "a great black maid" who "toyed wantonly" with him, and who "would not have denied me que je voudray, yet was I afeared and time was lacking. At which afterwards I was troubled, lest she should speak of what I had done, and her fellows make game of me when we were gone on the road" (4:11). The desire for sex, the fear of sex, and the fear of sexual ridicule link the Pepysian account of failure to seduce the maid to a counterpoint at the end of the novel when Powell replays, also at Dogdene, that classic of folk comedy: the man of power who proves to be sexually impotent—and tries to conceal the fact.

Attempting a climb in society, to match a climb to power in the City, Widmerpool has become engaged to a socialite named Mildred Blaides. Some years younger than she, Widmerpool is appalled at her "modern" suggestion that it would be wise for them to spend a weekend together before marriage. As the youngest daughter of Edward VII's friend Lord Vowchurch (and the sister-in-law of General Conyers), she awes Widmerpool. Jenkins, meeting her as a boy, had been struck by her flashy slang, glamorous ways, and raffish attitudes. Now Jenkins is as much shocked by the idea of Widmerpool's engagement to such a glamorous woman as Widmerpool is by her aggressive sexuality. In anxiety Widmerpool invites Jenkins to his club, hoping for advice, even as to how he should register for a clandestine weekend at a hotel. You might try registering as "Mr. and the Honourable Mrs. Smith?" Jenkins suggests dryly (4:61). In the end, Mildred arranges the "trial marriage" by getting them invited together to a weekend at Dogdene and by suggesting that Widmerpool visit her room that night.

The next morning she breaks the engagement. Widmerpool has failed again in the field of love. Apprised of the story, Jenkins is amused later at Lady Molly's to hear Widmerpool evasively allude to the prudential reasons why he has decided, after all, against matrimony (4:214).

During World War I Dogdene had been turned into a hospital for wounded officers; and there the lowest of them, a car salesman in civil life named Ted Jeavons, had met both Molly, the Countess of Sleaford, whom he was to marry after she became a widow, and Widmerpool's fiancée, Mildred Blaides, then a nurse. But Dogdene is more than a locus for temporal intersections: it is a symbol of the great English family and its roots. The geometric leap in density of character that baffles the reader who begins with *At Lady Molly's* is accompanied by the introduction of a nephew of the first Lord Sleaford, Chips Lovell, who is a colleague at the film studio where Jenkins now works as a scriptwriter. A gossip columnist by inclination, Chips Lovell is given the encyclopedic knowledge of genealogy (5:59) that Evelyn Waugh in *A Little Learning* suggests Powell himself had at Oxford (202) and Lovell appears in the nick of time, for rarely has a novel so needed an expert in family entanglements.

At Lady Molly's might be called The Book of the Tollands, for the most numerous and important of its new characters are members of the Tolland clan. This family may turn out to be the greatest, as it now seems to be the largest, family in English literary history. At least twelve Tollands are acutely characterized, from the "baby" Priscilla (who has not yet made her debut, but who has already attracted the matrimonial eye of scriptwriter Chips Lovell) to her stepmother, the family doyen who presides over the family in her townhouse while writing volume after volume of biography.[12] "Lady Warminster, eccentric herself, showed a decent respect for eccentricity . . . so that the Tollands were left largely to their own devices. Life at Hyde Park Gardens might be ruthless, but it was played out on a reasonably practical basis, in which every man was for himself and no quarter given; while at the same time a curtain of relatively good humour was usually allowed to cloak an inexorable recognition of life's inevitable severities" (4:208). Since Lady Warminster is the sister of Lady Molly, all of the younger Tollands visit Lady Molly's; and, indeed, Jenkins first discovers the hospitality at Lady Molly's when Chips Lovell, after a day at the studio, takes him along on his own quest for Lady Priscilla Tolland.

The door is opened by a butler who has been loaned to Lady Molly by her nephew Erridge, the titular head of the Tolland family. The butler is on loan because Erridge is closing his vast family country house, Thrubworth, to become a tramp and see how the other half lives. George Orwell went "down and out in Paris and London" for similar motives, his guilt at being a member of the privileged class figuring among them; and Erridge shares Orwell's reaction to social ills; he suffers with them.[13] But with Erridge we come to yet another problem.

Usually, the English novel is easier to read than the Russian novel, the reader not having the problem of contending with four or five names for each character; Widmerpool is always either Widmerpool or Kenneth. But English novels about the aristocracy can grow complicated. The name Erridge comes from the title, Viscount Erridge, that Erridge (as firstborn son) inherited at birth, and the nickname Erry is natural enough for members of his family. But he can also be called Alfred Tolland, joining Christian and family names, or Alf Warminster, since he became the Earl of Warminster on the death of his father. Powell is aware of the danger of confusing the reader—probably English readers as well as American[14]—and the narrator always calls him Erridge, but social realism demands that the family call him by the title under which he grew up (Erridge); that people who disapprove of that "pompous" practice, Lady Molly for one, call him Alfred, that strangers call him Lord Warminster; while those between, such as Chips Lovell, call him Erry Warminster on one page (5:195) and Alf on the next. With Erridge, such realism is worth any demand it may make on the reader, for he joins Widmerpool as one of the novel's great characters. We may console ourselves by reflecting that the name chosen also defines the speaker's position in relation to Erridge, the speaker's position in the social web.

Jenkins comes to meet Erridge through a miscalculation by J. G. Quiggin. Quiggin is open about disliking people who do not have "all the right ideas"—in current idiom, people who are not "politically correct"—and Jenkins is one who does not; but Templer's former wife has grown bored again, this time with Quiggin; and they have invited Jenkins, as a scriptwriter with possible connections to Hollywood, to the country to discuss securing Mona a role in a movie. They are residing in a cottage in Thrubworth Park, and Quiggin is annoyed when Erridge the owner drops by to invite them all up to the house the next day. Quiggin says Jenkins has to leave. When Jenkins replies that he does not have to return to work on Monday, that the studio is closed because of a strike, Erridge gets the mistaken impression that Jenkins, being out on strike, must have "all the right ideas."

Since Quiggin is maneuvering to get Erridge to underwrite a left-wing magazine of the arts that he wants to edit, he can express his irritation only obliquely. And the visit to Thrubworth precipitates two new changes of partner in the cosmic dance.

At Lady Molly's focuses on the family as Jenkins—gathering "scraps of information" about the Tollands as one does in life—meets them one by one. At Thrubworth he first meets Lady Isobel when she and her sister Lady Susan breeze in to announce Susan's engagement to Roddy Cutts, a Tory member of parliament. "Much as I hate the Tories," Quiggin says, "I've heard that Cutts is one of their few promising young men" (4:140).

The sight of Isobel marks a change in the rhythm of time for Jenkins: "Would it be too explicit, too exaggerated, to say that when I set eyes on Isobel Tolland, I knew at once that I should marry her? Something like that is the truth; certainly nearer the truth than merely to record those . . . inchoate sentiments of interest of which I was so immediately conscious" (4:136).

At almost the same time Jenkins becomes imperfectly aware of another shift, when Erridge sends his surly butler for champagne to celebrate Susan's engagement and Mona seems delighted. Though at the time it seems to Jenkins absurd to suspect that Templer's exwife Mona would see in so taciturn a hermit as Erridge hope of relief from boredom, by the end of the volume she and Erridge have gone off to China together, leaving Quiggin behind.

Among the crystallizing scenes in *At Lady Molly's* is an apotheosis of those amiable drunk-comedy scenes that stretch back in literature at least as far as Plato's Symposium. Thought to be a Milquetoast by some, scored for his ignorance by intellectuals such as Mark Members, Ted Jeavons is revealed to Jenkins during a pub crawl to be an amiable, modest, and amusing chap. Over the table in a nightclub recently opened by Umfraville, he sings "If You Were the Only Girl in the World":

"People don't think the same way any longer," he bawled across the table. "The war blew the whole bloody thing up. . . . Always feel rather sorry for your generation as a matter of fact, not but what we haven't lost our—what do you call 'em . . .

"Illusions?"

"Illusions! That's the one. We've lost all our bloody illusions. Put 'em all in the League of Nations, or somewhere like that. Illusions, my God. I had a few of 'em when I started. You wouldn't believe it. Of course, I've been lucky. Lucky isn't the word, as a matter of fact. Still people always talk as if marriage was one long roll in the hay. You can take it from me, my boy, it isn't. . . . Molly and I are very fond of each other in our own way. Between you and me, she's not a great one for bed. . . . Still, you have to step out once in a way. Go melancholy mad, otherwise. Life's a rum business, however you look at it, and—as I was saying—not having been born to this high life, and so on, I can't exactly complain." (4:179)

The story Jeavons is leading up to is that of an affair he had had during the war with a once glamorous girl, whom he discreetly does not name; nevertheless, Jenkins is able to identify her as the woman to whom Widmerpool is now engaged, Mildred Blaides. As Jeavons finishes the tale, Widmerpool enters with his fiancée.

Powell does not allow coincidence to rest there. The party to celebrate Jenkins's engagement to Lady Isobel brings out the eldest of the Tollands, Uncle Alfred, Erridge's namesake, who is an "Old Boy" from Le Bas' house. Indeed, it was after sitting beside Uncle Alfred at one Old Boy dinner that Jenkins had resolved, he now recalls, to attend no more reunion dinners. Coincidence might be said to swirl through the social no-man's-land that is Lady Molly's house: here Widmerpool first meets his own fiancée, and here Erridge meets the novelist St. John Clarke (4:124) with fatal effect for Quiggin. Quiggin had hoped to be Clarke's heir, but Clarke leaves his money to Erridge as one more likely to use it for the Left. Ironically, Erridge, disillusioned with the Left after his return from the civil war in Spain (5:197), uses the money instead to repair Thrubworth (5:227).

That Erridge resembles George Orwell in certain details, as several critics have remarked, is true, but the radical peer—the aristocrat by birth who adopts the viewpoint of the peasant or worker—is a familiar English type; and the rest of the English have always found the type amusing. Sir James Barrie in his play *The Admirable Crichton* (1902), for instance, portrays a radical peer in the character of Lord Loam, who forces the servants to eat "upstairs"—sitting down with the family—

once a year to show his egalitarian spirit, much to the disapproval of his butler, Crichton. "Can't you see, Crichton, that our divisions into classes are artificial, that if we were to return to Nature, which is the aspiration of my life, all would be equal?" That Lord Loam is wrong, that nature ordains a class system as the butler maintains, the play then sets out to "prove." And Erridge moves in that direction.

Casanova's Chinese Restaurant

Considered as a separable novel, *Casanova's Chinese Restaurant* is one of the more successful. As the word *Casanova* in the title might suggest, its theme is love—love comic and tragic (5:157), but married love. Jenkins's marriage to Lady Isobel Tolland takes place, but between chapters: the focus is on the marriages of a music critic named Maclintick, who commits suicide when his wife deserts him, and a musical composer named Hugh Moreland, who has married the former mistress of Sir Magnus Donners, but is at the point of leaving her for the sister of Lady Isobel when the suicide occurs. Love partnerships are broken and reformed in the cosmic flux, as husbands and wives dance to the music of time, "in seemingly meaningless gyrations, while partners disappear only to reappear again, once more giving pattern to the spectacle." And the Chinese restaurant of the title points to the spot in London where, in 1926, Jenkins came to know the two husbands, Maclintick and Moreland.

Only the first volume of The Music of Time has a more Proustian envelopment of theme. Jenkins sights a bombed-out pub (between 1947 and 1950 we assume, since he feels "glad the place had not yet been rebuilt")—with only the word *Ladies* still decipherable on the lintel of a "gateway to some unknown, forbidden domain, the lair of sorcerers." The doorway to the ladies' room leads now into an abyss of rubble. Suddenly "there came from this unexplored country the song . . . of the blonde woman on crutches . . . whose voice I had not heard since the day . . . Moreland and I had listened . . . the afternoon he had talked of getting married" (5:1). That talk had occurred in the early 1930s, at a period when Jenkins still loved Jean Templer. A more voluntary effort of the memory carries him back to the mid-1920s where the story began. (As a technique new to The Music of Time, after four volumes of simple chronological sequence, this use of the time shift opened new possibilities of form; volume 6, *The Kindly Ones,* takes us back to 1914.)

An index to *Casanova's Chinese Restaurant* is the song "Pale Hands I Loved beside the Shalimar," which poses a melancholy but appropriate question, "Where are you now?" Moreover, the song moves from the implication of the loss of love to the thought of love's infidelity, "Who lies beneath your spell?" In 1926 or 1927, in the pub, Jenkins had met not only the music critic Maclintick, but the violinist Carolo, a former child prodigy (of North Midlands origin despite the Italianate name). As the novel ends, Carolo lies "beneath the spell" of Maclintick's errant wife, Maclintick lies dead, and Moreland has returned to his wife, Matilda, after being for a time "beneath the spell" of Jenkins's new sister-in-law Priscilla.

A reproduction of Bernini's statue "Truth Unveiled by Time" is also introduced in the first scene, and it too tends to preside over the novel. Why Quiggin can be irritated despite being praised (5:196) becomes apparent when we learn to whom Clarke has left his money. Why Maclintick's suicide should make Moreland's wife happier becomes apparent when we learn of the breakup of his supposed affair with Priscilla. "What Matilda thought, what Priscilla thought remained a mystery. All sides of such a situation are seldom shown at once, even if they are shown at all" (5:221). And what is to become of these marriages in difficulty because time has already unveiled too much truth, time may or may not reveal.

Jenkins's marriage to Erridge's sister Lady Isobel Tolland seems to have been a society wedding to which at least Templer (6:102), Widmerpool (6:233), and General Conyers (6:208) are invited. In the previous volume, General Conyers had taken time out from playing "Ave Maria" on the cello and reading Freud to comment on marriage, as Widmerpool is released from its threat and as Jenkins moves toward it: "What was it Foch said? War not an exact science, but a terrible and passionate drama? Something like that. Fact is, marriage is rather like that too" (4:234). Since the marriage of General and Mrs. Conyers seems as happy as any Jenkins knows, the words instill some apprehension. But the marriage of Jenkins is less the center of attention in *Casanova's Chinese Restaurant* than the marriages of Moreland and Maclintick.

All of the marriages are puzzling in one way or another. The Maclinticks seem to be engaged in an unending quarrel (5:188, 209)— "To be married to either of the Maclinticks can not be much fun" (5:157)—but, instead of being relieved to be rid of his wife, time reveals that Maclintick's dependence on her is so acute he cannot survive her loss. The first odd feature of Moreland's marriage is that it links a rather conservative young man to a notorious young lady, for gossip has identified actress Matilda as the former kept-woman of Sir Magnus Donners. Meeting her, Jenkins discovers a candor and realism that make her character seem to be what Moreland needs in a wife; and it is, after all, only the prospective husband whose pride might object to "damaged goods." Three or four years of apparently happy matrimony elapse; then Jenkins and his wife discover at Moreland's concert that all is not well with the Morelands.

"Is it fun to be married to anyone?" Matilda asks. The shock of Maclintick's suicide induces Moreland to end his incipient affair with Priscilla and return to his wife, Matilda. What adds to the dimension of this coincidence is Matilda's revelation that, before consorting with Donners, she had been married to Carolo, who has now in a sense saved her marriage by breaking up Maclintick's.

Not only character but geography is simultaneously preserved and transformed. The Mortimer in London, for instance, seems a blend of two pubs, the Fitzroy Tavern and The Portland. Cecil Gray in his memoir recalls last seeing a novelist friend "when I was standing outside a public house called 'The George,' at the corner of Mortimer Street and Great Portland Street. . . . I thought he looked ill, and two or three days later he was dead. And then I remembered suddenly that the last time I had seen Robert Nichols before his death a couple of years earlier was in precisely the same place—a strange coincidence. And the last time I saw Philip Heseltine before he died was in 'The Portland,' about twenty yards away. That neighborhood is, for me, thickly populated with ghosts" (Gray 1948, 285). As for *Casanova's Chinese Restaurant,* a name that delights Jenkins with its "unequivocal blendings of disparate elements" that "linked not only the East with the West but the present with the past" (5:29), one element of its composition may be the famed Eiffel Tower restaurant, which, despite its French name, came into its glory under the management of Rudolf Stulik, who came from Vienna and spoke with a thick German accent.

Casanova's Chinese Restaurant is given historical counterpoint by Edward VIII's marriage to the American divorcée Wallis Simpson, an appropriate totem as a double divorcée about to take on her third partner. Widmerpool, appropriately "in" with the Wallis Simpson crowd of American businessmen, anticipates a bit smugly entering court circles after the marriage (5:127). The king's sudden abdication as the volume ends—"to marry the woman I love"—strikes Widmerpool as almost a personal betrayal (5:195).

The Kindly Ones

The Kindly Ones opens on the day of the assassination of Archduke Francis Ferdinand at Sarajevo, 28 June 1914, and closes 25 years later, some weeks after the signing of the Russo-German Non-Aggression Pact on 24 August 1939. The narrative begins with the news that Jenkins's father must go to war and closes when Jenkins in turn finds a way to go to war himself. Or, it opens with a demonstration of the leadership ability of General Conyers and the ease with which he confronts sect leader Dr. Trelawney; resumes the quadrille when Jenkins and his wife, Moreland and his wife, and Templer and his wife act out a pageant in the castle of Sir Magnus Donners; and comes to a close with the death of Uncle Giles—and further surprising revelations about the nature of love, from Uncle Giles and from Jean Templer.

Like many memoirs of upper-class childhood, the chapter dealing with Nick Jenkins' "discovery" of World War I is focused on the servants. Among the principals in the household of Captain Jenkins are the cook Albert and the parlor maid Billson; and again the theme is love, in this case Billson's unrequited love for Albert. Albert, stolidly averse to love, direly likens the suffragettes to the Amazons; and, when he announces that he has decided to retire, Billson's frustration comes to a climax. Stonehurst, the house the Jenkinses are renting at the time near a military camp, is haunted, some tales have it; and although such evidences as exist "might have been disregarded in a more rationalistic family; in one less metaphysically flexible, they could have caused agitation" (6:5). The Jenkins family and most of the servants take calmly the stories of ghosts. When General and Mrs. Conyers arrive for dinner and Billson is expected to serve the mousse, however, her nerves have been wracked by sighting ghosts. When she arrives at the dinner table to announce her own resignation, she is nude.

No book in The Music of Time gives more attention to Jenkins's family. The mother remains a shadowy figure, but Captain Jenkins is brilliantly characterized, with General Conyers as his foil. Captain Jenkins "hid in his heart a hatred of constituted authority. He did his best to conceal this antipathy, because the one thing he hated, more than constituted authority itself, was to hear constituted authority questioned by anyone but himself" (6:38). On the other hand, twice on the afternoon that informs this chapter General Conyers "earns" his position of authority by showing himself to be a man of action.

The first is on the occasion of Billson's nudity: "No one afterwards was ever very well able to describe how he transported her along the passage . . . the shawl always decently draped round Billson like a robe. The point . . . was that action had been taken, willpower brought into play" (6:61). The second occasion involves Dr. Trelawney. "There was something decidedly unpleasant about him, sinister, at the same time absurd, that combination of the ludicrous and alarming soon to be widely experienced by contact with those set in authority in wartime," Jenkins recalls of Dr. Trelawney (6:190). He trots into view across the hills near Aldershot in 1914 followed by his nature-boy disciples in long white robes, only to be stopped by the sight of General Conyers. "The Essence of the All is the Godhead of the True," Trelawney exclaims; and the enlightened general surprisingly replies in kind: "The Vision of Visions heals the Blindness of Sight" (6:64).[15]

Looking back over history, Nicholas Jenkins sees Dr. Trelawney, for all his "religious, philosophical—some said magical—tenets . . . of which he was high priest, if not actually messiah," as the emblem of a confused era: "one of those fairly common strongholds of unsorted ideas that played such a part in the decade ended by the war. Simple-lifers, utopian socialists, spiritualists, occultists, theosophists, quietists, pacifists, futurists, cubists, zealots of all sorts . . . were then thought of by the unenlightened as scarcely distinguishable one from another: a collection of visionaries who hoped to build a New Heaven and a New Earth through the agency of their particular crackpot activities, sinister or comic, according to the way you looked at things" (6:28). The intellectual sickness of a society, and the loneliness of its sentinels whose tradition was slipping away, are telescoped pictorially as Jenkins recalls seeing as a child, in the sunset, "Dr. Trelawney and his flock roaming through the scrub at the same moment as the Military Policeman on his patrol was riding back in the opposite direction. . . . This meeting and merging of two elements—two ways of life—made a striking contrast in physical appearance, moral ideas and visual tone-values" (6:29). Powell, it is obvious, shares General Conyers's interest in both the ideas and the tones.

Although Trelawney's idiom is that of Aleister Crowley, elements of Arthur Machen (1863–1947) may also go into his composition. Machen—a Welsh-born student of the occult and a member (with W. B. Yeats) of the Rosicrucian Order of the Golden Dawn—was either a neighbor or a family acquaintance of the Powells. "I saw him often when I was a boy," Powell recalls,[16] and it is as a boy that Nick Jenkins first sees Dr. Trelawney. Decades later, Moreland reveals that he too had been fascinated as a boy by the figure of Dr. Trelawney (6:83). And perhaps the physical-culture disciples of Dr. Trelawney owe something to those of Georgi Gurdjieff (that "eccentric, filthy, funny, phoney, tender, wise . . . and charismatic" magician of lost souls in the 1920s" (Calder-Marshall, 106–36). Whatever the ingredients of Dr. Trelawney, his mystic or pseudoscientific lore—countered well by General Conyers—helps demonstrate the general's ability to cope with an esoteric problem. Perhaps Powell aims here at an ironic commentary on the scandalous failures of politically appointed British generals in World War I; for the passage concludes with Uncle Giles's arrival and the news of the assassination at Sarajevo—which Uncle Giles typically and absurdly ascribes to the hazards of automotive transport.

The title *The Kindly Ones* takes us back to Greek myths that Powell sees as still powerful because of the patterns of human experience to which they give shape and symbol. The three avenging sisters the Erinyes, or the Furies—who are appeased by being addressed as the Eumenides, or the Kindly Ones—are first encountered by Jenkins in Miss Orchard's class for officers' children near Aldershot. Young Jenkins identifies them with the suffragettes that have so alarmed Albert: "They inflicted the vengeance of the gods by bringing in their train war, pestilence, dissension on earth; torturing, too, by the stings of conscience. . . . So feared were they, Miss Orchard said, that no man. . . fixed his eyes upon their temples. In that respect, at least, the Furies differed from the suffragettes" (6:2–3). They symbolize the emancipated women in the novel who turn its conclusion into another tortuous round of musical beds. But so far as the lives of the children and their parents are concerned, Uncle Giles with his news of the assassination at Sarajevo is the first "harbinger of the Furies" (6:70).

Evelyn Waugh claims the title "is self-explanatory: the Eumenides accomplish their task of vengeance, begun in 1914, completed in 1939, by the destruction of English civilisation."[17] But it is not certain that Powell has so grim a thesis in mind; it would be more like him to play on the ambiguity, as in the first association of "the kindly ones" with women.

The second chapter introduces Moreland in a conversation as brilliantly ideological as any in Aldous Huxley. From an antithetical background, one devoted to music, Moreland has had experiences similar to those of Nick Jenkins—even to encounters with Dr. Trelawney. Powell then advances the clock 10 years to the period of Hitler's victory at

Munich. Jenkins and his wife, not having seen the Morelands since their involvement with Priscilla, visit them in the country, and the four are invited by Sir Magnus Donners to his castle nearby. The "driver" he sends for them turns out to be Peter Templer, and the evening is highlighted by their decision to pose in tableaux of the Seven Deadly Sins for Donners's camera. Jenkins is appropriately cast as Sloth, but the highlight is Lady Isobel's depiction of Pride with Lady Ann Umfraville. "Here, before us, in these two was displayed the nursery and playroom life of generations of 'great houses': the abounding physical vitality of big aristocratic families, their absolute disregard for personal dignity . . . that passionate return to childhood, never released so fully in any other country, or . . . class" (6:128–29).

The dramatic climax comes when Templer, portraying senile Lust with Anne, drives his new wife Betty into jealous hysteria. At this moment Widmerpool arrives in his own new costume, that of an officer of the Territorials. After what seems a rather stilted chat about finance with Sir Magnus (6:137), he drives the Morelands and the Jenkinses home. Time is to unveil that the artificial talk had another role, to get Templer to gossip about certain financial details (6:174). Time also unveils another consequence of Templer's play for Anne; and by the end of *The Kindly Ones*, Anne has left Sir Magnus—and Matilda has left Moreland.

In the third section of the novel, six paths that have crossed before intersect near the sea, where the Jenkins family cook has become the proprietor of a small hotel. Nick Jenkins goes there on receiving a telegram that his Uncle Giles has died in the hotel. As Jenkins sorts through his uncle's possessions, revelations of time come as to who is to be Uncle Giles's heir (it is Mrs. Erdleigh, the fortune-teller, who is living nearby), as to Uncle Giles's status (contrary to gossip, he had received a bona fide military commission), and as to his secret life (in the bottom of his trunk is a copy of *The Perfumed Garden, or the Arab Art of Love*). More surprising is the presence in the same hotel of Dr. Trelawney, who between shots of heroin and brandy gets stuck, in a wildly farcical scene, in the hall bathroom (6:183).[18] Most surprising is the discovery in the dining room of Bob Duport, not seen for 15 years, who is here by the sea to avoid his creditors. Unaware that Jenkins has had an affair with his wife, Duport tells him that Jean left Templer and returned to him only to get a free trip to South America and another man. Jenkins is crushed by the revelation that when he thought Jean was only betraying her husband she was also betraying him, and with the most repulsive of Duport's associates, Jimmy Brent.

Recalling a chapter in *The Perfumed Garden,* "On the Deceits and Treacheries of Women," Jenkins quietly gives Duport the book as a token from Uncle Giles, who died a bachelor.

The final section leads us to the outbreak of World War II and to the efforts of Jenkins to activate his reserve commission and enter the army. Neither General Conyers nor Widmerpool can help him, although Widmerpool is less than frank about his limitations: "'You come and ask me for advice about getting into the army, Nicholas,' he said, 'and because I spare the time to talk of such things . . . you think I have nothing more serious to occupy me than your own trivial problems. That is not the case. The General Staff of the Wehrmacht would be only too happy to possess even a tithe of the information I locked away before we quitted the Orderly Room'" (6:230).

At Lady Molly's, however, Jenkins meets Ted Jeavons's modest brother (an obscure staff officer but in a position of power), who promises him action in a week or two and keeps his promise. Jenkins's commission is activated, and he is assigned to an infantry regiment in Wales. The Seven Deadly Sins of Society have invoked the Furies of Purgation and, like Orestes, Jenkins accepts their chastisements as "part of a required pattern the fulfillment of which was in some way a relief" (7:2).

The Valley of Bones

The Valley of Bones, the seventh volume of The Music of Time, begins with Jenkins's introduction to his regiment in the autumn of 1939 and closes with his departure from the regiment as the German armies near Paris in June 1940. Except for a brief leave when Jenkins visits his wife and gets briefed on Tolland family gossip, the cast of characters is completely new and totally Welsh. The focus is on the drama of life an infantry company; the captain and his officers, the sergeants and their men form a miniature society of their own. Here, nevertheless, the old pressures of love and power continue to exact their toll.

The day Jenkins arrives in Wales is Saturday, and next morning the regiment is marched to church where the Welsh chaplain takes his text from Ezekiel (and gives the volume its title):

> The hand of the Lord was upon me, and carried me out in the spirit of the Lord, and set me down in the midst of the valley which was full of bones, and . . . behold there were very many in the open valley: and, lo, they were very dry. And he said unto me, Son of man, can these bones live?

> And I answered, 0 Lord God thou knowest. . . . Come from the four winds, 0 breath, and breathe upon these slain that they may live. So I prophesied as he commanded me, and the breath came unto them and they lived, and stood up upon their feet, an exceeding great army.

The chaplain is from the mining valleys of Wales, not the urban "waste land" of T. S. Eliot: "Oh, my brethren, think on that open valley . . . a valley, do I picture it, by the shaft of a shutdown mine, where, under the dark mountain side, the slag heaps lift their heads to the sky. . . . They are our bones, my brethren, the bones of you and of me, bones that await the noise and shaking" (37–38).

The mighty army has come together; the question is whether it will live. The officers of Jenkins's unit, most of them Welsh bankers, had in peace been as dead men; the question is whether they will come collectively alive. At the end of the volume, it is obvious that they have; fore-runners have met the enemy at Dunkirk and taken his measure—but not without a price. A man from Jenkins's platoon has been killed; his brother-in-law Robert Tolland has also been killed; and Isobel has given birth to a son. War has accelerated the rhythm of life, but the rhythm remains.

Removal from the social matrix of earlier volumes has several effects. One surprise is that, presumably in the name of military realism, Powell for the first time "listens in" as soldiers tell an off-color joke (7:55) and talk obscenely (7:178). As surprising to readers accustomed to the earlier society is the isolation of Jenkins from anyone with whom we are familiar. Among the new characters is his platoon sergeant, Pendry, a man who withers away inarticulately for love and ends as an apparent suicide. Another is Lieutenant Bithel, an engagingly unsuccessful con artist.

More important to Jenkins, however, is his company commander, Captain Gwatkin (who turns out to be distantly related to the debutante Barbara Goring {7:187}). Gwatkin is determined to be a good officer and he has a number of virtues: he is sensible, humane, conscientious, and reasonably intelligent. But he blunders from mishap to catastrophe, alienating the well-disposed and conciliating the inherently vicious. He is fatally handicapped by his very determination and by his ignorance of human nature. In the end, he is relieved of the command of his company, and he finds no comfort in love. Infatuated with a barmaid in North Ireland, he overlooks Jenkins's suggestion that her character might not be of the best, and in the gardens of Castle Mallock, commemorated by

Byron and Thackeray, he finds her in the arms of another man, a soldier in his company.

In the third of the four chapters—a quadrille structure is maintained in seven of the 12 volumes—Jenkins is posted to Aldershot for a two-week training course and finds himself back on the fringes of the society we know. Marching beside Jimmy Brent, he painfully learns more about Jean Templer's perfidies (7:30). His single weekend away from Aldershot is spent in the country, where Isobel is awaiting the birth of their child, and there the novel resumes its web of marital interweaving. The ultradignified Lady Frederica is now engaged, he discovers, to the infraraffish Umfraville, one of those bizarre "human relationships easier to accept than to rationalize or disentangle" (7:145). Umfraville tells Jenkins the story of how his first wife, Dolly, had eloped with Buster Foxe (7:153), Stringham's stepfather, just as Commander Foxe himself arrives, looking "immensely distinguished . . . in naval uniform." Robert Tolland has married Stringham's sister Flavia; and Buster has come to implore Flavia's assistance in stopping Flavia's mother from divorcing him to marry the actor Norman Chandler (who had discovered the statuette *Truth Unveiled by Time*). But Buster arrives at the moment Robert receives an urgent call to report back to duty—unknown to them that evening, the German army is set to invade Holland—and Lt. Odo Stevens, a narcissistic salesman of costume jewelry in civilian life, arrives with a brooch for Priscilla, whose husband has been at sea for some time. The threat is there, in her strange encouragement of Odo, of another ruptured marriage.

Serial polygamy, as one sociologist has called the "new" pattern of marital living, is to be perceived as much in British upper-class circles as in Hollywood, and its drifting lovers are seen to be no happier—at least as observed by Jenkins from the vantage point of his own apparently solid marriage. Certainly the changing of partners is seen as a characteristic of modern life, if not of life itself. Changes may not be made quite as casually as in quadrille, yet the fact that the choice of mate so often remains inexplicable—Jean's choice of the fat Brent, Frederica's of the wild Umfraville, Conyers's of the astringent Tuffy Weedon, and Priscilla's of the obscene Odo—makes human lives seem like electrons whose quanta leaps cannot be predicted. The Music of Time probes the unknown quantity, as if Powell would analyze the character of the Wife of Bath by seeking the common denominator of the four husbands she survived.

When the fourth part of *The Valley of Bones* brings us back to North Ireland, we witness the dispersal of the infantry company Jenkins knew. He himself is posted to division headquarters, where he discovers that he has become Widmerpool's underling. "I had no reason to suppose you would be the most efficient," Widmerpool says with his usual crass pomposity, "but since none of the others had any more legal training . . . I allowed the ties of old acquaintance to prevail . . . subject to your giving satisfaction, of course." The volume ends rather ominously—"I saw that I was now in Widmerpool's power"—though not bleakly, since the general to whom Widmerpool is in turn subordinate seems hardly a man to admire the Widmerpools of the world.

The Soldier's Art

The second volume of the war-novel trilogy within The Music of Time covers the years 1940–42 and begins with Nicholas Jenkins a lieutenant attached to the headquarters of a British infantry division, commanding its defense platoon. By coincidence Widmerpool and Stringham are also attached to the headquarters unit, and the focus is on the struggles for power up and down the echelons of command. The situation is congenial to neither Jenkins nor Stringham, and they eventually escape, Jenkins after a visit to London on a quiet day of the Blitz—which leaves three of his friends killed by bombs.

The title *The Soldier's Art* is of distinguished literary provenance. We can trace it back at least to Shakespeare's *King Lear,* when the old king, half mad, is followed into a storm by his friend Edgar, who in order to approach him feigns madness. The scene ends, as they enter a hut, with Edgar's enigmatic and ominous words:

> Child Rowland to the dark tower came;
> His word was still
> "Fie, Foh, and fum!
> I smell the blood of a British man." (3:4:173)

After rereading *King Lear* in the 1850s, Robert Browning was inspired to write one of his better poems, the enigmatic "Childe Roland to the Dark Tower Came." In that dramatic monologue a knight is depicted crossing a grisly landscape to a mortal but otherwise uncertain combat. The only living thing he comes upon is a "stiff, blind horse, his every bone a-stare":

Seldom went such grotesqueness with such woe;
I never saw a brute I hated so;
He must be wicked to deserve such pain.
I shut my eyes and turned them on my heart.
As a man calls for wine before he fights,
I asked one draught of earlier, happier sights,
Ere fitly I could hope to play my part.
Think first, fight afterwards—the soldier's art;
One taste of the old time sets all to rights.

But this effort of the memory to find sustenance in past time is in vain.
"Not it!" the knight exclaims, as recollection brings up only the faces of
friends disgraced or hanged as traitors.

"Better this present than a past like that," the knight reflects as he
resumes his journey, uncomforted, into desolation. The sentiment he
expresses is that of Stringham, who reads the passage from Browning
aloud to Jenkins as they stand on a street corner just before the climax of
World War II (8:221). Stringham is the happy warrior, but his years of
dissipation have left him so wasted physically that he has been denied
entrance into glamorous fighting units such as the commandos and the
paratroops. When reunited with Jenkins, he is a private soldier serving
as a waiter in an officers' mess.

The former governess who cured Stringham of his alcoholism had also
introduced him to the poems of Browning. When Jenkins protests that
he personally is "never sure" what he feels about Browning—presumably because of the glibness of some of Browning's moralizing—
Stringham insists that "there's a lot in what he says." Moreover,
Stringham identifies with Browning's knight. Jenkins, suspecting this,
tentatively follows Stringham's reading with a query: "Childe Roland to
the Dark Tower Came?" Stringham replies, "Childe Stringham—in this
case" (8:221).

Of Jenkins's acquaintances during this dark period of the war, the
period of the Blitz, many turn to the great Victorian writers as to wells
of moral surety from a world where, as Yeats puts it, "the best lack all
conviction." Victorianism reborn might almost be considered a minor
theme of the volume. It is General Liddament's shock that Lieutenant
Jenkins does not share his enthusiasm for the novels of Anthony Trollope
and his discovery that Jenkins reads Balzac in French instead (8:47) that
leads to Jenkins's salvation: the general recommends him to the Free
French as an interpreter. Although Jenkins fails his examination with a

Major Finn (a character much like Stringham in that he resists escalation of his own rank), while in Major Finn's office he meets Pennistone, who tacitly promises to rescue him from the Infantry Officers Replacement Pool to which Widmerpool would have consigned him on his own departure to higher things (8:106).

Widmerpool had reproached Jenkins earlier for trying to get Stringham a better position. " 'I have always been told,' said Widmerpool, '—and rightly told—that it is a great mistake in the army, or indeed elsewhere, to allow personal feelings about individuals to affect my conduct towards them professionally. . . . Why should Stringham have some sort of preferential treatment just because you and I happen to have been at school with him? . . . War is a great opportunity for everyone to find his level. I am a major—you are a second-lieutenant— he is a private'" (8:72–73). Powell at this point suggests clearly that in battle, where the playing field levels and a soldier is tested, Stringham may turn out to be the better soldier.

During Jenkins's absence on leave, Widmerpool has Stringham transferred to a Mobile Laundry Unit; and we learn that Stringham has the loyalty to his superiors that is another part of the knightly tradition. One night he finds his commanding officer Lieutenant Bithel drunk on the street. He telephones Jenkins for aid in getting Bithel, who loves the army and drinks because he knows his position to be insecure, back to the officers' quarters before the police can spot him.

Ironically, when Jenkins comes to Stringham's aid, the three men in the blackout bump into Major Widmerpool. Widmerpool dismisses Jenkins as the air-raid alert sounds: "Stringham and I will get this sot back to bed. I'll see this is the last time the army's troubled with him."

The sight of Widmerpool by flashlight has set Stringham to musing: " 'It's interesting to recall, sir,' he said {to Widmerpool} 'the last time we met. I myself was the inert frame. It was you and Mr. Jenkins who so kindly put me to bed. It shows that improvement is possible, that roles can be reversed. I've turned over a new leaf. Stringham is enrolled in the ranks of the sober, as well as the brave'" (8:185). The volume closes as Stringham cheerfully sets forth, carrying his volume of Browning, apparently destined for service in North Africa where a rear-echelon laundry, in the fluidity of desert war, may easily find itself on the front line.

A possible model for this phase of Stringham's life can be seen in the career of a contemporary of Powell's at Oxford, Alfred Duggan, whom

Evelyn Waugh recalls in *A Little Learning* as an Oxford student who was always drunk:

> Little could have surprised me more forty, thirty, or even twenty years ago than the revelation that Alfred was to become the industrious, prolific historical novelist who is honoured today. . . . He was very rich then with the immediate disposal of a fortune greater than any of our contemporaries. He was, moreover, the stepson of the Chancellor of the University, Lord Curzon. This connection irked the authorities, who otherwise would have summarily sent him down. . . . Whether in the saddle in the late mornings or at "the 43" [Mrs. Meyrick's night club] in the early mornings, Alfred was always tight; never violent, always carefully and correctly dressed, always polite, he lived in an alcoholic haze. . . . Lord Curzon discerned his quality [however]. His memory was exceptionally retentive and in the shadowy years when he continued to drink very heavily and was seen sitting, apparently stupefied, turning the pages of an historical work in the library at Hackwood, his brain, like an electronic device, was in an inexplicable way storing up recondite information which became available when he heroically overcame this inherited disability. (Waugh, 202–3)

Stringham is not destined for literary distinction, as Alfred Duggan was, though he is, next to Moreland, the most articulate of Jenkins's friends. Nor is it Powell's style to make Stringham the center of the grand heroics that shower medals of honor on the brave and the lucky. Stringham's destiny is to be taken prisoner of war with the fall of Singapore and to die in a Japanese prisoner-of-war camp. That in the battle for Singapore Childe Stringham may have redeemed his wasted life we never know.

In form *The Soldier's Art* is the first volume in the series to have a three-part structure: one day of Jenkins's leave in London is sandwiched between two periods of duty as a staff officer at an infantry division headquarters. The first of these sections focuses on the abuses of power at the headquarters, abuses which Jenkins observes. Widmerpool, the adjutant general of the division, is of course at the center of the intrigue; he prevents a corporal in Jenkins's defense platoon from going to officers training school because he is a good clerk; and he schemes to get his own candidate made commander of a new reconnaissance unit. The larger intrigue ends in Widmerpool's discomfiture when Sunny Farebrother, now Widmerpool's "opposite number" at a higher headquarters, steps back into Jenkins's life after 20 years to reveal that his own candidate has secured the coveted post (8:195). Farebrother has suavely and ruthlessly used Widmerpool's own words against him, and the volume ends with Widmerpool temporarily deflated, his machinations exposed. Some relief is brought to Jenkins and to Widmerpool, respectively, at the end, however, with the news that Germany has invaded Russia and that the general whom Widmerpool now has most reason to fear will be leaving to command a corps.

Like several of the previous volumes, *The Soldier's Art* traces the mysterious and therefore not wholly traceable path of a suicide. A vulgar captain in charge of physical training, an officer but no gentleman, finds Stringham's cool demeanor and cultivated accent offensive in the officers' mess; and Stringham is hounded without mercy. But it is the captain who is found hanging in the cricket pavilion: "Never thought Biggy would have done that. In the cricket pav, of all places, and him so fond of the game" (8:228).

The central section of *The Soldier's Art* takes us through only the first day of Jenkins's leave, a quiet day in London during the Blitz; but during the day we have the first death of friends attributable to enemy action. It opens with Jenkins dining with Moreland at the Café Royal, and Chips Lovell is with them for a while. In town unexpectedly, Chips hopes to meet his wife, Priscilla, later at the Café de Madrid, where Bijou Ardglass is celebrating her fortieth birthday by giving a party to which Priscilla has been invited. Chips hopes to effect a reconciliation.

Chips has barely departed for the Madrid when Priscilla arrives at the Café Royal on the arm of Odo Stevens, the commando with whom she is having an affair. The sound of a distant explosion, possibly that of a German tip-and-run raider dropping a single bomb, punctuates the conversation only indistinctly; yet Priscilla grows nervous and leaves in agitation, almost breaking relations with Stevens on the spot. She returns to Lady Molly's, apparently hoping Chips will find her there, preferring Molly's family bastion to the nightclub atmosphere of the Madrid.

Later Moreland and Maclintick's wife (with whom Moreland is now living) take Jenkins to their apartment, and the talk is again punctuated with the sound of a distant explosion. Moreland's new lodger Max Pilgrim enters to tell them that the Madrid, where he was playing that night, has been bombed and that Chips Lovell is dead. When Jenkins tries to phone Molly to inform her, he fails to get through. Taking a taxi to Lady Molly's, he discovers that a bomb has just struck the rear of her house, leaving the facade intact, and that Priscilla is dead. Husband and wife, each in the mood for reconciliation, each having gone where the other should be found, are killed in one quiet evening. Separate bombs falling on widely separated areas of London have ended another pattern. Was Priscilla's inexplicable fidgetiness at the Café Royal after the first muffled sound the result of some psychic contact with her husband? Powell leaves us with the possibility. The strange patterns of life continue, and patterns close, not all with satisfying conclusions.

But Lady Molly has also been killed by the second bomb, and the patterns will never be the same.

The Military Philosophers

The "war trilogy" (as Anthony Powell calls this subset within The Music of Time) concludes with *The Military Philosophers*. Jenkins, in his new role as liaison officer to Allied military commands, is in the heart of London during the three years (1942–45) covered by the volume, except for a brief visit to field headquarters on the Continent. Widmerpool again is contiguous, but the focus is on Peter Templer and Odo Stevens, both of whom parachute to join alligned but bickering partisan factions in the Balkans. Templer finds death, and Stevens the clouded medals of a hero.

To the soldier in the foxhole, who does not know what is going on in the war though he has a frontline seat, so to speak, knowledge seems to lie in the rear—not on his periphery, where the action is, but at central control. And the trajectory of Jenkins has taken him steadily toward the center. There the wisest of military men should be, but the title *The Military Philosophers* is at least in part ironic.

As the novel opens, Jenkins is night-duty officer, as a member of the general staff in Whitehall (a name that in England seems to combine the connotations of Pentagon and State Department); and he seems to be near the heart of British military intelligence. Indeed, a teletype is delivering just-decoded news of a potentially important break in the war: the Russians are allowing Polish troops to cross their frontier into Iran. This exodus may result in the doubling, at least, of Polish forces associated with the British army; yet it is odd in view of the earlier Russian "liquidation" of thousands of Polish officers in the Katyn Forest, an event about which there is only a growing sense of certainty, not certainty itself.

Powell's point seems to be that, even at the heart of things, uncertainty reigns. Whitehall is, of course, an immense international nerve center; and Jenkins is not exactly at the heart of Whitehall. But the volume opens on the day when he, fortuitously, is ushered into a bombproof command room deep under Whitehall, where security clearances are so high that even Captain Jenkins is twice alluded to as a security risk. And there—in command of the situation, fresh from a cabinet minister's office (and from drafting memoranda that would be read by Churchill) and prepared to explain the complexities of the new Polish situation to all—is Colonel Widmerpool.

In one of those patterns of coincidence that are integral to Powell's ultimate purpose in The Music of Time, both Sunny Farebrother, a parachutist now, and Peter Templer, about to be dropped on a secret mission in the Balkans, join them for Widmerpool's briefing. His information that the new Polish integer in the puzzle, General Anders, is a bit of a swashbuckler awakens the old irony: "Still, I'm no enemy to a bit of dash. I like it" Widmerpool maintains (9:17).

The comedy thus continues at the heart of things but shaded with tragedy. The time is 1942, the Balkans have been occupied by the German army, and liaison is needed with the partisan factions within countries such as Yugoslavia. Odo Stevens adds to the complexities by joining the communist partisans within Prince Theodoric's country (Tito's faction?); Templer (like Evelyn Waugh) joins the conservative or royalist faction (Mihailovich's?). But Odo the stout is going to glory (Military Cross and Bar); Templer, as a result of a Widmerpool decision, is going to his death.

The solemn presiding deities are, presumably, Lord Alanbrooke and Field Marshal Montgomery; but on Jenkins's level the tone is seldom far from the comic. The book opens with a reference to the myth and symbols of the Nibelungs: "The curtain had obviously just risen on the third drama of The Ring—Mime at his forge—the wizened lieutenant revealed in his shirtsleeves, crouched over a table, while he scoured away at some object in an absolute fever of energy" (9:2). It is with ironic deflation that Jenkins notices that the lieutenant is actually polishing not the sword of Siegfried but his own Sam Browne belt.

The spit-and-polish aspect of military decorum is personified, of course, by Widmerpool, who meets his match, when it comes to the intricacies of protocol and red tape, in the person of professional staff officer Blackhead. On the other hand, the network of personal relations that has been seen as a part of the Establishment proves to be of military utility when it enables Jenkins to expedite the training, in England, of restless Belgian partisans (9:195) who are threatened by the field marshal: "I'll shoot 'em up. Is that clear? I'll shoot 'em up" (9:179).

As officer in charge of liaison with the Belgians and Czechoslovaks, Jenkins meets an array of characters who bewilder the casual reader. Later, in 1944, he is promoted to major and charged with French and

Luxembourg liaison as well. He finds Welsh-Breton links with the Free-French liaison officer Kernével, and an attempt is made to interweave other groups: Horaczko of Polish liaison marries Margaret Budd in the end, for instance, and setting the boys agog in the Free-French and the Polish legations is a niece of Charles Stringham.

Pamela Flitton, daughter of Stringham's sister Flavia, is first seen as a staff-car driver from the Woman's Transport Auxiliary (ATS); and although she leaves that boring job later to work in Egypt, her sullen beauty shuttles through the whole novel. Umfraville is the first to peg her correctly: "Giving men hell is what Miss Flitton likes. . . . I know the sort" (9:74). Jenkins comes to see in Pamela "a woman whose sexual disposition was vested in rage and perversity" (9:128). Pamela enters with the suggestion that she has had an affair with the nephew of her mother's second husband, the American Milton Wisebite (9:72); but the stories of her affairs are legendary. Running through them, however, is a pattern: an "unvarying technique of silence, followed by violence" (9:74). Like many stunningly beautiful women, Pamela is also attractive to other women, such as Lady Norah Tolland (9:76) and Lady McReith (9:99) whom she similarly mistreats.

The men with whom Pamela Flitton is thought to have had affairs—including Peter Templer (9:82), Prince Theodoric (9:102), and Bob Duport (9:190)—constitute a list that suggests nymphomania, a word Powell does not use. Instead, he sees Pamela as a figure of myth, allied to the myth of Venusberg, and as a scourge for Widmerpool. When told "the name of the girl in red who came in late," Widmerpool is interested: "So that's Pamela Flitton? . . . I've seen her before. With some Americans at one of Biddle's big Allied gatherings" (9:100). Though it is "unlikely Pamela had ever visited Widmerpool's underground office . . . she herself could be envisaged as one of the myriad incarnations of Venus, even if Widmerpool was not much of a Tannhäuser" (9:203). Still, Widmerpool does somehow stumble "on the secret entrance to the court of the Paphian goddess" and another affair develops.

After V-E Day, Jenkins notices in the paper that "Colonel K. G. Widmerpool, OBE," has become engaged to Miss Pamela Flitton. At an embassy victory party, we are treated to a view of the conflict between Widmerpool and his fiancée that forebodes a life of marital pain. She arrives late, wearing the "oldest, most filthy garments she possessed" but looking "very pretty, in spite of her disarray."

"I think you ought to meet the Ambassador, dearest."

"Stuff the Ambassador."

"You really oughtn't to say things like that, darling. . . . Nicholas and I think it very amusing, but someone else might overhear. . . . I shall have to go now. I am late already."

"Late for what?"

"I told you—I'm dining with the Minister."

"You're giving me dinner."

"I only wish I was. Much as I'd love to, I can't . . . Besides, I'm sure you told me you were dining with Lady McReith."

"I'm going to dine with you."

From this struggle of wills, Widmerpool attempts to extricate himself by pointing out that "Nicholas used to be a friend of your uncle, Charles Stringham." " 'Yes,' she said, 'and Charles isn't the only one he knew. He knew Peter Templer too—the man you murdered'" (209–11). Widmerpool's attempts to evade this charge succeed only in showing how his swing to the left politically, and his sympathy for the communist partisans, may indeed have been a factor in Templer's death. But in another way, Pamela is to blame for his death, for it was she who made it clear to Templer, whose first wife deserted him and whose second was in an asylum, that he was "not so hot extra-matrimonially either," just before he insisted on participating in that dangerous mission behind the German lines (9:23, 188).

Some philosophy is needed to get a person through such a life, but in *The Military Philosophers* Maj. David Pennistone, at Whitehall with Jenkins, is the only ostensible philosopher. In practical areas Pennistone's philosophy is also exercised in shepherding temperamental liaison officers from Allied countries. Pennistone is devoting his spare time, however, to "writing a book about Descartes—or possibly Gassendi" (9:6), a book ultimately published under the title of *Descartes, Gassendi and the Atomic Theory of Epicurus* (10:240). By the end of the war, Pennistone's interest in philosophy is reported to be so fatigued that he plans to join Colonel Finn in Paris in the cosmetics business (9:237). It is Dicky Umfraville who alludes to the saying of that philosophic general Marshal Lyautey "that gaiety was the first essential in an officer" (9:140). Pennistone would not disagree, but he seems more stoic. " 'Not all the fruits of Victory are appetising to the palate,' said Pennistone, 'An issue of gall and wormwood has been laid on'" (9:197).

Part of the "gall and wormwood" comes with the victory celebration, with the news of Stringham's death in a Japanese prisoner-of-war camp (9:204). Part of it comes with the award of medals to representatives of countries who entered the war only after Allied victory had been assured. One of these, a South American, even arrives late to the victory service in St. Paul's Cathedral. Jenkins finds room for him among the liaison officers he has shepherded to St. Paul's and is afterward offered a ride back to Whitehall. Out of the car that comes to meet the latecomer step two ladies looking "incredibly elegant," the younger reminding Jenkins of Jean Templer. The colonel introduces Jenkins to his wife. But not until she begins to laugh and exclaims "Nick . . . You look so different in uniform" (9:233) does he recognize Jean Templer and her daughter Polly Duport.

Books Do Furnish a Room

Twenty years after the first volume of The Music of Time was published, the tenth appeared as *Books Do Furnish a Room.* When the narrative begins Jenkins is 40 and has returned for a visit to his university; when the volume closes, he is 42 and has returned for a visit to his public school. We move from the winter of 1945 to December 1947. Discharged from the army, Jenkins returns to the London publishing world of *What's Become of Waring,* accepting a position as subeditor in charge of book reviews for the new magazine *Fission,* which is "to strike the right note for the Atomic Age. Something to catch the young writers coming out of the services" (10:36). Initially, the magazine, far from splitting up the world, as its name might imply, draws characters—and the novel—together.

J. G. Quiggin, the literary critic who appeared as an Oxford undergraduate in *A Question of Upbringing,* returns to Jenkins's circle as cofounder with Sir Howard Craggs, now married to Gypsy Jones, of the publishing firm of Quiggin & Craggs. The company is sponsoring the "modern" periodical *Fission.* Though the firm has inherited the good will of the Vox Populi Press and other left-wing publishers, *Fission* is to be less dogmatically leftist, as befits the late 1940s. The sudden death of Erridge, the wealthy Earl of Warminster, whose sister is married to Jenkins and who is the patron of *Fission,* threatens its economic foundations: "The magazine was to be Warminster's toy to do more or less what he liked with" (10:36). And we find that Widmerpool, as a Labour

MP and a backbencher in the House of Commons, is also interested in *Fission:* "He wants an organ for his own views" (10:95).

The new financial backer of the magazine turns out to be Rosie Manasch (10:101), who is having an affair with one of the contributors, Odo Stevens, just returned from the theater of war where Templer was killed. Odo wishes to publish his memoirs. Also getting memoirs in order for publication by Quiggin & Craggs (with excerpts to appear in *Fission*) is the don Sillery, now Lord Sillery, who has been threading his way through Jenkins's life since *A Question of Upbringing*. In short, the magazine serves to draw familiar characters together again in reasonable ways, thereby enabling Powell to return to the extended comic episode form of the earlier volumes, a form that the war-trilogy volumes tend to dissipate into anecdotage.

Books Do Furnish a Room introduces fewer new characters than any of the war-trilogy volumes, but three of them are important; and each is linked to *Fission:* Books Bagshaw, Ada Leintwardine, and X. Trapnel.

Before his death, Erridge appointed Books Bagshaw editor of *Fission*. Several stories circulate as to how Books Do Furnish a Room (Books for short) Bagshaw got his nickname—all of them disreputable. But the phrase (perhaps tossed off in a pub one evening, Books *Do* furnish a room) stuck. Here it is rich with ironic relevance, for like Peter De Vries' title *No, But I Saw the Movie,* it conveys an attitude toward culture that is both respectful and nugatory. Yet Bagshaw's ambivalence about literature makes him more, rather than less, promising as an editor.

"There was a chap called Max Stirner," Bagshaw would argue with friends like Moreland. "Stirner believed it would be all right if only we could get away from the tyranny of abstract ideas." But according to Jenkins, "Whatever Bagshaw thought about abstract ideas when drunk, he was devoted to them when sober. He resembled a man . . . familiar with the name of every horse listed in *Ruff's Guide to the Turf,* who has now ceased to lay a bet, even feel the smallest desire to visit a race-course" (10:31). Bagshaw is thus an authority on the factions of the Left while remaining objective enough to use his knowledge to ease the course of *Fission.* And it is Bagshaw who hires Jenkins as book editor.

Jenkins and Bagshaw meet by chance at the railway station of the university where Bagshaw has just gone to recruit an executive secretary for *Fission.* We see Ada Leintwardine first in Sillery's rooms. She has come to collect a volume of Sillery's diaries, which she is helping to edit for their eventual appearance as *Garnered at Sunset: Leaves from an*

Edwardian Journal. "A masterpiece of dullness," Bagshaw later said of the published work (10:210). Sillery implies to Jenkins that Ada is part of his spy network, but her family name is that of a village near Offa's Dyke on the border of Wales, not far from where the House of Powell came to prominence, and we see that her tart common sense disconcerts Sillery, pleasing Jenkins. Her role in Powell's novel is not large, but it is cohesive; for one thing, she is the only known friend of Widmerpool's wife.

But Bagshaw's biggest triumph as editor is to snare for *Fission* X. Trapnel, the author of *Camel Ride to the Tomb,* the outstanding novel of the year. Christened Francis Xavier, Trapnel has perhaps taken a hint from Francis X. Bushman, star of silent films, to drop his first name and give himself an "X" of distinction. Trapnel's long overcoat and his swordstick with a death's-head on its handle also capture the imagination. In contrast to Bagshaw's mind, his is subtle. Bagshaw argues: "All I said was, Trappy, that personally I preferred Realism— Naturalism, if you wish. . . . That's how Tolstoy came in. It's like life." Trapnel replies (in words Powell himself has used), "But Naturalism's only 'like' life if the novelist himself is any good. If he isn't any good, it doesn't matter whether he writes naturalistically or any other way. What could be less 'like' life than most of the naturalistic novels that appear?" (10:215–16).

What makes Trapnel most interesting is his internal contradiction, his confusion as to his own myth:

> Trapnel wanted, among other things, to be a writer, a dandy, a lover, a comrade, an eccentric, a sage, a virtuoso, a good chap, a man of honour, a hard case, a spendthrift, an opportunist, a raisonneur; to be very rich, to be very poor, to possess a thousand mistresses, to win the heart of one love to whom he was ever faithful, to be on the best of terms with all men, to avenge savagely the lightest affront, to live to a hundred full of years and honour, to die young and unknown but recognized the following day as the most neglected genius of the age. (10:144–45)

Trapnel seems misplaced in time—as do so many of Powell's favorite characters—for his time is "the Eighteen-Nineties, the decadence. . . . One could not help speculating whether an eye-glass would not be produced—Trapnel was reported to have sported one for a brief period, until broken in a pub brawl" (10:106). He is a connoisseur of pubs, his favorite for a while being The Hero of Acre (10:156). His background is mythic, too, for Trapnel vaguely suggests that his Middle Eastern childhood was occasioned by his father's peregrinations there on secret service work. His career as a novelist has perhaps been influenced by "the resemblance between what a spy does and what a novelist does, the point being you don't suddenly steal an indispensable secret that gives complete mastery of the situation, but accumulate a lot of relatively humdrum facts, which when collated provide the picture." Later, it turns out that Trapnel's father had been a jockey "whose professional career had been made largely in Egypt" (10:229).

Trapnel's panache had been the product of myth. The last words of *Books Do Furnish a Room* are those of Dicky Umfraville, who when asked if he has heard of a jockey called Trapnel, says: "Heard of him, old boy? When I was in Cairo in the 'twenties, I won a packet on a French horse he rode called Amour Piquant" (10:241).

What makes X. Trapnel's excursion into love especially "piquant" is that, when he first meets Pamela Widmerpool, she ignores him; and he is repelled by her lack of good manners. Yet at the christening party for *Fission* given by Rosie Manasch, love blossoms when Pamela arrives and admits she has read and liked *Camel Ride to the Tomb*.

Later, when Trapnel in despair asks Jenkins how he can see her again, Jenkins facetiously suggests he might return the quid that he borrowed from Widmerpool that night for his taxi home. And the next comic episode takes us, by way of a dinner at the House of Commons with Jenkins's brother-in-law Roddy Cutts, to Widmerpool's flat nearby. When the three men arrive they hear the water running full blast in the bathroom. The assumption is that Pamela is bathing, until a neighbor appears and informs them that Pamela has departed, carrying a walking stick, with a man carrying her suitcases and the Modigliani that Stringham had left her.

By brazen coincidence, Jenkins also happens to be present months later when Widmerpool, having traced Pamela and Trapnel by means of private detectives, arrives with a list of denunciations of Trapnel. "First . . . you borrow money from me. . . . Then you lampoon me in a magazine of which I am one of the chief supporters. . . . Finally, my wife comes to live with you." Mixing the absurd with the deadly serious, as is Widmerpool's way, he proceeds to analyze the situation as he sees it: "You can keep my pound . . . I make you a present of it. . . . Secondly . . . . Your so-called parody is a failure. Not funny. Several people have told me so. . . . You may fear that I am going to institute divorce proceedings. Such is not my intention. Pamela will return in her own good time. I think we understand each other" (10:201–2). Nothing could seem more absurd than Widmerpool's understanding anybody; but, by the end of the novel, Pamela has returned to him.

The mechanism of her return is aesthetic, or more accurately a struggle of wills aesthetically colored. Pamela wants Trapnel's new novel *Profiles in String* to end differently: "I'd rather you burnt it than publish it as it stands. In fact you're not going to" (10:196)

In the book's final episode, Bagshaw phones Jenkins to ask his aid in getting Trapnel home from a pub. Trapnel, suspecting that Pamela has left him, and talking with brilliant extravagance, is trying to postpone the return, obviously afraid of what he will find. But they have not yet reached Trapnel's flat when the discovery is made: the manuscript of *Profiles in String* is floating down the Maida Vale Canal. Trapnel, in a baroque gesture, sends his famous death's-head swordstick flying into the canal after it. The odor in the lonely flat later reminds Jenkins of Maclintick's flat, and he thinks of Maclintick's suicide. "Trappy will never take that step," Bagshaw assures him, correctly. "He's too interested in his own myth" (10:228).

During the two years of *Fission*'s existence, Jenkins has been working on his own book, *Borage and Hellebore,* a study of the seventeenth-century antiquarian Robert Burton. *Books Do Furnish a Room* is striated with allusions to Burton's famous *Anatomy of Melancholy,* which first appeared with a longer title: "An Anatomy of Melancholy, What it is, with all the Kindes, Causes, Symptomes, Prognostickes, and severall cures of it. . . . With a Satyricall Preface. . . . Anno Dom. 1621" (10:2). Most of Powell's characters are somehow marked by "Burton's 'vile rock of melancholy, a disease so frequent, as few there are that feel not the smart of it'" (10:54). Burton felt that even the botanical world must feel the smart of love as "two trees bend and . . . stretch out their bows to embrace and kiss each other . . . sick for love, ready to die and pine away" (10:230). Erridge is "a subject for Burton if there ever was one" (10:28), but so are Moreland and Trapnel, Widmerpool and Pamela.

Pamela is first seen in church at Stringham's wedding, where she vomits into the baptismal font (10:48). She then outrages the family at Erridge's funeral by slamming noisily out of the middle of the funeral service and vomiting into one of Erridge's five-foot-high Chinese vases (10:82). Yet in the end Powell brings us sardonically into a kind of sympathy with the girl. "She wants it all the time, yet doesn't want it," Trapnel muses in his desolation. "She goes rigid like a corpse. Every grind's a nightmare. It's all the time, and always the same" (10:225). Jenkins wonders if "the Furies that had driven her into the arms of Widmerpool by their torments . . . at the same time invested her with the magnetic power that mesmerized Trapnel, operated in a manner to transcend love or sex, as both are commonly regarded. Did she and Widmerpool in some manner supplement each other, she supplying a condition he lacked—one that Burton would have called Melancholy?" (10:195–96). Borage and hellebore are reputed herbal cures for the melancholy of love that has no cure.

No cure but death—and Pamela above all "seemed an appropriate attendant on Death" (10:46). From being a promising young novelist, Trapnel is reduced to a literary hack, doing bits and pieces for the cinema and radio as well as for literary magazines. *Books Do Furnish a Room* concludes in Victorian-novel fashion, with a review of the characters; but it is less the fates of the characters that are traced than of the books they have written. Odo Stevens's memoir of the war in the Balkans is thought derogatory to the Communist party, and Gypsy Jones attempts to "liquidate" it by destroying the two known manuscripts. But landing on his feet as always, Odo has a third copy and arranges a better deal for *Sad Majors* with another publisher. Guggenbühl, who had become a Fellow at the university apparently on the strength of his book *Kleist, Marx, Sartre, the Existentialist Equation,* cements his position there with another academic treatise, *Bronstein: Marxist or Mystagogue?* His change of name to Vernon Gainsborough is presumably also designed to establish him in the English landscape.

Only Moreland, who has resisted Bagshaw's plea for an article about existential music, fails to produce the book he contemplated, *The Popular Song from Lillibullero to Lilli Marlene* (10:120). Trapnel, whose *Profiles in String* is lost, does not write another novel, and his critique *The Heresy of Naturalism* never gets written. A very bad novel entitled *Sweetskin,* with passages salacious enough to be thought obscene, like *Lady Chatterley's Lover,* after the preliminary injunction becomes a Quiggin & Craggs best-seller. While Jenkins's *Borage and Hellebore: A Study,* with, we presume, its more genuine contribution to our understanding of human nature, or love's melancholy at any rate, enters the world quietly the following December, *Fission,* having provided the pattern for the novel, stumbles out of existence.

Temporary Kings

Nicholas Jenkins is listening to the singing of a Venetian gondolier in the opening scene of *Temporary Kings,* both amused that the Venetian is singing with joy a Neapolitan song (*Funiculi-Funicula*) and sobered by the reflection that the aged singer might be the same one he had heard in Venice with his parents 40 years before. Now, in 1958, an international festival of the arts has also brought to Venice two Americans, a university professor named Russell Gwinnett and a film producer named Louis Glober. Opposites in almost every respect, Gwinnett and Glober are both drawn richly and truly, redeeming the occasional flaws in Powell's earlier portraits of Americans.

Gwinnett is American gothic, descendant of a Welsh signer of the Declaration of Independence, Button Gwinnett of South Carolina; Powell describes him as "at once intensely American and allergic to American life" (11:49). Reticent yet candid, naïve yet shrewd, generally knowledgeable about the English life he is dedicated to studying yet ignorant about its subtler details, Gwinnett wins Jenkins's sympathy, and needs it, for he is engaged in research for a biography of the elusive X. Trapnel. "Let's hope he treats Trapnel's own Romanticism in a Classical manner," a mutual friend remarks. Since Gwinnett shares Edgar Allan Poe's preoccupation with death—or stands, as Jenkins puts it, "halfway between Henry Adams and Charles Addams" (10:84)—there is cause for concern.

Gwinnett has come into possession of Trapnel's cryptic Commonplace Book, which reveals more about Trapnel's affair with Pamela Widmerpool and the manuscript of his last novel, thrown into the canal by Pamela, than Jenkins had known (11:189). He thus holds a key to Trapnel's life. On the other hand, although he had resided in London, an admirer of Trapnel when Trapnel was still alive, he had never managed to meet him, not knowing how easy it would have been (11:23). Confronted with a welter of conflicting stories about Trapnel, Gwinnett must rely on those who did know him, such as Jenkins and Pamela Widmerpool.

The other American, the son of Jewish immigrants who changed the family name to Glober, has roots so shallow that his patriotism surprises us; Jenkins delights quietly in Glober's being "at once pseudo-American and intensely devoted to American life" (11:99). Glober, with the profile of a young Byzantine emperor, a quiet laugh, and good manners, had as a publisher attracted Jenkins's interest in London 30 years before. Jenkins had helped him in the purchase of his first Augustus John.

The international press now calls Glober a playboy-tycoon, "a noted rider, shot, golfer, yachtsman," race-car driver, film producer—but he is still secretly a collector of pubic souvenirs. The former owner of the John painting revealed that after "Glober did me on the table," he "insisted on a cutting from my bush . . . he said he always did that after having anyone the first time (11:72). Neither American much likes the other, yet both the diffident scholar and the flamboyant film producer are liked by Jenkins. And both are drawn toward the sexual maelstrom that is Pamela Widmerpool.

Growing older and like Gwinnett obsessed by death, Pamela wants to try being a film star and hopes the last novel of X. Trapnel, translated into a film script, may be the vehicle (11:149). In the pattern we have come to expect, Glober, who may produce the film, has "something of Trapnel about him—a Trapnel who brought off being a Complete Man" (11:74)—and Gwinnett grows to resemble Trapnel more the more he studies him (11:201).

A larger pattern emerges with the appearance at the Venice Film Festival of Polly Duport, as the star of a new Thomas Hardy film. In a sense the four schoolboys of *A Question of Upbringing* cross paths again, exchanging partners. Although Peter Templer and Charles Stringham have died in the war, Polly is Templer's niece, Pamela is Stringham's niece, and Widmerpool arrives in pursuit of Pamela. When first seen by Jenkins, however, Pamela is being pursued by Glober; and she leaves Venice, indeed, leaves the world in pursuit of Gwinnett. Polly and Pamela are linked in other patterns: Polly "lived almost as a nun" (11:52) and Pamela seems to have some yearning for the religious life, comic or pathetic (11:158). Also about the time Pamela takes up the pursuit of Gwinnett, Glober meets Polly, and "it was an instantaneous click." Not that Pam cared: "She was already mad about that other American" (11:220–21).

The title of the volume comes from the oratory used to persuade Jenkins to attend the festival, where, Mark Members assures him, he will be treated like a king. "One of those temporary kings in *The Golden Bough*," Jenkins asks rhetorically, "everything at their disposal for a year or a month or a day, then execution? Death in Venice?" The title encompasses more than the regal feeding of the intellectuals and their privileged access to normally unvisited Venetian palaces. Jean Templer's daughter Polly reveals that her stepfather might be considered a king, having become military dictator of his country in South America (11:235). Glober, too, the movie king who has won and lost several fortunes, is to meet his final death within the year in a racing car on the Riviera. But the shock Powell seems to prepare us for most royally is the arrival in Venice of Lord Widmerpool.

After losing his seat in the House of Commons in the Tory victory of 1955, Widmerpool was elevated to the House of Lords by the outgoing

Labour government. But he is only a Life Peer. With his death the line itself becomes extinct; there will be no peerage for a son to inherit, but then he has no son. Moreover, his figurative assassination by Lady Widmerpool after 12 years of marriage is foreshadowed by a painting usually hidden from the public in the Bragadin palazzo in Venice, Tiepolo's *Candaules and Gyges*. Appropriately, Pamela and Glober, both houseguests of Jacky Bragadin in Venice, are supine on the floor, corpse-like, contemplating the painting on the ceiling when Jenkins and Gwinnett arrive. The painting (invented by Powell) depicts Candaules, King of Lydia, unclad and supine awaiting his wife at the moment when she glances aside to see Gyges, the king's chief officer (who has been coerced by the king into a voyeur's role) sidling away. In the myth's sequel the queen, shocked at her husband's exposure of her in the nude, confronts Gyges with a choice: kill the king and marry me or be killed. Gyges takes the first option and lives to rule Lydia well for 40 years (11:87). Pamela's fascination with the myth is only fully explained when she effects the symbolic execution of Candaules—Widmerpool, as Hugh Moreland defines him—near the end of the volume.[19]

While chapters 1–3 cover three successive days in Venice, the last three chapters record events spread over the following year in London. Gwinnett, on sabbatical leave to write his book, arranges to room with another Trapnel authority, Books Bagshaw, now converted into the television personality Lindsay Bagshaw. Bagshaw's eccentric ménage includes two nubile stepdaughters who take a fancy to Gwinnett, and when Pamela finally tracks him down at Christmas time and is discovered nude in the hall, locked out of Gwinnett's room, a row ensues. Gwinnett leaves the next day.

"To express how things fell out is to lean heavily on hearsay," Jenkins admits (11:190), but as the winter progresses he pieces together clues as to Gwinnett's progress: "We had a talk. . . . I was not sure he was up to tackling so picturesque a figure as Trapnel" (11:215). At a military reunion dinner he also learns a bit more about Stringham's death in a Japanese prison camp after the fall of Singapore—"Stringham . . . behaved very well there" (11:206)—and of the developing "Widmerpool case." Rumor has it, he learns at a literary luncheon at the Soviet Embassy, that Widmerpool is to be tried for espionage or treason, perhaps given 25 years in prison (11:215), but few facts have reached the papers.

Truth is revealed with time, but what quickens the rhythm to an almost unbearable degree is a charity production of Mozart's *Abduction*

from the Seraglio given at the home of Rosie Manasch and her husband,
Odo Stevens. "Am I to be suffocated by nostalgia?" Moreland demands.
"Will that be my end?" Jenkins talks to Polly Duport, thinking of his old
love for her mother, Jean, while Glober, who has brought Polly, talks to
Jenkins's wife, Isobel. Moreland is acutely aware that his former wife,
Matilda, now Sir Magnus Donners's widow, is there and demands to
know if Jenkins has noticed, hanging on the wall, "Barnby's drawing . . .
of Norma, that little waitress at Casanova's Chinese Restaurant? All this
and Mopsy Pontner [who sold the John to Glober] too. I can't bear it."
But at that moment, Carolo, Matilda's first husband, arrives as substitute violinist, and Audrey Maclintick, Moreland's current mistress, forces
recognition on him—"I lived with the man for three years, didn't I?"—
quickening Moreland's progress to the grave. When the clairvoyant
Myra Erdleigh also turns up, with Jimmy Stripling, and reminds Jenkins
of their first meeting—when (under the wing of his Uncle Giles) she had
foreseen his marriage to Isobel—and of their second—at Peter
Templer's, when her planchette board had broken up the party with its
eerie predictions—even Jenkins grows appalled: "Better reminiscence
should stop there," he thinks (11:243), echoing Stringham's (and Childe
Roland's) last words. As the party ends, Jenkins hears that Moreland has
blacked out. "I told you nostalgia would get me," Moreland laughs on
his way to the hospital.

The orchestration that began with wondering where the hands are
now, the "Pale hands I loved . . ." is drawing to a close. The crescendo is
reached on the terrace before Stevens's house, when Glober, unwittingly
perhaps, offers the Widmerpools a ride home in his vintage car and
Pamela (who had once had an affair with Stevens) accosts first Polly—"I
hear you're going to be the star in Louis's new film" (256)—and then
Glober, regarding his "little cushion" of pubic souvenirs. Failing to rattle
either Polly or Glober, she turns on Widmerpool: "Anyway it's a cheaper
hobby than his" (11:256–59).

Myra Erdleigh, who had been chatting about the occult with
Moreland, now attempts to intervene, as if aware of how lethal emotions
are becoming: "My dear, beware. You are near the abyss" (260). Her
effect is uncanny. Pamela pauses, for a moment. "Court at your peril
those spirits that dabble lasciviously with primeval matter . . . sperm of
the world . . ." (11:260–61).

Pamela goes into a frenzy. "He thought I didn't spot he was watching
through the curtain. . . . Watching your wife being screwed. Naturally it
wasn't the first time. It was just the first time with a blubber-lipped

Frenchman, who couldn't do it, then popped off." She reveals that
Widmerpool has been "playing games" with a former mistress of
Trapnel, too (from whom she has just received Gwinnett's new address),
and that Widmerpool escaped the charge of treason only by betraying
his dead communist friend, the "blubber-lipped Frenchman" who died in
his wife's bed while he watched. Goaded to violence, Widmerpool
attacks her physically, is staggered by Glober's fist, and then hustled
away. The departure of Pamela was "most mysterious," Moreland reports
later, with "some parting shot to the effect that none of us would ever
see her again" (11:261–66).

The last chapter is brief. Jenkins visits the hospital to see Moreland, and
they discuss Widmerpool as a modernization of the myth of Candaules.
They muse on the fate of his queen. Pamela had visited Gwinnett's hotel
later that night: "You really think she took the overdose, told him, then
. . . . Literally dying for love" (11:270). Moreland links power-seeking to
voyeurism in a philosophic ramble, Widmerpool to Donners, Pamela to his
own lost love Matilda. On Jenkins's last visit to the hospital, Moreland
mentions an Elizabethan play, *Cambises, King of Percia: a Lamentable Tragedy
mixed full of Pleasant Mirth,* which he enjoys because it "does summarize
life." Finally, he thinks with cheerful rue of an opera he might have composed, "about Candaules and Gyges perhaps" (11:275–76).

"That morning was the last time I saw Moreland," Jenkins concludes.
"It was also the last time I had, with anyone, the sort of talk we used to
have together. Things drawing to a close, even quite suddenly, was hardly a surprise" (11:276:77).

As Jenkins walks back across Westminster Bridge, observing a parade
of vintage cars, wondering if one might be the car driven by General
Conyers in 1914, his path intersects that of Widmerpool, who is walking
crisply along the Thames. At that moment, a car with Glober and Polly
Duport is passed by another carrying Odo Stevens and Jimmy Stripling.
The hooting horns are read by Widmerpool as a mockery of himself, and
he glares at the cars with "enraged surprise." The encounter unavoid-
able, Jenkins exchanges a few banalities. "In the Upper House . . . I shall
continue . . . to expose the bankruptcy of cold-war propagandists," Lord
Widmerpool says. Jenkins thinks he sounds "more than a little
unhinged" and offers, as they part, a final "platitude about the evening's
drawing in" (11:280).

The September Song symbolism behind the platitude is lost on
Widmerpool, who years after they met is hurrying doggedly on as his
"evening draws in." But *Temporary Kings* has been put together so

beautifully that Powell's success in drawing things to a close, "even quite suddenly," in one more volume of The Music of Time seems to pass finally into the realm of the probable. We close the volume with confidence that Powell, like Jenkins, will "get home before dark."

Hearing Secret Harmonies

The last volume of The Music of Time opens at the home of Nicholas and Lady Isobel Jenkins on an estate in the west of England, where they are living in partial retirement. Ducks are flying, and sounds of dynamite come from the distant cliff that marks a quarry, a cliff that recalls in its craggy asymmetry the Assyrian temple in Deacon's painting *The Boyhood of Cyrus*.

The dynamics of nature are restoring the dance: a hawk hovers and falls, ducks rise in disciplined flight. Death is in the air, but the focus is on the young, the successors, and the would-be young. A niece of Isobel's has brought a call from Isobel's sister Blanche to ask if she and Nicholas can put up on their grounds the caravan in which their niece Fiona is traveling. Though Fiona is the daughter of Susan, not Blanche, Fiona has jettisoned her parents, and Susan and Rodney Cutts—whose engagement, celebrated by Erridge, led to his elopement to China with Quiggin's wife in *At Lady Molly's*—have not found parenthood easy. Fiona is a wild, rebellious, child of the 1960s; her use of drugs and alcohol has brought embarrassing publicity to Cutts, still a Conservative member of parliament. Word has come of reform, sobriety, a new leaf, Blanche says, and Fiona and her friends will be only passing through. Hospitality is extended.

The caravan, or motorized home (a successor to the gypsy wagon of earlier centuries), carries not only Fiona but a tough young woman named Rusty and two young men, the foursome crossing England apparently from megalith to megalith. The leader, whose will has brought Fiona to sobriety, Scorpio Murtlock, has discarded his given name for one denoting his astrological sign, and Murtlock, suggesting "warlock" perhaps, also points to Scorpio's role.

Dressed in a blue robe, "sweeping out of his eyes handfuls of uncared-for black hair," Scorpio is issuing orders when Nicholas and Isobel stroll down to see how the campers are faring. Both women are wearing T-shirts with the word *Harmony* printed across the chest, and *Harmony* (with many an ironic variation) is the final theme, as the title of the novel suggests.

The title, *Hearing Secret Harmonies,* at first seems to come from lines by Thomas Vaughan, the seventeenth-century Welsh alchemist and brother of metaphysical poet Henry Vaughan. Jenkins hears the words from the lips of Mrs. Erdleigh (who like Scorpio did not believe in death), who speaks "of how the 'liberated soul ascends, looking at the sunset towards the west wind, and hearing secret harmonies'" (12:36). Later, when Jenkins meets Anglican scholar Canon Fenneau, who knew Scorpio as a child in his church choir and also knows Mrs. Erdleigh, we learn that Vaughan was apparently quoting more ancient sources. Canon Fenneau is pleased to learn of the residue left at Jenkins's estate:

> Camphor? I am glad to hear of that. Camphor traditionally preserves chastity. With regard to Trelawney, I hope Scorpio has purged away the more unpleasant side. Harmony is the watchword. . . . An element of Gnosticism emphasized the duality of austerity and licence, abasement as a source of power, also elements akin to the worship of Mithras, where the initiate climbed through seven gates . . . imagery of the soul's ascent through the spheres of the Planets—as Eugenius Philalethes says—hearing secret harmonies. (12:134)

But Harmony in the caravan is to be found only under the leader's will. "We could make a bonfire," Fiona suggests. "Too near the solstice," Scorpio replies (12:12). Isobel's invitation to dine at the house is also rejected by Scorpio: "This is a day of partial fast." Isobel suggests they might hunt crayfish in the pools of the river that runs down to the pond, where the hawk hovers and ducks take ordered flight. Soothsayers of old specialized in "reading" bird flights, Jenkins suggests, in ornithomancy. "What message do the birds foretell?" Scorpio asks. "I was thinking of the Roman augurs too." "They also scrutinized the entrails of animals for prophecy," Scorpio adds ("with a certain relish"). Jenkins spars back: "Sometimes—as the Bard remarks—the sad augurs mocked their own presage." But Scorpio ignores him (12:20). "The shining amulet, embossed with a hieroglyph, that hung round [Scorpio's] throat from a necklace of beads, splashed into the water" as he takes charge of the hunt for crayfish: "There is no killing—death is an illusion" (12:14).

Scorpio does demonstrate what seem to be occult powers when a retired farmer wanders by in search of his dog, Daisy. Scorpio amazes the farmer (and surprises Jenkins with his apparent knowledge of local topography): "Seek the spinney by the ruined mill. . . . If you find her make an offering . . . burn laurel and alder in a chafing dish" (12:22). Later the farmer reports that Daisy had indeed been found by the ruined mill. "The words just came," Scorpio says. But Scorpio is himself surprised when, planning the next day's travels, he asks Jenkins the way to the next megalith, and Jenkins reveals there are a pair of local stones on a neighboring farm known as the Devil's Fingers with druidic associations of their own. The next morning, without farewell, the caravan is gone.

The Devil's Fingers site is threatened by a hoped-for expansion of the quarry, we learn, as local antiquarians, nature lovers, archaeologists, and preservationists (with Isobel in the foreground) convene to protest. One farmer near the threatened land is expected to be in attendance, but does not arrive. He had been out before dawn that morning, hunting rabbits using the lights of his land-rover, when suddenly the lights had revealed a stag's-head dance, men and women naked, leaping and swaying around the Devil's Fingers. The farmer took shelter in his home and refused to emerge. Later we learn that Widmerpool had joined Scorpio's dance, that the blood found at the site is from a gash he received, and that the ritual had been an attempt to revive the spirit of the "dead" Dr. Trelawney. Since Scorpio has already reminded Jenkins of Trelawney (though Scorpio's disciples are robed in blue and Trelawney's had been robed in pastel shades), Jenkins puzzles over the relations of both to psychic powers.

Jenkins is reading a translation of Ariosto's *Orlando Furioso* and pondering one of the greater mysteries of love when the next chapter opens: "Orlando (Charlemagne's Roland), a hero, paladin, great man, had gone off his head because his girl, Angelica, beautiful, intelligent, compassionate . . . had abandoned him for a nonentity." The English duke Astolpho, to save Orlando from the living death of madness, mounts a hippogryph and flies to the moon to seek in the Valley of Lost Things— lost kingdoms, lost riches, lost reputations, lost days—the missing wits of the great Orlando. "Astolpho was surprised to come across a few of his own lost wits, simply because he had never in the least missed them." But he also finds those of his old comrade-in-arms and, after the return spaceflight, enables Orlando to resume the Heroic Life.

It is the year before American astronauts land on the moon, Pennistone had just published a book on Cyrano's flight to the moon, and Jenkins notes that Astolpho had seen Time at work on the moon, "Ariosto's Time." "Although equally hoary and naked, he was not Poussin's Time. . . . sitting down while he strums his instrument . . . a trifle sinister, nevertheless . . . genial, composed. / Ariosto's Time (a writer's time) is . . . restless," collecting dog tags on the double to dump them in the waters of Oblivion, only a few to be salvaged by swans for the Temple of Fame (12:33). Just before closing *Orlando Furioso* to turn his attention to the news, Jenkins notes a stanza linking the images of kestrel and mallard to a man of magic powers—"So by degrees this Mage begins to fly"—and it brings back that day of crayfishing, the mysteries of Scorpio's relations to Dr. Trelawney.

> I tried to rationalize to myself this coincidental passage. There was noth-
> ing at all unusual in mallard getting up from the water at that time of
> day, nor a kestrel hovering over the neighbouring meadows. . . . It was
> the word Mage. Mage carried matters a stage further. . . . One of the
> firmest tenets—so Moreland always said—in the later teaching of Dr
> Trelawney was that coincidence was no more than "magic in action."
> There had just been an example of that. *Orlando Furioso* had not only pro-
> duced that evening a magical reconstruction of considerable force, it had
> also brought to mind [the] revival of Trelawneyism . . . among young
> people. (12:34–35)

On the news, to heighten the coincidence, is Lord Widmerpool, tele-vised nationally as the recipient of further honors, central figure in the installation of the new chancellor of an English university. In mortar-board and gold-brocaded robe, Lord Widmerpool rises to begin his acceptance speech, with what we assume will be the usual clichés and unctuous false modesty, when angry students splash him with red paint. To most recipients of such a welcome, embarrassment would ensue, but after 50 years we know that Widmerpool will not attempt to rise above it; he will make himself invisible by pretending that it did not happen or that it happened for the good, a part of the counterculture movement of which he of course approves. "Not the smallest resentment," Widmerpool begins his speech. "Even glad this has taken place. Let me congratulate those two girls on being such excellent shots with the paint pot" (12:46). He goes on to denounce the establishment of which he has just become chancellor.

The girls are the twin daughters of J. G. Quiggin, Amanda and Belinda, members of Scorpio's commune. Jenkins learns more about them when he meets Gibson Delavacquerie, perhaps at one time Matilda's lover (12:51), one of the few recipients of a Donners-Brebner Fellowship (like a Rhodes Scholarship), which brought him from the Caribbean to Oxford in Sillery's time and then into employment with Donners-Brebner in the field of public relations. Time and the war ended the fellowship project, the trust now being used to fund the Donners Literary Prize for the best biography of a contemporary figure.

Matilda has coerced Jenkins into joining the Donners Prize Committee by offering a viewing of the photographs Donners had taken in the 1930s of Jenkins, Isobel, Templer, Moreland, and others at Stourwater Castle in their tableaux of the Seven Deadly Sins. Acting as secretary of the committee is Delavacquerie, knit of sensibility and toughness ("Firmness in any sphere, he says, "is ultimately the only thing anyone respects"). Businessman as well as poet, Delavacquerie does not meet the guru Scorpio Murtlock, but both remain to the end vessels of strength and of mystery. Scorpio twists the mystic strands of earlier volumes into a knot of alchemy, astrology, cabalism, esoteric Buddhism, catatonic druidism, and even herbology—in tune with the vegetarian and vegan movements of the time. Delavacquerie supplies the tact and common sense that keep the committee functioning.[20]

Powell does not satirize Scorpio's movement any more than he satirizes Widmerpool: he merely juxtaposes the impromptu taunts and provocative banners of Scorpio's followers with their idealistic slogans and deviant practices. Scorpio has used his creed to form a cult and the cult to form a commune, and at the moment Widmerpool is unwittingly the major victim.

Widmerpool has tried to ride every wave driven in by history, but always after the crest has passed. Ego centered, he is neither able to keep a good ear to the wind nor to predict waves of the future, but when he sees one at hand his instinct is to ride it. Venture capitalist in the late 1920s, Fascist in the late 1930s, fellow traveler in the late 1940s, now, in the 1960s, he seeks desperately the crest of counterculture foaming up on the beach. A late-life convert to alternative life-styles, wearer of *Harmony* T-shirts and medallions, Lord Widmerpool turns the official residence granted him as university chancellor into an open house, welcoming especially downtrodden undergraduates ("Call me Ken"), and Scorpio knows how to take advantage of hospitality. Overnight the chancellor's residence becomes a commune where drugs and sex rituals radiate "harmonious vibrations."

The Donners Prize Committee holds an annual awards dinner, and Lord Widmerpool has been invited to this year's dinner; ironically, the committee, with some misgivings, is to honor an American professor Gwinnett, who has just turned out a biography of the late novelist X. Trapnel. Fearing Widmerpool may sue for libel, dealing as the biography does with his former wife, Pamela, who committed suicide apparently for love of some one else, Delavacqurie approaches Widmerpool and, with some surprise, encounters no obstacle. But one condition: Widmerpool is to be invited to the banquet and allowed to bring two guests.

Given that Gwinnett, as a young scholar in London to study X. Trapnel, "took" Widmerpool's wife away from him, that Gwinnett, feeling overmanipulated, fled back to America and that the forsaken beauty chose to take her overdose in his seedy London hotel room, the meeting of Gwinnett and Widmerpool now imposes more than a little strain. Rising belatedly to address the banquet, Widmerpool tries to show himself a man of the times, insisting that his honour—quaint word—has not been damaged at all. He tacitly forgives both Trapnel and Gwinnett in announcing his conversion to youth and love: "I take pride in ridiculing what is—or rather was—absurdly called honour, respectability, law, order, obedience, custom [and] for bringing home to so large an audience the irrelevance of such concepts in this day and age . . . the wrongness of marriage . . . the wrongness of education, the wrongness of government, the wrongness of the manner we treat kids like these" (12:111). Widmerpool is a proud convert to a spirit that has already begun to seem a little comic. With apt timing, the "kids"—Quiggin's twin daughters, whom Widmerpool has brought to the banquet— choose that moment to detonate their stink bomb.

Perhaps a year later, Jenkins is surprised to discover that one of his nephews has agreed to hold his wedding reception at Stourwater Castle. The very name brings a flood of memories of the mime of the Seven Deadly Sins 30 years before, when tycoon Sir Magnus Donners, having heard Jenkins, Moreland, and others were in the neighborhood, had sent Peter Templer over to pick them up (*The Kindly Ones*). The scenes staged for Donners's camera that night had seemed a turning point at the time, and now the "models" and their stand-ins or avatars reassemble.

After Donners's passing, Stourwater Castle became a girls school, which the bride-to-be had attended. During vacation months it is available for wedding receptions. With its fourteenth-century moat and dungeons, and the machicolations added centuries later, it seems an ancestor of the great country houses such as Thrubworth (now, after Erridge's death, being converted by Jeremy Warminster into a biological research center) around which the lives of the characters have revolved. Dancers, 30 years on, as if in a final assembly of their generation, gather for the wedding. Umfraville and Flavia Stringham are there. Even the bride's grandfather had been at school with Jenkins and Stringham—until he was expelled for suspected homosexual behavior. He had written a mash note to Templer, apparently expressing admiration and devotion that seemed to the authorities suspiciously intense, but may have been the mere seedling of a poetic faculty beginning to bloom. In coming across the note, Widmerpool had, in the interests of "duty," he later laments, delivered it into the hands of the school tribunal. Akworth, now Sir Bertram Akworth, had been expelled, and now he is attending his granddaughter's marriage to Jenkins's nephew.

Flavia is there as godmother of the bride, Clare Akworth, Umfraville there as . . . but the web of relationships grows so complex that a summary can do it no justice. The 11 earlier volumes of The Music of Time extend their strands through the chapter and the richness, even for Jenkins, becomes overwhelming, as nostalgia had overwhelmed Moreland with almost fatal intensity in *Temporary Kings.*

Widmerpool alone seems absent from the assembly. But it turns out that his mother's cottage in the woods near Stourwater became home to Scorpio's disciples after his resignation led to his loss of the chancellor's house. So across the girls' hockey field Widmerpool comes trotting, at the head of the blue-robed followers of Scorpio. Lagging behind is another aged disciple, filthy and unshaven, who turns out to be the Bithel drummed out of the army by Widmerpool 20 years before. A drop-out from society after the war, Bithel has been adopted by Scorpio, who senses in him rare psychic powers. And Scorpio has forced Widmerpool to do unspeakable acts of penance for his crime against Bithel.

Recognizing her former comrades, Fiona stops the column by shouting to Barnabas Henderson (the fourth caravan companion of chapter 1). Impulsively, Fiona invites them all to the wedding reception in Stourwater Castle. Recognizing Akworth there, Widmerpool prostrates himself in the Great Hall to atone for his mistaken sense of "duty." In a great slow-motion scene the bride and groom reappear to take their departure and Jenkins hears Stringham's sister Flavia (who apparently was approaching Widmerpool to express "the detestation she felt for him and all his works") emit a gasp as Widmerpool, going down on his knees before Akworth, causes her to fall almost on top of him. Others raise Flavia and carry her to the sickroom.

"Are we going out to see them off?" Isobel asks, coming up at that moment. "Did somebody faint near where you were standing?"

"Widmerpool's mother-in-law," Jenkins replies. "Her son-in-law is a subject she feels strongly about" (12:231).

But Jenkins survives the deluge of coincidence, and in the last chapter, at home alone, he has begun a bonfire to dispose of the summer's detritus, kindling the pyre with twists of old newspaper. One scrap catches his eye, the headline of a review of a dual exhibition at Barnabas Henderson's new art gallery in London. Jenkins remembers missing the opening but finding his way to the gallery a few weeks later, in the chill afternoon, wending around workmen who are repairing the street. The encircling past has joined a retrospective of the art of Bosworth (once Edgar) Deacon—brought back to life by a discerning critic (following a hint of Sickert's decades before)—and a collection of seascapes, mostly Victorian, once despised but treasured by Duport and "stored" for a time in Templer's Maidenhead home.

To compound the emotional tumult, Jean Templer herself arrives, now widow of the assassinated South American general, perhaps dictator, Carlos Flores, and former wife of Duport. Tended in his wheelchair by his daughter Polly (starring in a current London production of a Strindberg play), Duport is revisiting his former collection before the last painting is sold. Jean has brought the Duport party to visit the exhibition the same afternoon.

Duport's seascapes recall Jean and Nick's lost love. "Do you remember the pictures in the dining-room, Nick? Peter's Maidenhead house was where we met." "And played planchette." "Yes—we played planchette." In Jenkins's memory the seascapes are vague: "Rather a job lot they had seemed to me that weekend. Even if other things had not been on my mind—that soft laugh of Jean's. . . . 'It's the bedroom next to yours. Give it half an hour. Don't be long.'" But more than fashion has changed. Though public kissing is now routine, Jean holds herself erect, and they part: "So nice to have met." "Yes, so nice" (12:256). Rarely has so much emotion been packed into such simple words.

Chandler is in the Duport party as director of the Strindberg play. Dawdling behind, he recalls how he had sold the statue *Truth Revealed by Time* to Mr. Deacon, a statue now perhaps in the Valley of Lost Things. As the crowd departs, Barnabas, the gallery owner, brings Nicholas to his basement office to reveal more. He shows Jenkins the Modigliani once owned by Stringham. Bithel has visited his gallery, bringing the Modigliani (left to Pamela by her uncle and inherited by Widmerpool at her death), having saved it from the ritual pyre of Widmerpool's things Scorpio had ordered after Widmerpool's death. Jenkins is astounded. Scorpio killed him, Bithel told Chandler, ordering Widmerpool, ill, off the floor where the disciples slept and out for a naked run through the woods in the predawn cold. Such runs along paths through dark woods are to instill *Harmony,* according to Scorpio. But Widmerpool suddenly called for a faster pace and spurted ahead: "I'm leading now." Rounding a bend, they come upon his inert body (12:269).

Jenkins stirs the dying fire as the day darkens in the west. Flakes of snow are beginning to fall. "The thudding sound from the quarry had declined. . . . ceased altogether at the long drawn wail of a hooter—the distant pounding of centaurs' hoofs dying away, as the last note of their conch trumpeted out over hyperborean seas. Even the formal measure of the Seasons seemed suspended in the wintry silence" (12:272).

One of the world's great novels has come to an end, the dance too, in "wintry silence."

Chapter Four

Later Works and Conclusion

Dialogue in Anthony Powell's novels is supple and witty, effective at revealing character without losing a sense of reality. Almost any chapter in *Afternoon Men*, for instance, reveals how little the novel depends on description and narration. His novels never fail to heed the advice of Henry James, "Dramatize! Dramatize!" Good advice to young novelists that Powell has quoted on more than one occasion. Moreover, Powell spent years in the 1930s writing film scripts that apparently satisfied film producers about Powell's sense of character in motion, his authorial "stage presence." Powell had the makings of a dramatist.

So when the idea arose of converting the novel *Afternoon Men* into a play, it was natural that Powell should be approached about rendering it into a form suitable for staging. The year was 1961, Powell was in the midst of writing The Music of Time and serving, in his spare time, as literary editor of the *Daily Telegraph*. He had to decline. The assignment was given to Riccardo Aragno, who produced an adaptation of the novel for the stage in eight scenes. But the production languished until a young American director named Roger Graef became interested. Casting was completed and a theater chosen.

On various trips to London in the spring and summer of 1963, Powell attended rehearsals of the play, came to know the actors ("an accomplished and delightful crowd"), and regretted that he had to miss the opening night at the New Arts Theatre Club on 22 August 1963. He and his wife had made reservations to fly to Venice for the start of a Hellenic cruise (*Strangers*, 106–15)

Afternoon Men had a four-week run, a modest success, and the theater became a new interest for Powell. Attending rehearsals of a play has given birth to many a playwright. Seeing what does work on a stage and what does not, how a change of phrase or gesture can electrify a scene that seemed irreparably flat, sharpens the dramatic sense. Then, too, as Powell admitted, "Among the hypnotic influences exercised by the Theatre none is more intoxicating than to hear one's own dialogue spoken on the stage" (*Strangers*, 116).

The sixth volume of the The Music of Time had just been published, *The Kindly Ones,* which leads the narrator to the brink of World War II. Looking ahead, Powell decided that The Music of Time should end not with the tenth volume, as had once been announced, but with the twelfth. The number of the books in an epic is 12: *The Iliad* had set the pattern; Virgil, Milton, Joyce, and other writers of epics had followed; and there was some appeal in such classical symmetry. The pattern of 12 fell easily, like the months, into four seasons. But Powell saw some danger in just grinding out the war-trilogy immediately ahead. "A brief change in employment might fend off risk of growing stale" (*Strangers,* 116–17). The result was the publication, in 1971, of two fine plays: *The Garden God* and *The Rest I'll Whistle.*

The Garden God

In the Roman pantheon Priapus is the god of gardens as well as the god of lust, an apparent incongruity that may have appealed to Powell. And the play *The Garden God* might be called a drawing-room comedy, but with its drawing-rooms outdoors, one gardenlike setting formed by an archaeological dig (referred to in the play as the Grotto of Priapus), the second provided by the terrace of a neighboring tavern, and the third by a hillside picnic spot near the Grotto. English archaeologists on a Greek island have unearthed a puzzle: what is an altar dedicated to the Roman god Priapus doing on a Greek island? Three of the principal characters are archaeologists, all in one way or another trying to solve the problem. All are privately concerned with sexual problems of their own, as are the attendant figures: a television "personality" named Bland who has come to the island in pursuit of an interview with a Greek tycoon named Aristarchos (echoes of Onassis), who remains only an offstage presence; a widow who arrives the day the action begins with her daughter, Lucinda (who has passed all of her medical examinations, but is more interested in medical research than practice); and the daughter's fiancé, Jonathan, a young photographer with ambitions to become a great photographer.

Archaeologists Kent and Nitherby unearthed the altar dedicated to the god Priapus at a spot visited for centuries by local islanders troubled with infertility or impotence, their presence thus validating an "unscientific" tradition. Kent and Nitherby are welcoming the arrival of an assistant, fresh from a dig in Northumberland, named Prudence

Smurthwaite. In Restoration fashion, their names can be treated as indicative. Kent is remarkable for his fidelity (like the Duke of Kent in *King Lear*), for 20 years faithfully in love with a woman he has not seen in all that time, a woman who married another, had a daughter, and was left a wealthy widow. Nitherby has loved only himself, while Prudence has prudently shielded herself from all sexual encounters. It is the arrival from Rhodes of Barbara Hunter and her party that sets the plot into motion, for Barbara, now widowed, is the woman Kent has loved in absentia for 20 years.

As an element of fantasy (in the Greek dramatic tradition), a deus ex machina appears by surprise. In the middle of the first act the figure of Priapus himself looms above the altar, as if the statue there had become animate, while the characters seem to go into a trance: "No doubt this pilgrimage to my grotto has been some amends for a thousand imperfections in all of you," intones the god sternly. Nitherby is chastised first as a "self-abuser" who claims to honor Priapus but has done so only in "a perverse and infertile form" or in "sordid encounters . . . the Arab boy in Tunis . . . your sole physical experience."[1] Nitherby's attempts to shift the blame to his "nature" and then to his mother are rejected.

Prudence is rebuked as an "unfruitful woman," her dislike of children no excuse. "Your third decade is upon you. . . . You did not give yourself. You were frigid and neurotic." Kent is surprised to find his idealistic fidelity also a cause for reproach: "That Swedish girl you picked up in Sicily? . . . You abandoned her on the slender pretext that she read Baedeker aloud in bed." His self-defense that he has really loved another for 20 years is also rejected: "What consequence is [it] to me whether or not you loved? My worship . . . heeds not love as you call it" (29).

This stern disassociation by Priapus of himself from Eros and Cupid forecasts the greater surprise of Bland, the television personality who because he propositions every other attractive woman he meets, loving none, thinks himself the most devoted of priapic slaves, "your veteran drudge." Promiscuity, he learns, is also a vice in the priapic decalogue. Sterility is a vice, as is abortion: "We must have none of that. Fertility, fertility and more fertility. That is the watchword" (27).

Priapus in myth is the son of Dionysus, god of wine, song, and revels, and in the second act, on the terrace of the tavern, the abstemious Prudence is introduced to the island brandy, urged on by Bland, the others to retsina and ouzo. On them all alcohol works to smooth the path to bed, or so it would seem, until we learn the next morning of Bland's expulsion from Prudence's room. And at the picnic the next day

Nitherby again eases into his ideal state: "Light headed yet thinking very clearly" (94).

Priapus in his first incarnation praises Lucinda's fiancé Jonathan for being "too sensible to be an age snob," and the third act completes the plot as mother and daughter swap potential mates.

The intergenerational tensions apparent earlier, as when Lucinda scolds her mother for glamorizing her sordid "goings-on" with an actor while still married, are matched by cross-generational attractions: Barbara for her daughter's fiancé, Lucinda for Kent, the man who loved her mother steadily for 20 years. In the end, Jonathan is torn between his hopes of making a career in photography and his attraction to Barbara. All have felt stranded on the island by the uncertainties of boat service to the mainland, or to other islands, but at the picnic two ships are seen arriving at the harbor below: the yacht *Avra,* carrying Aristarchos and his "new chick," perhaps stopping off on its way to Haifa or Istanbul (92), and the ferry *Lesbos,* bound for Athens. Bland urges Jonathan to catch "the chance of a lifetime" for a photographer and board the yacht as part of his "team." Barbara urges him to join her on the *Lesbos,* bound for love.

As Barbara and Jonathan go off together to pack, Kent turns to Barbara's daughter Lucinda and discovers that she intends to stay on the island—in the interests of medical research, she implies. Prudence and Nitherby, left to clean up after the picnic, are staying as well, united in their devotion to work, their dedication to archeology.

The last word of dialogue echoes Molly Bloom when Lucinda says that she has never been in love before, but "People always tell you it's wonderful." Kent replies, "It has its moments," and Lucinda says, "Yes." She crosses the stage to kiss him. "KENT, for a second, is astonished. Then he takes her in his arms. The laughter of PRIAPUS is heard, loud and long."

The Rest I'll Whistle

A manor house on the borders of Wales is the setting for Powell's second play, all scenes indoors. The house dates back to the fifteenth century and, as a historic landmark, has a custodian who admits tourists at two shillings a head on as few days as he can manage.

The title comes from Shakespeare's *King Lear* (3.2.163). The Duke of Kent, having arrived at Gloucester's castle (in his role of messenger to Lear's wayward daughters), is ordered to the stocks by Regan's husband, the Duke of Cornwall: "There shall he sit till noon." Regan finds that not punishment enough: "Till noon? Till night, my lord, and all night too!" The servants are dismayed that such a noble man should be treated like the "basest and contemn'dest wretches For pilferings and most common trespasses," and the Earl of Gloucester, left alone with Kent, offers to intercede. "Pray do not, sir," Kent replies. "I have watched and travelled hard. Some time I shall sleep out, the rest I'll whistle."

It is Kent's denial of self-pity (Don't grovel, I'll pass the time OK) that highlights the moral toughness of both the play and its protagonist, Mark Ludlow: "Here am I a scholar of some standing where the Dark Ages are concerned—though not the smallest fame—who has to eke out a precarious livelihood by presiding over this . . . 15th century manor house, a period in which I take only the most limited interest . . . at the mercy of every tourist whose eye falls on the sign 'Trefwardine Court: Ancient Monument' . . . . Not one in a hundred appreciates the architecture . . . . What they rave about is the Art Nouveau sundial, erected in 1911 by the retired stockbroker who saved the house from falling down."[2]

Of sterner fibre yet is Ludlow's daughter Ankaret, who has run out of funds in London and returned to take shelter briefly. In the first act Ludlow confirms his suspicions that a well-reviewed current novel *The Rest I'll Whistle* by "Janet Boggs," is actually by Ankaret. He has recognized the picture of the "rural antique dealer," the heroine's father, as a very unflattering portrait of himself (*Whistle,* 114). Ankaret admits it.

> LUDLOW: Do you suppose the book is autobiographical?
>
> ANKARET: First novels usually are.

The housekeeper informs Ludlow that the American has been back again, seeking to gain not only admission but a talk with him about the seventeenth-century metaphysical poet thought to have once stayed in the house, Henry Vaughan. A bit of a ham, Ludlow turns into Henry II: "Will no one rid me of this turbulent Professor of English? Oh, that four trusty knights, owing me fealty, might hack him to pieces as he sits bowed over his typewriter, dilating upon semantics or the plot structure of *Moby-Dick*" (*Whistle,* 104).

But Grover Rasch, though an American and a scholar, is not a professor. Being of independent means, he is a scholar by inclination, free to avoid the chores of teaching and committee work and devote himself to his passions. He has already published a work on the history of medieval swords, *The Metamorphosis of Excalibur,* and is pursuing his new fascination with the mystical poets of Shakespeare's time. He is even carrying with him part of the manuscript of his next book, on the metaphysical poet Henry Vaughan.

Staying at the Black Lion Inn in the neighboring village, he has already befriended the housekeeper's son Ken, offering to help him, financially, to escape the dominion of his mother (and the shadow of rumor that he killed his drunken father) and find happiness in London. Ankaret, clever in manipulating Rasch, learns of his oedipal "generosity" and strikes a bargain: if she works her father into letting him spend the night in the Vaughan Room, he will pay for her escape—a ticket to New York.

The Vaughan Room is so called because of a verse etched into the glass of the window there and the supposition that Vaughan may have etched it himself while a guest in the room three centuries before. Which is why Rasch wants to spend a night, or preferably a week, there, feeling that the ambiance will help his understanding of Vaughan.

> If a star were confin'd into a tomb
> Her captive flames must need burn there;
> But when the hand that lock't her up, gives room
> She'll shine through all the sphere.

Ankaret, reading the verse on the glass, in childhood has identified with the imprisoned "star," which helps explain her need to escape. But she has not pursued this reading of Vaughan. Rasch, in the third act, in the Vaughan Room, quotes to her, in part to explain himself, from one of Vaughan's more famous poems:

> Man hath either toys or care,
> He hath no root, nor to one place is tied;
> But ever restless and irregular
> About this earth doth run and ride. (*Whistle*, 168–69)

Being told that Ankaret has never read that or any other of Vaughan's poems, Rasch reproaches her.

The arrival the same day of Ankaret's mother, Brenda, whom Ankaret has never met, complicates things at first. Twenty years before she had eloped with a man named Leopold, leaving her infant daughter behind, and now she has returned, ostensibly because a reading of *The Rest I'll Whistle* has alarmed her. The story of a heroine abandoned by her mother, suffering in childhood a disturbing episode with her father and later pursuing a sordid and degraded life in London, has aroused her maternal conscience and she has come back to "save" her daughter (*Whistle*, 146–47). But when Ludlow proclaims he will prevent both her plan and Ankaret's departure for America with Rasch, keep her there, Brenda reveals that Ludlow is not Ankaret's father: "When you went to Spain that time" (*Whistle*, 161)—to do research for his book on "the horsehoe-arch in Visigothic ecclesiastical architecture" [*Whistle*, 129])—she had an affair with Leopold.

At first suspecting that Brenda, a former actress, is improvising a new role, Ludlow remembers being struck at the time that the dates had seemed "a little inexplicable" (*Whistle*, 162). And Leopold's eyes? But if Ankaret is not his daughter, the cross-generational attraction that the two have felt for each other is no longer technically incestuous—a word too crude for Powell to use.

A demonstration duel with Rasch turns serious, and Rasch is disarmed, which both have agreed is (to the medieval mind at least) a fate more disgraceful than death. Rasch departs on the milk wagon the next dawn with Ken, with hints as to his bisexuality (*Whistle*, 139, 169) remaining as vague and uncertain as the hints of childhood molestation or incest suggested in Ankaret's novel (*Whistle*, 115, 117, 157), when its heroine, like Ankaret, had lived alone with her father. That such questions are left unresolved may disturb some. Not Powell apparently. At the end Ludlow, who has yet to finish reading Ankaret's novel, asks her how the book ends:

ANKARET: She goes back to live with her father.

LUDLOW: As I suggested.

ANKARET: As you suggested.

The only true test of a play, of course, is whether it succeeds on the stage, and neither *The Garden God* nor *The Rest I'll Whistle* appears to have been produced. Both seem witty and well-formed, with themes of interest and sharp dramatic tension, suitable for stage production in all respects except possibly one: the archaeologists and scholars who dominate the casts may seem to producers to be a bit rarified, eccentric, without much popular appeal. Yet neither play can be dismissed as a closet drama—that is, a play designed for the library, not the stage, like Byron's *Manfred* or Goethe's *Faust*. Both of Powell's plays are fine examples of a novelist's turning at last to the theater and producing distinguished work.

To Keep the Ball Rolling

"What is one to do, sir, when the major work of a lifetime has been completed?" For Powell in 1976, with The Music of Time behind him, a need still existed, at least one: to clarify the picture. Many a critic had equated Powell with his narrator Nicholas Jenkins. Because Jenkins in the novel marries Lady Isobel Tolland, who has nine siblings, at least one critic even assumed that Powell's wife, Lady Violet Pakenham, in fact the third of four daughters, had nine siblings as well. Distinctions needed to be drawn between fiction and fact, most of them more subtle. Other motives must have been involved, but the result was the publication of four volumes of memoirs: *Infants of the Spring* (1976), *Messengers of Day* (1978), *Faces in My Time* (1979), and *The Strangers Are All Gone* (1982). In 1983, Powell reissued the four volumes in abridged form in a single edition titled *To Keep the Ball Rolling*.

Critics, like readers generally perhaps, have a tendency to read fiction as autobiography—a natural tendency, since most great fiction in our time has been at least partly autobiographical. Cyril Connolly never wrote a great novel, but he wrote novels, knew novelists well, and knew that they could not write good fiction without in some way drawing on personal experience. But he also knew that novelists are doomed if they depend entirely on experience: "To write an autobiographical novel is to live on capital, hence only permissible when, like Proust, you know you will not live to write about anything else."[3]

During the 25 years it took for The Music of Time to emerge, Powell had been steadily vexed by the "question, tedious to myself, but congenial to readers of novels," of the extent to which the narrator should be identified with the author (*Faces,* 13). Not even the best biography a century hence could disentangle such threads as well as the author himself. After facing the restraints imposed by narrative logic, Powell, was confronted with a new challenge, that of creating a parallel image, this time of the real milieu, with a new system of restraints imposed by a new form. The time had come for memoirs.

Powell's retrospective title for the four volumes, *To Keep the Ball Rolling,* is taken from Joseph Conrad's novel *Chance* (1910). In the opening chapter of that novel, the narrator has just passed his marine board examinations, receiving the certificate qualifying him to sail as a mate ("The finest day of my life"). But he has worked the Thames docks seeking a position in vain. The narrator asks Marlow what he should do:

"Why don't you go and speak to Mr. Powell in the Shipping Office."
To keep the ball rolling I asked Marlow if this Powell was remarkable
in any way.

"He was not exactly remarkable," Marlow answered. . . . "It's very difficult to become remarkable. People won't take sufficient notice of one,
don't you know."[4]

When the narrator later finds Mr. Powell in the labyrinth of the shipping
office and is asked his name, he hands over his new certificate, "so that
he could read *Charles Powell* written very plain on the parchment."
Minutes later Mr. Powell, wordlessly shoving over the certificate, implies
to a skipper who has arrived seeking a mate that the young man beside
him, though inexperienced, may be related, therefore dependable, and
the young man get his first post as a ship's officer. Other "chances" may
await Charles Powell, but Anthony Powell's point is made.

The title *To Keep the Ball Rolling* focuses on the implication that we
would ask about "Powell," or Anthony Powell's life, only as a last resort,
or to keep the conversation from dying altogether. It seems a kind of
apology for writing memoirs at all. A further suggestion is that Powell's
own life may not have been remarkable: it is the art that is remarkable.
But of course beneath that is another suggestion, that in the denial of
curiosity something of interest may have been overlooked—perhaps
because people paying little attention had failed to remark it. The eye of
a John Aubrey (Powell's favorite antiquarian) might have found such a
life remarkable enough.

Infants of the Spring

The title of the first volume of Powell's memoirs, *Infants of the Spring,*
comes from Shakespeare's *Hamlet* (1.3.14–43). Laertes, about to return
to the university in Paris, warns his sister, Ophelia, to beware of Prince
Hamlet:

> Perhaps he loves you now . . .
> but you must fear . . .
> his will is not his own
> . . . for on his choice depends
> The safety and health of this whole state. . . .
> And keep you . . .
> Out of the shot and danger of desire. . . .
> Virtue itself scapes not calumnious strokes.
> The canker galls the infants of the spring

Too oft before their [blossoms] be disclosed,
And in the morn and liquid dew of youth
Contagious blastments are most imminent.
Be wary then; best safety lies in fear.
Youth to itself rebels, though none else near.

Within the volume Powell may clarify the title when he focuses on memories of fellow Etonian Cyril Connolly, who "—like others of his generation—recalls Laertes' comment that 'the canker galls the infants of the spring'" (*Infants,* 129). In part Connolly's most famous book, *Enemies of Promise,* with its argument that success and adulation in childhood is the enemy of expectations in maturity, may be on Powell's mind. But Powell's context suggests more that Connolly's childlike absorption with himself even in maturity—the intensity of his interest in every detail of his own experience that forced his friends to participate in the rings of gossip surrounding his life—may be the true "canker." Egoism (the self-centeredness quite natural in a child) may be like the worm in Blake's poem that, left to fester, kills the flower that might have been. From egoism and self-adulation, "the infants of the spring," however innocent, are in danger. If there is a "moral" to be drawn from the *Infants of the Spring,* that may be it. "Youth to itself rebels, though none else near."

But Powell writes no moral homily: the title merely suggests what any reasonable person might infer, looking back over childhood, several childhoods and their sequels. The dedication of the book—"For my grandchildren"—suggests that Powell is writing memoirs with an eye on the future.[5] Indeed, the final volume of memoirs concludes in a tone foreign to Powell's usual detachment, with committed advice about behavior in the future, if not quite in the same terms as Laertes' advice to Ophelia.

The opening of *Infants of the Spring* is more like that of a biography: it begins not with early memories but with a family tree and a chronicle of the events leading up to the life around which the memories are to accrue. The chapter of genealogy, a subject important enough to Powell at all times and to be expected here, is a product of research rather than memory. Going back to the twelfth-century Welshman Rhys ap Gruffydd, Powell adds much to our knowledge of the Powells and the Dymokes and the King's Champions, who gave distinction to the family in later centuries.

Of particular interest is Powell's speculation on the treatment of the Marmion side of his ancestry in Sir Walter Scott's poem *Marmion* (1808):

Had not Walter Scott, whose writings were evoking a romantic hurricane
throughout Europe, chosen the name "Marmion" as prototype of the
great nobleman of high romance? Proud and sinister, melancholy and
fearless, Lord Marmion's path is a shambles of slain enemies and seduced
nuns. . . . The period in which Scott places the poem . . . is that of [the
battle of] Flodden (1513), but the fiefs attributed to its hero-villain—
Fontenay-le-Marmion in Normandy, Lutterworth in Leicestershire,
Tamworth Castle . . . and, of course, Scrivelsby in Lincolnshire—were the
actual holdings of the historical Marmions.

This "gothic mirage," as Powell calls it, led his great-grandfather
Dymoke Wells—"discernible at all levels as a man of romantic tempera-
ment"—to "put in a claim to the barony of 'Marmyun' in 1819 . . . fol-
lowed up by another, to perform the office of King's Champion at the
Coronation of George IV. . . . Neither was successful. . . . Dymoke
Welles (again resembling Philip Powell) went bankrupt" (20–21).

   "Go, Bid the Soldiers Shoot," chapter 4, is devoted to events following the outbreak of war in 1914 when Powell was eight. Joining the
family in "Yorkshire for the summer holidays of 1915," the brigade staff
"housed in a requisitioned hotel," he first came to know his father's adjutant Capt. Thomas Balston, years later his guide in London—which raises a question of form for the memoir writer: whether to mention such a
figure at each reappearance in time or "to . . . briefly summarize his lifetime relations . . . ? There is something to be said for, and against, both
methods. A mixed chronology is perhaps preferable; each case treated on
its own merits" (59). Later contacts with Balston are left for later chapters, later volumes.

   About this time Powell was sent to a prep school in Kent favored by
parents in the services, so that many of his classmates were the sons of
generals. He was struck, on first visiting the school with his father, when
the headmaster, to demonstrate some point about the student body,
called out "Yorke" and a boy stepped forward who had hardly any military connection at all. The boy was to become one of Powell's best
friends, the novelist Henry Green, then known as Henry Yorke. Why of
all the boys had he been called forward? They could never explain the
coincidence.

   Memories of Eton resonate in the chapters "The Wat'ry Glade" and
"The Game and the Candle"—the first title from Gray's "A Distant
Prospect of Eton College," used before in the anthology *The Old School*
(1934), and the second presumably referring to the Eton wall game and
the *Eton Candle,* polar elements of athlete and aesthete. Harold Acton

and Brian Howard, guiding spirits of the Society of Arts and its now famous periodical the *Eton Candle*,[6] are treated respectively with affection and disdain. And in dealing with other friends, such as the stepsons of Lord Curzon, Powell drops a clue about certain origins of his art. Powell, Hubert Duggan (the younger stepson), and Denys Buckley had become known (from the name of their housemaster) as "Goodhart's bloody trio."

> Hubert Duggan's demeanour at school . . . contributes something to a character called Stringham in my novel. On the other hand, Buckley bears no resemblance whatever to Templer, represented as the Narrator's other companion at tea. Templer . . . a trifle like John Spencer, a friend at another house, always dressed in the latest mode. . . . one of the several temperamentally unmilitary figures known to me who died in action; major in the Welsh Guards. (98)

Another chapter, "Arcades Ambo," deals with two men who were contemporaries at Eton but who did not become friends for another decade or more, Cyril Connolly and George Orwell, the latter then known as Eric Blair. "Since the days of his forebear who had served with my own in the Marines, the Connollys had been soldiers and sailors; usually attaining respectably senior rank. Connolly's father had retired as only a major, but he was also an authority on conchology and had compiled a cook book" (120). Connolly gets the survey treatment, his life considered as a whole: "What, in short, was the point of Connolly? Why did people put up with frequent moroseness, gloom, open hostility? Why, if he were about the neighborhood, did I always take steps to get hold of him? The question is hard to answer" (128).

Eric Blair he did not come to know well until a year or two after *Down and Out in Paris and London* (by George Orwell) was published in 1933, when Powell was "impressed by its savagery and gloom," not by any inkling that the author might ever become "a close friend." It was Connolly who revealed that the author, "George Orwell," had been with them at Eton, when known as Eric Blair. In the mid-1930s, as friendship with Orwell developed, Powell came to respect his decency and courage. When Orwell was dying of tuberculosis in 1949, it was Powell who enlisted Evelyn Waugh and other friends to provide what cheer hospital visits could provide.

"The Close and the Quad" takes us to Oxford and Balliol, to one tutor whose critique of an essay made Powell see "in a flash the importance of structure," and to another, Kenneth Bell, "wartime Gunner

major with an MC . . . apparently a hearty of hearties, but in fact full of
unexpected powers of discrimination" (150). It was Bell who did the
most to teach him the art of writing, paying "attention not only to history, but to the manner in which an essay was written" (152). Here we
also meet don F. F. Urquhart, known as Sligger, and Powell raises the
question as to who "is" the Oxford don Sillery in The Music of Time.
When the first volume, A Question of Upbringing, was reviewed, "two
Cambridge papers said that the don . . . called Sillery was obviously
modelled on a well-known Cambridge figure. Nevertheless, Sillery has
time and again been 'identified' with Urquhart. Here seems an opportunity for stating that Sillery and Urquhart, apart from both being
dons, were persons of altogether different sort." And Powell goes on to
elaborate.

It was Hubert Duggan's older brother Alfred who first invited Powell
to the Hypocrites Club at Oxford, and that luncheon did much to
change his life, or to begin the change. The Hypocrites Club drew students of a particular flair and artistic temperament from different colleges and mingled them: several good friends later were met here.
Among the additions Powell makes to earlier memoirs of the Hypocrites
is a distinction between "A Ninetyish aestheticism of a musty sort . . . by
no means defunct in Oxford of those days" and that associated with former members of the Eton Society of Arts. "Aesthetes of a type unrevised
since the turn of the century were not Hypocrites material [while]
Harold Acton . . . himself making fun of the old-fashioned aesthete—
might reasonably be . . . classed [as an aesthete] by the undergraduate-
in-the-High. . . . Nor were Byron and Waugh that sort of aesthete,
though both affected a style of dress . . . that probably so denoted them
in their colleges" (155–56).

The chapter "Cymbals in Naxos" is devoted to friends made at
Oxford outside the Hypocrites circle. One was Alfred Duggan, wastrel
stepson of Lord Curzon, who was to amaze Powell in 1950, when as
novel-review editor of The Times Literary Supplement he was handed a
well-written historical novel by "Alfred Duggan" and did a double take:
"the unbelievable . . . had taken place. Alf Duggan had begun a new
career." Others were Wyndham Ketton-Cremer, who received some
fame later for a book on his ancestral home of Felbrigg and for biographies of Horace Walpole and Thomas Gray; George Kolkhorst, a don
whose warm Sunday mornings deepened Powell's acquaintance with
John Betjeman and Evelyn Waugh; and Pierse Synnott, later secretary of
the Admiralty, through whom he met Maurice Bowra. The chapter con-

cludes with two excursions from Oxford, one by car to the Royal Military College at Sandhurst with Hubert Duggan, Robert Byron, and a few others, where the group interrupted a dance and Byron at least got thrown in the lake, an episode that became in Sandhurst legend a battle with hundreds of Oxford invaders.

The other account, of his first tour of Europe and other continental travels, provides interesting commentary on his second novel, which some critics believe to have been placed in Riga, capital of Latvia:

> The town described in *Venusberg* is a mixture of Helsinki (where we lived in a hotel facing a "modernismus" railway station . . .) and Reval [Tallin], the Estonian capital across the Gulf of Finland, where I spent a weekend. The architectural admixture of this ancient Hansa city, with the modernity of Helsinki, apparently produced an approximation to Riga, capital of Latvia, which I did not visit. (172)

"In the summer term of my first year at Balliol, Synnot brought Maurice Bowra, then Dean of Wadham, to my rooms in college." So begins the last chapter, "Skins: Thick, Thin and Changing." The don who most affected Powell's later years—war veteran, iconoclast, wit, disdainer of foes—Maurice Bowra seems to have had the networking facility of Sillery, and a thick skin. Henry Yorke the thin skin? "Through connections of his own Yorke had almost immediately registered as a Bowra friend, and we used obsessively to mull over Bowra parties and Bowra lore. Yorke also had an introduction (probably through his mother . . .) to Lady Ottoline Morrell at Garsington; a house to which he soon brought me too" (185–86). Both Bowra and Yorke get rich treatment here, but summary treatment (Yorke until his death in 1974), being discussed only briefly in later volumes.

Messengers of Day

The second volume of Powell's memoirs, *Messengers of Day,* deals with his postschooling, premarital years, with coming down to London in 1926 at the age of 21 and entering both the publishing world on the edge of Bohemia and the world across London of debutante balls. It is Bohemia that gets the most attention. Portraits of Evelyn Waugh (in the period of his first marriage and divorce), the combative Sitwell trio, Cyril Connolly, Henry Lamb, Augustus John, and others make *Messengers of Day* absorbing reading for those acquainted with the period, interesting and informative for those not.

Other portraits are less sympathetic: of his employer Gerald Duckworth ("If the virus of bibliophobia is dormant in the blood there is nothing like a publisher's life for aggravating the condition"), of the popular novelist Warwick Deeping (who visits Henry Lamb in the hospital, finds that he is reading Milton, and comments: "Strange old-fashioned stuff"); and of the sinister Aleister Crowley (offering the memoirs of his mistress, *My Hymen*, to Duckworth's for an outlandish advance).

Early love affairs are hinted at but few details are given. Powell obviously does not see the "memoir" form as equivalent to the "confession" form of Rousseau. One "small, dark, elegant" beauty is said to have rejected his suit (*Messengers*, 142–44), but her identity remains obscure, sadly, when the emotional experience seems to have motivated the writing of *Afternoon Men*.

The breakup of Waugh's first marriage, to Evelyn Gardner in 1930, foreseen by Balston but not Powell, proved Balston more intuitive, he confesses, or more experienced in matters of matrimony. Powell set off late in 1930 on a motor trip to Berlin with John Heygate, and Heygate was called back to England by Evelyn Gardner, leaving Powell in Berlin with no clue as to what was really going on. The Waugh marriage split, and Powell was to experience a rift with Waugh that lasted until Waugh's second marriage, to Laura Herbert in 1937, and the development of a friendship with Alexander Dru, who in 1943 married Laura's sister (123–33) Powell visited Germany again in 1932 when Heygate was working for a film company outside Berlin, "and some relics of this glimpse of the film industry . . . found a place in *Agents and Patients*" (154).

Instead of being treated in individual chapters, Rosa Lewis, hostess of the Cavendish Hotel, and Constant Lambert, the composer, are treated in depth as they were encountered in various times in Powell's life. Both were brilliant in quite different ways: Lambert, as enthralling a talker as Powell was to know, and Lewis, unflappable in her loves and detestations. A former beauty, possibly mistress of the Prince of Wales, with a "very aristocratic mien," Lewis talked "old-fashioned cockney" and cared not who was present. She once invited Powell to drop in for a drink after his day at the war office and, when he arrived, drew him around the bar, introducing him to all as "Bimbash Stewart," utterly mystifying Powell until he learned that Stewart, a bimbashi, or captain, in the Egyptian army, had died the year after he was born.[7]

These memoirs close as Powell drifts away from the publishing world ("Twilight in Henrietta Street"), after a motor tour of Spain, toward the possibly more complex world of matrimony and war.

Faces in My Time

The title of the third volume of Powell's memoirs comes from *King Lear* (2.2.99). The Duke of Kent, in disguise, is halted in his abuse of the knave Oswald ("Thou whoreson zed! thou unnecessary letter. . . . A plague upon your epileptic visage") and defends himself to Regan's husband, the Duke of Cornwall:

> I have seen better faces in my time
> Than stands on any shoulder that I see
> Before me at this instant.

Since one of the faces before him is that of the Duke of Cornwall, the Duke's sarcasm is not unexpected:

> This is some fellow
> Who, having been prais'd for bluntness, doth affect
> A saucy roughness. . . .
> He cannot flatter, he!
> An honest mind and plain . . .

Angrily, he orders Kent into the stocks.

Kent of course is alluding to men he had known in younger years, superior in memory to any he now surveys, echoing the note of lonely, defiant courage that Stringham admires as he reads aloud passages from "Childe Roland" (in *The Soldier's Art*). It is at the same time a tribute to the past and an expression of doubt, recurring to aging men, that the younger generation can possibly have the right stuff.

Dealing with the prewar and war years, 1934–45, *Faces in My Time* opens with comments on Powell's prewar novels, expressing his own dissatisfaction with *Agents and Patients* for not being "exploratory" enough, not advancing enough in technique. In the age in which it appeared, an age dominated by fellow-traveling writers, the main criticism of the novel had been not that it was mainstream but that it lacked "seriousness." The problem of seriousness in fiction "always poses complex problems," Powell replies, "though one might bear in mind Nietzsche's conjecture that the individual when closely examined is always comic" (*Faces,* 2).

"O saisons! O chateaux!" the opening chapter focuses on his marriage. Between falling in love in late September 1934 and the ceremony in early December, only a couple of months elapsed. Details of the courtship and marriage are now perhaps less riveting than Powell's conclusion: marriage is of all relations the least predictable.

> People can be close friends for years; cohabit, sometimes under the same roof, for decades; meet and marry on sight. All are equally chancy once the knot is tied. . . . it might be added that, by the age of close on twenty-nine, I had never asked another woman to marry me . . . and, after nearer fifty than forty years, to speak unequivocally, have never wished to be married to another woman. In consequence, taking a risk in the matter seems something not always to be condemned. (13)

The Powells, after a honeymoon in Greece, took a house in London on Great Ormond Street (used for the title of the second chapter), and there or in the neighborhood (Regents Park) they came to know Elizabeth Bowen and Dylan Thomas, while Powell worked for Warner Bros. in a London suburb, there coming to meet Terrence Ratigan. The next chapter also gets its title from a street of residence, North Palm Drive in Beverley Hills near Hollywood, where they traveled in 1937 in hopes of his finding employment as scriptwriter. Contacts with California movie stars and producers were of peripheral interest compared with contacts with Ernest Hemingway and F. Scott Fitzgerald (46–71).

After their return to London, the Powells found larger quarters at Chester Gate. With some expectations of a larger family, Powell also abandoned attempts to write for the cinema, turning instead in his spare time to reviewing. Portraits of Graham Greene and Malcolm Muggeridge, all concerned with London journalism at that time, appear in this volume of his memoir along with details of the Powells' summer trips to France in 1938 and 1939, when the clouds of war were darkening the horizon.

"What's the Drill?" "Cambridge Waters" and "Kierkegaard in Whitehall" focus, respectively, on Powell's entry into the army in Wales and his experiences as an infantry platoon leader in the Welch Regiment (*The Valley of Bones*); on his being sent to a politico-military course at Cambridge University (where John Hayward had taken refuge from the London blitz with his friend Gerry Wellington) (110–30); and on his improved assignment in 1940 to British military headquarters in Whitehall, where he came to know Alexander Dru, translator of Kierkegaard (131–54), and to absorb the background for *The Military Philosophers*.

Minor characters in a novel can sometimes be taken straight from life, as Powell remarked earlier, and in the next chapter, discussing his return to liaison duties, he admits to some: "The Czech military attaché, Colonel Kalla, appears in the *The Military Philosophers* more or less 'as himself' under the name of Colonel Hlava; the Belgian military attaché, Major Kronacker, also not much altered, as Major Kuchérman; but the Belgian Colonial Officer, Major Offerman, is a composite picture of Major Clanwaert" (160).

The Strangers All Are Gone

The title of the final volume of the memoirs, *The Strangers All Are Gone,* carries a touch of melancholy, with its implication that acquaintances have departed. By 1982, the year in which the volume was published, a great many of Powell's had.

This volume covers roughly the decades between the war and the writing of the memoir (1945–80), though Powell, as indicated before, wrestled with the problem of organization and sometimes needed to go backward or forward by decades to make various stories coherent. But again the internal structure is primarily individual. "Reflation; Haunts of Ross and Brooke," the first chapter, puns on the names of its primary subjects, two men Powell came to know after the war, Julian Maclaren-Ross and Jocelyn Brooke, both of whom he respected highly as writers and neither of whom lived to fulfill his promise. An outline in Maclaren-Ross's *Memoirs of the Forties* suggests that had he lived he would have written a sequel with a chapter entitled "Anthony Powell Plays Happy Families," which Powell supposes would have crystallized a visit to his home when Maclaren-Ross played a card game with Powell's son Tristram, who was later to produce a television program featuring Maclaren-Ross, *Writers during the War* (1964), which was introduced by Jocelyn Brooke (*Strangers,* 13).

Brooke's 1953 article praising *Afternoon Men* had led to their correspondence and quickly to friendship. This early praise was a favor Powell reciprocated after Brooke's death by bringing together three of his volumes of fictionalized reminiscences in *The Orchid Trilogy* (1981) and writing an introduction analyzing Brooke's merits as a writer of power and originality.

"Rustication: Chantries and War Memorials" deals with the acquisition of an estate called the Chantry by the Powells after the war and their move to Somerset where he found good neighbors in descendants of the Horners of Mells, whose family chapel memorializes the Asquiths and Tennants of the family fallen in battle and whose home sheltered in his age Monsignor Ronald Knox. Powell came to value Knox's friendship and Evelyn Waugh, to write his biography.

"The London Charivari" records his friendship with Malcolm Muggeridge and the politics of running the magazine *Punch* after Muggeridge took over as editor. His own tribulations as literary editor of *Punch* are viewed in retrospect with shrewd amusement.

"Fit for Eros," the fourth chapter, reveals a side of Powell some readers might find incongruous with his conservatism. It relates his experiences after volunteering as a witness for the defense in the famous "trial" of *Lady Chatterley's Lover,* a novel by a writer he did not greatly admire, D. H. Lawrence, but whose right to express sexual feelings was one Powell wanted to defend. Other writers also sometimes thought subversive or pornographic, such as Apollinaire and Casanova, also found in this conservative novelist a liberal ally.

"Transatlantic Reconnaissances," about his trips to America in the 1960s, and "Thespian Moods," about his experiences in the theater with *Afternoon Men,* we have touched on before. "Heyst's Magic Circle," taking its locus from Conrad's *Victory,* relates Powell's experiences in the Orient on being invited to Japan in 1964.

Rupert Hart-Davis, a publisher of independent spirit and, after the publication of his scholarly volume *The Letters of Oscar Wilde,* recognized widely as a prince of editors, is portrayed in the chapter "Men of Letters." Also pictured here are Kingsley Amis, who became a friend even before the publication of *Lucky Jim,* a novel here given a fine defense by Powell; Robert Conquest, in whom Powell may have found some of the Anglo-American spirit of his character Russell Gwinnett; and V. S. Naipaul, whose wit and good sense may have contributed something to Powell's portrait of Caribbean exile Gibson Delavacquerie in *Hearing Secret Harmonies.*

"The Writer and Society" treats, with ironic skill, the temptations put before writers in the postwar period, luring them to divert energy from art to conferences, talks, and public appearances. The pleasure of travel and the adulation of audiences led many a talent astray after the war. Sensing the danger, Powell was able to resist, resist until, lured by a promise of royal treatment, Venice beckoned. Here we get the background of his trip to a writers conference in Italy in 1968, influential in the writing of *Temporary Kings.*

The last chapter in this last volume of Powell's memoirs focuses on trips to India in 1966 and 1968, with Sir Mortimer Wheeler, the archaeologist, as guide, and on the complexities of Shakespeare's life, the connecting thread being the theme of calm in the midst of transience. "Grave Goods," the chapter is entitled, but the tone is less that of Gray's churchyard than of Browning's Childe Roland. "As the eighth decade gradually consumes itself, shadows lengthen, a masked and muffled figure loiters persistently at the back of every room." But Powell cites Wallace Stevens to the effect that as "[d]eath is the mother of beauty," the fulfillment of one's desires and dreams comes only with death. "Anyway that was what Wallace Stevens thought; others too" (194).

The world's impulse is to act. Better to remain calm: "all epochs have had to suffer assaults on commonsense and common decency, art and letters, honour and wit, courage and order . . . even if sworn enemies of these abstractions . . . seem unduly numerous in contemporary society." Have faith, courage, and proceed firmly even into apparent desolation like Childe Roland. Good terminal advice. And the memoirs conclude with a veiled allegory: "Vasari says that on a winter day in Florence, when snow was deep on the ground, one of the Medici sent for Michelangelo to build a snowman in the courtyard of the Medici palace . . . one can scarcely doubt that the finest snowman on record took shape" (201). In this muted Florentine hyperbole Powell implies an understanding that even the finest of art works, the greatest of novels, may be transient, snowflakes in cosmic time. The four volumes of his memoirs end, as did The Music of Time, with a quiet echo of Shakespeare's "The rest is silence."

O, How the Wheel Becomes It!

Powell's first novel in nearly 10 years, *O, How the Wheel Becomes It!* was published in 1983. The ironic story of an English man of letters, G. F. H. Shadbold—poet, novelist, critic—the novel opens with Shadbold's reflections on Ophelia's words "O, how the wheel becomes it!" (*Hamlet*, 4.5.172). Ophelia, abused by Prince Hamlet, becomes increasingly incoherent as she enters a hall at Elsinore, singing a ballad:

> They bore him barefac'd on the bier
> (Hey non nony, nony, hey nony)
> And in his grave rain'd many a tear.

When her brother, Laertes, suggests she may be out of her wits, she continues with another nonsense refrain: "You must sing 'A-down a-down, and you call him a-down-a.' O, how the wheel becomes it! It is the false steward, that stole his master's daughter."

The "wheel" she mentions is conventionally thought to be the refrain in line 2 of the ballad, something that comes round again in a song. Enigmatic, admittedly, but Shadbold argues that Ophelia is really alluding to some predecessor of the roulette wheel, that she therefore means that chance becomes it.

The thematic focus in *Oh, How the Wheel Becomes It!* shifts to the emotions of jealousy and envy as exemplified in this aging man of letters, Geoffrey Shadbold. In Powell's memoirs, mulling over the differences between American and English character, he had considered the remark of an American friend, a friend also of Ernest Hemingway and Cyril Connolly, surprised at "Connolly's occasional peevishness about acquaintances who seemed to be doing rather too well . . . : 'But I *like* my friends being successful,'" the man remarked. Later Powell reflected on the words as being more American than English: "I don't feel at all confident that I could produce more than a few persons known to me in my own country who could truly echo that sentiment" (95).

Perhaps few novels on either side of the Atlantic fail to touch on envy or jealousy at one point or another, so deeply entwined are these twin emotions in the human condition, all nationality aside. Powell, however, more than once in earlier novels touches on them with more than normal interest. Here he neatly singles out as exemplar Shadbold, a man of letters who is—late in life when serenity might be expected—almost consumed by envy and jealousy.

Shadbold is a man of many gifts: verbal felicity, powers of observation, an excellent memory, all the equipment needed to make a successful poet or novelist, one would think, all but character. Shadbold has no consistent view of life, no set principles, no inner compulsion to make his views known to the world. Nothing to keep him writing if, say, his fortune were suddenly to be made elsewhere.

With Shadbold's gifts writing came easily, and he produced in youth a volume of verse, "the slimmest of slim volumes," *Unweeded Gardens.* "How he managed to get this collection of juvenilia into print no one knew."[8] He himself disparaged it in later years as derivative. Coming to maturity in the mid-1920s and becoming a schoolmaster after leaving the university, he tried to be original. "Everyone these days writes a novel about their school experiences . . . I'm changing the pattern and writing a play." The play, *Irregular Conjugation,* "was performed by Shadbold's pupils, and led to [his] sack from that particular school," later being published by an esoteric press in a very limited edition (6). Novels followed, *Trip the Pert Fairies,* "mostly conversations in the

Peacock tradition," and *Thumbs;* but none sold at all well. "A short study of one of the Cavalier poets (Denham, Suckling, possibly Lovelace) commissioned by an inexperienced publisher for a series of minor poets, was taxed with gross inaccuracy by a reviewer (the sole one)" and promptly disappeared (7).

Writing reviews of books by others Shadbold found to be more profitable, and he soon abandoned creative labors for critical ones: reviews, articles on literature, lectures, radio talks, and later television appearances, from all of which he pieced out a living. In time through such piecework and public appearances he had even made a name for himself as an all-around man of letters. And his second marriage to a popular writer of detective novels had removed any fear of poverty.

When he is invited to lunch in London by a publisher, he accepts the invitation as a matter of course. Then the bombshell. Some years earlier the publisher, fascinated by both of those baroque periods, the 1890s and the 1920s, had asked Shadbold for his advice about a novel published in the 1920s by a friend of his, dead in the war, Cedric Winterwade. It was a question of possibly republishing Winterwade's only novel, *The Welsons of Omdurman Terrace.* Shadbold remembered having read the novel when it came out and being almost happy to perceive that it was not excellent: subject matter derivative of Wells and Gissing, style embarrassingly vulgar and pedestrian. His advice had been in the negative. Now the publisher has a new proposition: a diary kept by Winterwade through the 1920s and 1930s, perhaps into the 1940s and his death in the war, has turned up in Australia. But with characters identified only in code, it needs editing, deciphering. As a friend of the writer and as one of the dwindling number of survivors who could decipher the diary, would he take on the task of editing it?

Motivated more by curiosity than desire to gild his friend's posthumous reputation, Shadbold agrees to look over the manuscript at least and carries it back to his place in the country. That a publisher had been so eager to republish *The Welsons of Omdurman Terrace,* not his own forgotten novels, had aroused Shadbold's envy, but now as he deciphers the diary and realizes that, though nearly illegible, it is beautifully written, jealousy awakens. Winterwade had had a true talent after all, but like that of Pepys, for diary writing.

The worst comes when Shadbold determines that a symbol used for one of the women Winterwade knew, a small crown, must represent Isolde Upjohn, a girl he himself had loved in vain in the 1920s, one he had even introduced to Winterwade. Shadbold had been only one of

Isolde's many suitors, he knew, but he remembered her resistance to being kissed in a taxi, her laughter and softness and beauty ("like a cover of *Vogue,*" someone said), and the grief he felt when she married a rich man and moved abroad. And now he discovers in the diary that Winterwade had known Isolde before Shadbold "introduced" them; worse, that she had asked Winterwade to take her to Paris for a weekend, where the two had found a room in a Left Bank hotel that Shadbold had once recommended to Winterwade as both picturesque and inexpensive.

The flickering hope that Winterwade might be writing wish-fulfilling fantasy is dispelled as Shadbold reads on:

> The whole episode . . . was set out in Winterwade's most accomplished vein. The experience had . . . been a good deal less than idyllic . . . Winterwade emphasized that fact with amused resignation. . . . If Winterwade had indulged in transports of bogus delight Shadbold could more easily have dismissed the descriptions as fiction. . . . Winterwide did not pretend that being in bed with Isolde Upjohn had been in the least a triumph of sexual felicity. Isolde had been cold, absent from the hotel for long periods, remote, yet Winterwade recorded a few orgasms before closing the dozen pages devoted to the Paris episode with a quotation from Swinburne: "I wrought my joys with tears and pain!" (35)

Shadbold was by then "too dispirited to sneer afresh at Winterwade's old-fashioned taste in poetry." Almost afraid to read further, he returns the diary to the publisher with an adverse report, saying that since he could not finish the manuscript he would accept a lesser fee.

Shadbold has been offered a substantial sum to talk about Jacobean poets to a literary society at a redbrick university and, in need of a change of scene, he accepts. There he finds himself, as foreseen, pitted against "an Eng Lit don at the university, who was not only patron of the Society, but . . . one of the former husbands of Prudence," Shadbold's second wife. The don's pedantry, aggressiveness, and pretensions are captured with comic precision—Lucky Jim could hardly do better—but Shadbold volleys well, having learned the jargon. Prudence had already made plans to visit the university to gather material for her next novel and, when after the lecture her name comes up, her ex-husband tries to score a point:

> "Although we are ever delighted to see Prudence, the aim of her visit struck me as a little old-fashioned . . . Nowadays emphasis in the detec-

tive novel is laid no longer on the pure mechanics of movement and dis-covery—maps of the district, plans of country houses, all that parapher-nalia beloved of the past. . . . Social comment . . . is the preoccupation of the better detective writers of today. You must surely agree the bourgeois world of Sherlock Holmes . . . is no more with us, Shad?"

"You forget, Horace, that in *The Priory School Adventure*—which I con-cede betrays snobbish overtones in the disappearance of a duke's son—the murdered German master's name is Heidegger, no doubt father or uncle of the Existentialist philosopher Martin Heidegger, from which ontological hint the story should surely be judged? . . . Not only that, but the maths master is referred to as Mr Aveling."

"I fail to see the significance."

"Clearly Edward Aveling. A little known interlude in the life of the lover of Karl Marx's daughter. You will remember the poor girl thought Aveling was going to marry her, but Aveling found a richer wife. . . . No doubt Holmes had a file on Aveling—perhaps on Marx too under M, next to Moriarty and Moran. Holmes's political awareness often comes through in the stories, though naturally he concealed it for his own rea-sons." (56–57)

The professor of English literature is outplayed at his own game.

But in the countervolley, when Horace tries to upend Shadbold with knowledge of a forgotten novel he "probably doesn't know," *The Welsons of Ordurman Terrace,* Shadbold discovers that the don plans to teach the novel and is seeking anything else that Winterwade may have written. Looming over him as he leaves is the threat of Winterwade becoming, for all his unpopularity in his lifetime, an academic classic.

But Shadbold's memory and intelligence have met the test, and he has confidence that he can handle the coming televised interview with Rod Cubbage. He has studied Cubbage in action and is aware of both his style and his tactics. Hard-hitting, aggressive, insulting, probing for a weakness, Cubbage then moves on to the surprise witness, the devastat-ing revelation, the kill.

The climax of *O, How the Wheel Becomes It* begins with a telephone call shortly after Shadbold's wife has departed to gather material for her next detective novel. "Geoffrey?" a feminine voice says. His friends call him Shad. No one has called him Geoffrey in 30 years. When he finds that the caller, Mrs. Abdullah, is actually the former Isolde Upjohn, he bare-ly stops himself from blurting out, "I thought you were dead." Isolde invites herself to his place to cook lunch for him, since his wife is away, but before she can reach the kitchen Don Cubbage arrives with his television crew, a day before expected, and takes over the house. And is taken over in turn by Isolde, or seems to be.

The Cubbage hard-driving interview style, left jabs all the way, begins as the television cameras are set up, but the uppercut has already landed: the arrival of Isolde. Shadbold, no dummy, has prepared himself for the style, but the persistent interventions of Isolde so rattle him that he loses composure, reveals too much. And promises too much. "By the end of the day Shadbold had admitted to an admiration for *The Welsons of Omdurman Terrace,* agreed that Winterwade had died a hero's death that he himself envied, and promised to do his best to find out the circumstances in which Winterwade's heroic end had taken place" (109). He has even promised on national television to write an introduction to Isolde's memoirs.

When later, in anguish, he tells Prudence about the interview, she insists that he has been a fool, that Isolde and Cubbage must have set him up. But now he feels he must edit Winterwade's diary after all and thereby gain some control of it. Things can be elided, colored, left "undeciphered," even suppressed. But his inquiries of the publisher go unanswered. Word from a former fellow soldier that Winterwade had actually been killed fleeing a military police patrol near a Bombay brothel is of little comfort.

Months later, at another luncheon at the Garrick Club, he learns that the manuscript of Winterwade's diary had been returned to Australia and that "Winterwade's son had destroyed it as unsaleable. Didn't want it cluttering up the house." Shadbold decides against having lunch: "Do you know I'm not feeling very well, Jason. I think . . . I'll . . . go back to the country this afternoon" (140).

The last chapter opens with Jason delivering the panegyric at Shadbold's memorial service. It is being held "in one of the City churches, though Shadbold had no particular associations with the City nor for that matter with churches" (141). Giving voice to many of his own prejudices and a few of Shadbold's qualities, Jason concludes with a verse from the 1890s:

> Though our thoughts turn ever Doomwards,
> Though our sun is well-nigh set;
> Though our Century totters tombwards,
> We may laugh a little yet.

Prudence, who had often stressed "her own matter-of-factness in the face of mortality," was "got up as if for skiing." But among the women dressed in mourning is one who "had evidently been a beauty in days gone by." As the book ends the publisher identifies her as Mrs. Abdullah, adding that his "new firm had somewhat reluctantly turned down her Memoirs . . . as being of not quite sufficient interest to promise any great sale" (143).

The Fisher King

Reviewers were not kind to *The Fisher King,* or rather they were kind in a patronizing way, doing the novel and their readers an injustice. Noting that Powell was 80 years old when the novel was published (in 1986) and discovering that the central figure is an artist aware that he is nearing the end, reviewers for the most part treated the novel as a valedictory: Powell's farewell to his art.

The Fisher King is perhaps a valedictory, but it shows no sign of fatigue, none of senility. A sign of age may appear it is true in a drifting of interest toward the problems of aging, but the book is more, as rich and complex an average-length novel as Powell has written. The love triangles about which it seems to center are merely a scaffolding on which to hang the real themes. More than a slice of life, the novel has striated levels of meaning while remaining at the same time in every sentence lucid.

The framework for the story is simple enough: varied passengers embark on the ship *Alecto* for a cruise up the coast of England to visit archaeological sites. It closes before the cruise ends, when the *Alecto* reaches its most northern port of call, its ultima Thule. On board are several lecturers in archeology, but they are not even of peripheral interest. The passengers go ashore to explore Hadrian's Wall, the Edinburgh vicinity, and the great Stone Circle on the Orkney Islands, but Powell eliminates all detail about debarkation and embarkation. A chapter closes on shipboard, the next opens the next day at the wall, the next in the middle of dinner the next day. The trivial is eliminated to concentrate on character and theme.

The initial focus is on a novelist who prides himself on superior powers of observation. Valentine Beals is leaning on the ship's rail, watching fellow passengers cross the staging area to embark, playing a game with himself, a sort of solitaire in which powers of observation and intelligence are the keys to matching the new arrivals with the passenger list, the score to be checked as further observation reveals to what extent he has identified them correctly. The passenger of most interest to himself is already aboard, a photographer named Saul Henchman.

The title *The Fisher King* may remind us of the passage in *Temporary Kings* in which Jenkins, invited to a festival in Venice, hesitates to accept. Mark Members, wanting him to attend the festival, assures Jenkins that he will be treated like a king. "One of those temporary kings in *The Golden Bough,*" Jenkins replies, "everything at their disposal for a year or a month or a day, then execution? Death in Venice?"

The king of photography in England is the aging Saul Henchman, recognized by Beals as an archetype of that mythological figure in *The Golden Bough,* the Fisher King. Henchman's life has been dedicated to art, but an art with its dry periods (not without fears of total desiccation), and he seems to accept its drying up—like his deposition as king of English photographers—with stoicism.

The ostensible theme of the novel involves the myth of the Fisher King, familiar to many people through study of T. S. Eliot's *The Waste Land,* as one of the passengers on the *Alecto* points out.[9] The myth comes into play as Beals makes another game out of finding correspondences between myth and reality, between the myth of the Fisher King and the history of Saul Henchman. Powell handles this artfully by having Beals open his game to the other members of his foursome, the exposition of the parallels thus extending through several conversations over the first half of the novel, growing richer and more complex without entering the realm of tedium.

The Beals quartet consists of four friends, more or less intellectual, who have elected to go on the cruise together. Beals had begun a career in business as a salesman, with his friend Middlecote in advertising. Beals then tried his hand at writing a historical romance, laced it with sex, succeeded, and found he could make more money writing "bodice-snatchers," novels with a historical setting and a good deal more sexual frankness than the inventor of the historical romance, Sir Walter Scott, dared permit himself. Beals accordingly has switched occupations, become an internationally known novelist, garnered fans and money, and developed an indifference to the fact that his novels are despised by intellectuals.[10] The novel to him is a trade, not an art, and he enjoys the research required.

Beals and Middlecote enjoy a certain amount of rivalry still, Beals outwitting Middlecote in cultural matters—identifying quotations, reading Latin inscriptions—and Middlecote countering with more up-to-date data about the world of business. During the war both had been in the navy. "Beals had served at sea in Naval Intelligence. . . . Middlecote had been in a destroyer escorting material of war for Russia"

(18). And their wives are different enough to be companionable: Fay Middlecote aggressive, knowledgeable, curious; Louise Beals reserved, reflective, intuitive. Conversation among the four, if sometimes tense, is always stimulating. And what they like best is discussing the more curious of their fellow passengers.

The center of attention is the ship's most mismatched couple, the aged photographer Saul Henchman, crippled and war-scarred, and his companion and photographic assistant Barberina Rookwood, a former ballerina in her early 20s, still beautiful. Beals has investigated Henchman's history, perhaps with a novel in mind, and is able to reveal how Henchman started as an apprentice and lent his camera at first intermittently to pornographic and sadomasochistic ends. Acquaintance with a village tart led to "a series of photographs of this girl lying naked on her back in a shallow pool among some beech woods. Absolutely everything on display, not a hair missing. . . . Round the naked lady were floating bits of garbage, empty beer bottles, a tin or two prised open, an old boot, possibly a dead dog." The row that followed the exhibition of these photographs Henchman surmounted with "complete self-confidence" (31).

What would distinguish Henchman in any art, Powell suggests without using the term, is genius. He is more observant, more intelligent, more articulate than the novelist Beals, as he several times demonstrates. His portraits excel not because he has greater technical knowledge— skill with lens and developing techniques—as Sir Dixon Tiptoft believes, but because he has learned to use words to manipulate subjects into exposing what his intuition perceives to be the selves they want hidden. Click. Anyone can click his cameras; Henchman selects, even creates the right moment. Such photographs have brought him an international reputation. And though shell-battered and condemned to crutches, Beals is utterly without self-pity, which takes strangers by surprise. On the other hand, no one would describe Henchman as nice. Brusque and rude, rather, and with at no great distance below the surface a streak of cruelty. Almost every passenger seems to experience it. When Sir Dixon looks at an eighteenth-century house and remarks that it makes him think of Adam (presumably Robert Adam the eighteenth-century architect, one of four well-known brothers) Henchman expresses "hearty agreement," and deliberately misunderstands him.

> "No—a bastard. . . . God was right to expel him. . . . Adam is not the sort of man one would care to have created oneself, legitimately or

illegitimately. Personally, I never wished to create anyone, even in days when that was feasible. In doing so I am inclined to think God undertook too grave a risk. It cannot be said to have come off well. Expulsion from Eden was the only possible outcome. . . . Everyone gets expelled sooner or later. Haven't you found that? . . . What seems so strange is that Adam apparently expected to be an exception. . . ."

"I meant the brothers. When you are taking a photograph of an eighteenth-century building. . . ."

"The brothers? Cain and Abel? As a child I was always on Cain's side. I should have done the same myself. I read a lot of the Bible as a boy, or had it read to me . . . I mean of course, the real Bible, not the appalling modern translations nowadays foisted on the English-speaking world. The Bible tells you how human beings behave. It always gives a useful standard of perspective. A realistic one."

"Perspective is just what I want to ask you about. The focus—"
(243–45)

Photography is just what Henchman does not want to talk about, and he has his will; Sir Dixon is thwarted again.

Robin Jilson is also interested in photography. Indeed, the worsening of his muscular disease having made work in a bank no longer feasible, he is relying on photography as a future source of livelihood. Seeing too that Barberina is taking an interest in the young man, perhaps also seeking a new way to torment her, Henchman offers to take Robin on as an apprentice, perhaps: "I have accumulated a few useful experiences . . . While we are on board together, I might be able to pass on a little of that" (95). His words are ambiguous and Barberina later expresses skepticism.

Brought up to be a ballet star by a grandmother with designs, even given a more glamorous name, Barberina had been sent at 16 to Henchman's studio to have some publicity shots taken. Some stories have it that she never left the studio, but sent for her toothbrush. At any rate, the ballet forsaken, she melted into a life of serving Henchman six or seven years ago. Her servitude is analyzed with relish by the foursome, Beals linking her to the myth of the Fisher King, the virgin maid who brings the king his bowl.

Other couples aboard the *Alecto* play supporting roles: Professor and Elaine Kopf from America, adding some pedantry to Beals's erudition, and Sir Dixon Tiptoft, a retired British civil servant, and his wife, who have come on the cruise with their daughter, Dr. Lorna Tiptoft. Mrs. Jilson and her pale son form another couple, traveling together for

Robin's health. Assigned to different cabins, they share quarters with two semidetached strangers, Lorna Tiptoft having been assigned to Mrs. Jilson's cabin, and an incongruous latecomer, a newspaper and business tycoon named Lamont, to her son's cabin.

Evidence accumulates to indicate that Lamont has come aboard sensing that Henchman has grown vulnerable. A rabid fan of ballet, the recently widowed—his wife died while they were on a business trip to New York—Lamont had once, briefly, been close to Barberina and perhaps wants to marry her. Henchman—who proves himself repeatedly the most observant and sensitive of the passengers, as well as the most eloquent and ruthless—is quite aware of the threat, as he is of Barberina's interest in Robin Jilson, who, like Lamont with his new heart problem, also seems in need of a nurse.

Below the quite adequate mythological structure seems to be the real theme. Talk. To put it that bluntly risks oversimplifying the theme, for "talk" is actually complex. Talk is the most obvious way people communicate, indeed the nexus of almost all personal relationships. But talk can be revelation or obfuscation, depending on the motives and skills of the speaker. And of course there is talk intended to be obfuscatory that gives the speaker away and talk intended to be revelatory that muddies the understanding. As the Fisher King needs to communicate with his people, but for a while cannot, so the passengers fall into a shifting spectrum, from those suffering from an inability to communicate to those insufferable because they cannot cease talking, from those who misunderstand most of what they hear to those who pretend misunderstanding to torment those they love or hate.

The ancient mariner in Coleridge's poem is cursed for the crime of wantonly destroying natural beauty (in the form of an albatross) with a penance, having to buttonhole passing strangers ("He stoppeth one of three") to relate his tale, or "confess" his crime and its consequences. On the *Alecto,* Mr. Jack plays the role of ancient mariner, traveling alone, haunting the bar, apparently desperate to relate anecdotes of his innumerable sexual encounters to anyone he can trap into listening. ("Have you ever fallen in love with a tart? I mean a real whore? Just after the war, I did.") Comic till the end, as successive passengers come to realize his unsnubability, Mr. Jack begins as an ancient mariner, compelled to speak forever of his sexual encounters, but turns during the course of the novel into another mythic type, a modern Don Juan, traced by Beals (who has done research for a novel dealing with Spanish history) from early Spanish legend through Molière to Byron and Mozart, changing over the centuries from laughing sexual predator to doomed, melancholy victim of sex. Why did we not see it earlier? Jack is a form of John as Juan is the Spanish for John. Sex has become an albatross from which Mr. Jack seems doomed never to escape, tortured still, however impotent he becomes with age.

Henchman, the most accomplished talker on board, uses talk to control Barberina, Lamont, Robin, Mr. Jack, and even Beals. Like that other compulsive talker Scheherazade of *The Arabian Nights,* fabled for telling stories with a hidden motive, to wear out the nights, Henchman is conscious of what he is doing, forcing on fellow passengers (with more than casual focus on Beals) his brutal tale of the King of the Black Isles.

Barberina's dancing has been stilled by her love for Henchman, her promising career abandoned; but in what the passengers recognize as the climax of the trip, at night when the ship's orchestra is playing bits of Tschaikovsky's *Swan Lake,* she enters the saloon where Henchman and Mr. Jack (Scheherazade and the ancient mariner) are having a nightcap and stuns her public with a private ballet, the dance her way of talking, of saying good-bye, a wordless symbol of farewell to Henchman. At the end he nods a silent acknowledgment.

In the last chapter Henchman reaches his ultima Thule, the circle of ancient stones on the Orkney Islands that still speak somehow, and even here the heroic has been defaced with graffiti, as he had known it would be. Scrawled, inarticulate expressions of protest against life? Or only of protest against death, of the inarticulate will to live, clutching at a sliver of immortality? Henchman swings along on his crutches ahead of the other pilgrims, with Mr. Jack now carrying his camera equipment, until he comes to a stone that stops him, the graffiti "incised not only in the largest lettering of any hitherto seen up to that point in the Circle, also executed with far the greatest skill."

G ISBISTER
1881

"Just look at the size of that name," Fay Middlecote says. "What a frightful thing to do." "I am looking at it. In fact I am recording its horror by photographic means," Henchman replies (249). When she suggests the carver may have been related to "Isbister, the portrait painter," Henchman puts her down by recalling that Isbister's first name was Horace and that "Isbister is also an Orcadian place-name. Excavations are in progress there at the moment. Accordingly, the epigraphist is likely to have been a local, rather than tourist. One pictures him returning day after day with hammer and chisel" (249).

In the end, everyone having been put down by Henchman, Henchman abandons the cruise to stay at the loch, perhaps with Mr. Jack, his new assistant. He has told them that he wanted to fish. Lamont is called back to London by news of what is possibly a ministerial appointment. Robin, suffering it would seem from muscular dystrophy, is taken in hand by Dr. Lorna Thorncroft, while Barberina, released by her art from servitude, continues on the cruise back to the south of England, perhaps to find her way back to ballet.

For a man of any age, *The Fisher King* would be a remarkable achievement.

Criticism: 1990–1991

Powell, as we have noted, reviewed books throughout his career. At times he was also active in supporting the republication of literary works he thought unduly neglected and in memorializing people he thought should be more widely known, contributing in this way introductions or essays to perhaps a dozen books. Sharing a concern of friends that these "ephemera" of the writer's life, scattered in newspapers, magazines, and anthologies, might be lost, he was persuaded to collect and publish them in book form, giving the ephemera, so to speak, a more permanent domicile.

Miscellaneous Verdicts: Writings on Writers 1946–1989 gives us 500 pages of superlative book reviews, essays, and brief memoirs. The reviews from the *Times Literary Supplement* had appeared anonymously, so that most of them are here identified as Powell's for the first time. And a few others in rare journals, such as the *Balliol Register,* had been virtually inaccessible.

A year later another volume of essays appeared, *Under Review: Further Writing on Writers 1946–1989* (dedicated to a member of a younger generation, Kingsley Amis). These essays and reviews, like those in the earlier volume, have been frequently quoted in earlier chapters of this study (the original publications cited); further illustration seems unneeded. Here they are more conveniently arranged: thoughts about the 1890s with Oscar Wilde and Max Beerbohm and "Earl Lavendar" Davidson, thoughts about American writers, thoughts about the writings of his friends, thoughts about continental diarists.

The picture of a venerable author in his eighties collecting and arranging the more perishable of his writings recalls a bit the image of a grandparent sorting stray photographs for a last album, with fond and worried thoughts of a grandchild who may someday be mature enough to want to leaf through the dust: This is the way life was, my dear, grotesque and beautiful.

Notes and References

"Anthony Dymoke Powell." The name to begin with offers some trouble with pronunciation even in England. There the young have no trouble with the first name, for they tend to rely on pronunciation to misspell it "Antony." The shorter "Tony" is easy enough on either side, but that points to the correct East-of-the-Atlantic pronunciation of Anthony (without the diphthong "th") as opposed to the American pronunciation (with the diphthong).

"Dymoke" is not to be pronounced "Diemoke," as I was once told by someone who knew Anthony Powell. Rather (Mr. Powell was kind enough to correct me), the "y" should be muted, as in "Dimmok."

And the family name of "Powell" is pronounced to rime (or rhyme) with James Russell Lowell (rather than with Gen. Colin Powell). Perhaps slightly bisyllabic, as in Noel. Indeed the spelling of the family name in many Welsh (or Welch) historical documents is "Pole" or "Poel." Yet even in England (at least in middle-class academic circles) blankness may be encountered if one expresses a fondness for the novels of "Antony Pole." "Oh, you mean Antony *Powell*!" Best perhaps to keep discourse civil and be flexible in such matters.

The notes that follow refer to reviews, articles, letters, or books by Powell unless otherwise indicated. With the exception of volumes in The Music of Time, references to works cited more than once are given in full below and thereafter cited parenthetically in the text, by abbreviated title and page number for works by Powell, by author last name and page number for other works. References to the 12 volumes of The Music of Time (all of which are from the first editions published by Heinemann in London between 1951 and 1975) are cited in the text by volume and page number (as 6:123).

Chapter One

1. *Daily Telegraph,* 26 June 1959, 14.

2. See Powell's "Reflections on the Landed Gentry," in *Burke's Genealogical and Heraldic History of the Landed Gentry* (London: Burke's Peerage, 1965), xxv–xxviii. Here the entry on the family is entitled "Powell of the Chantry," 596–97. The Bodleian Library in Oxford has separately bound tearsheets entitled "The Powell Family of Llowes and Clyro in Radnorshire; and Brilley in Herefordshire, 1581–1800, by Mr. A. D. Powell." The tearsheets are from the *Radnorshire Society Journal* (1941) 62–67, bear the note "Sent to the Bodleian by Capt. A. D. Powell," and are stamped "26 Jan. 1942."

3. *John Aubrey and His Friends* (London: Eyre and Spottiswode, 1948), 20.

4. *Times* (London), 5 January 1960, 11.

5. *Punch,* 3 February 1954, 187. In The Music of Time, Captain Jenkins is also invalided out of the army in 1928 (6:126).

6. *Daily Telegraph,* 22 May 1959, 14.

7. *Daily Telegraph,* 4 March 1960, 16.

8. *Daily Telegraph,* 22 September 1961, 18.

9. Anthony West, *New Yorker,* 16 February 1963, 159.

10. *Infants of the Spring* (London: Heinemann, 1976), 47.

11. *Daily Telegraph,* 12 October 1962, 19.

12. *Daily Telegraph,* 23 March 1962, 19.

13. Samuel Lodge, *Scrivelsby: The Home of the Champions, with Some Account of the Marmion and Dymoke Families* (London, S. Stock, 1893), 42.

14. Samuel Pepys, "23d April 1661, Coronation Day," *Diary and Correspondence* (Philadelphia: McCay, 1887), 1:177.

15. Quoted by Lodge, 146–47. See also Sir Walter Scott's long narrative poem *Marmion.*

16. Lodge, 115. An attenuated form of the ritual was reinstituted in the twentieth century.

17. *Daily Telegraph,* 21 September 1962, 18.

18. Norreys Jephson O'Conor, *Godes Peace and the Queenes: Vicissitudes of a House, 1539–1615* (Cambridge, Mass.: Harvard University Press, 1934), 125.

19. "The Wat'ry Glade," in *The Old School: Essays by Divers Hands,* ed. Graham Greene (London: Jonathan Cape, 1934), 149. Referred to hereafter in the text as "Glade."

20. Henry Green, *Pack My Bag* (London: Hogarth Press, 1940), 156. (Referenced hereafter as Green 1940.)

21. Cyril Connolly, *Enemies of Promise* (London: Longmans, Green,1938), 317–19. See also John Lehmann, *The Whispering Gallery* (London: Routledge and Kegan Paul, 1955), 105–96. Eric Blair, better known to the world as George Orwell, was at Eton with Powell, but they did not become friends until later.

22. Henry Green, *Blindness* (New York: Dutton, 1926), 9. (Referenced hereafter as Green 1926.)

23. Harold Acton, *Memoirs of a Aesthete* (London: Methuen, 1948), 90–101, 111, 119, 154. Powell and Acton also had an ancestral connection, a great-aunt of Powell's having married Sir John Acton, "an English cavalry officer in the Army of the Two Sicilies." *Punch,* 12 December 1956, 730.

24. See also *Infants of the Spring,* plate 16, a photograph of top-hatted students on a carriage: "Electioneering for an Eton master, 1923: Robert Byron, Hubert Duggan, on box holding reins; John Spencer . . . AP [Anthony Powell] in back."

25. Cyril Connolly, *Sunday Times* (London), 15 July 1956, 5, and Powell, *Punch,* 30 October 1957, 518.

26. Evelyn Waugh, *A Little Learning* (London: Chapman and Hall, 1964), 201. Hereafter cited in the text as Waugh.

27. Christopher Hollis, *The Road to Frome* (London: Harrap, 1958), 65.

28. *Messengers of Day* (London: Heinemann, 1978), 4, 9.

29. Beverley Nichols, *The Sweet and Twenties* (London: Weidenfield and Nicholson, 1958) 50, 57.

30. Evelyn Waugh, "Urbane Enjoyment Personified," *New York Times Magazine*, 30 November 1952, 72.

31. *Daily Telegraph*, 27 May 1960, 18.

32. *Daily Telegraph*, 5 August 1960, 14.

33. Osbert Sitwell, *Noble Essences* (London: Macmillan, 1950), 149–50; Powell, *Daily Telegraph*, 3 May 1963, 20, and 18 May 1962, 18.

34. Evelyn Waugh, *Vile Bodies* (Harmondsworth: Penguin, 1955), 30.

35. *Daily Telegraph*, May 18, 1962, 18.

36. *Punch*, 19 September 1956, 346.

37. See also Arthur Calder-Marshall, *The Magic of My Youth* (London: Hart-Davis, 1951), 106–36.

38. *Punch*, 31 July 1957, 138; 16 October 1957, 460; and 16 November 1955, 585; *Daily Telegraph*, 30 October 1959, 18.

39. W. K. Rose, ed., *The Letters of Wyndham Lewis* (London: Methuen, 1963), 244–45.

40. Watson Lyle, "Modern Musicians—II—Constant Lambert," *Bookman* 81 (March 1932): 342; Watson Lyle, "Constant Lambert, 1905–[1951]," *Composers Today* (New York, 1934): 157–59; and Hermon Ould, "English Music of the Year," *Bookman* 80 (December 1931): 181. In a similar fashion, the musician Moreland is "taken up by" the fashionable Mrs. Foxe in The Music of Time (5:133).

41. *Afternoon Men*, new ed. (London: Heinemann, 1954), 2.

42. Cecil Gray, *Peter Warlock* (London: Jonathan Cape, 1934), 223–28; Harry T. Moore, *The Intelligent Heart: The Story of D. H. Lawrence* (London: Heinemann, 1954), 212–19.

43. Jocelyn Brooke, *Aldous Huxley* (London: Longmans, Green, 1954), 15; Aldous Huxley, *Antic Hay* (London: Penguin, 1948), 49–54.

44. *Daily Telegraph*, 27 July 1962, 16.

45. Cecil Gray, *Musical Chairs* (London: Home and Van Thal, 1948), 289–96.

46. *Daily Telegraph*, 18 March 1960, 15.

47. Adrian Daintrey, *I Must Say* (London: Chatto and Windus, 1963), 13, 29, 155–56.

48. Nina Hamnett, *Is She a Lady?* (London: Allan Wingate, 1955), 28–35, 128f; her portrait of Powell is reproduced in *Messengers of Day*. Powell discusses Hamnett only briefly in *Punch*, 3 August 1960, 18, and in the *Daily Telegraph*, 18 March 1960, 16.

49. *New Statesman*, 22 December 1956, 812.

50. Maurice Richardson, *Books and Bookmen*, November 1978, 30.

51. An official photograph shows both fathers in uniform for the state

funeral of George VI in 1910: "Capt. Philip Powell (Welch Regt., adjutant 13th London Rgt.)" and "Lt. Col. the Earl of Longford (commanding 2d Life Guards escort)." Reproduced in *Infants of the Spring,* plate 12.

52.   She was surprised to learn years later, when her son Tristram Powell produced a documentary film on the life of Katherine Mansfield, that the New Zealand novelist had preceded her by a few years at the same school. *Within the Family Circle* (London: Heinemann, 1976), 171.

53.   *Times,* 3 December 1934, 17.

54.   *Faces in My Time* (London: Heinemann, 1979), 34–45.

55.   *Times,* 22 February 1946, 8.

56.   *Venusberg,* new ed. (London: Heinemann, 1955), 180–81.

Chapter Two

1.   "Time's Laughing Stocks." *Times Literary Supplement,* 29 June 1962, 476, and "The Early and the Later Powell," 13 July 1962, 509.

2.   V. S. Pritchett, "London Letter," *New York Times Book Review,* 12 January 1958, 22.

3.   Untitled review of John Hargrave's *Harbottle, Cherwell* (Oxford), 31 May 1924, 123–24. Signed A. D. P.

4.   In the neoclassic vein, when Powell does touch the beauties of nature, the touch is cool, as in this view of the Camberley countryside: "The grass looked parched. Some charred gorse marked the limits of a heath fire. The unspeakable pines gave off a medicinal odour." (From *What's Become of Waring* [London: Heinemann, 1953], 200.)

5.   Richard J. Vorhees, "The Music of Time: These and Variations," *Dalhousie Review* 42 (Autumn 1962): 313.

6.   Several critics have treated Powell with hostility for describing Verlst as a Jew. James Tucker, in *The Novels of Anthony Powell* (London: Macmillan, 1976), defends Powell by attributing the comments on Verlst as Jew to the protagonist, Atwater (13–14). Unhappily, such reasoning could end our sympathy for Atwater without ending the argument. Since Verlst is the only character seen as successful with money, he also becomes Atwater's foil by virtue of the novel's structure; he appears much less a character than as a symbol of success. Atwater is weedy and thin; Verlst has the look, almost, of an officer in the Guards; Atwater works in a museum, Verlst buys works of art; Atwater loves Susan, Verlst takes her off to America. But in the 1920s, when *Afternoon Men* must have been begun, before Hitler turned the clock back, Jews were so widely accepted in British society that a critical view of an individual Jew did not automatically imply the intolerance it would later. One might also note Powell's dedication of *Casanova's Chinese Restaurant* to the chairman of the Anglo-Israel Bank.

7.   "The roast-beef-English atmosphere" of the boxing arena Comrades' Hall (in Camden Town, London) is said to have made it a favorite with Roy

Campbell, Nina Hamnett, and others of the Heseltine circle. See Hamnett's *Is She a Lady?* 49–54.

8.   With her Chinese tea-gowns, books with such titles as *God's Failures,* exotic liqueurs, kindly and misguided patronage, and aristocratic absence of sham, the character Naomi Race may owe something to Lady Ottoline Morrell.

9.   Possibly a touch of Evelyn Waugh enters Pringle's portrait at this point. In *A Little Learning,* Waugh confesses that, while in despair as a school-master in Wales, he once left a farewell note (among his clothes, and in Greek) as he swam out to sea, only to be stung by jellyfish to the point where life on shore seemed more desirable (Waugh 1964, 230).

10.   *From a View to a Death,* new ed. (London: Heinemann, 1954), 12.

11.   *Agents and Patients,* new ed. (London: Heinemann, 1955), 3–4.

12.   The shop (and Commodore Venables) seem based in some measure on the Varda Bookshop run by "The Beautiful Varda," as she had been billed on the stage by C. B. Cochran. "As well as beauty, Varda possessed a sharp and witty tongue. 'The only woman I know with a male sense of humour,' Constant Lambert used to say." Lambert lived in one of the two small flats (the other inhabited by Peter Quennell) above the Varda Bookshop (c. 1926–28). "Michael Salaman . . . set Varda up in the bookshop . . . out of a disinterested admiration for beauty and wit, combined with his own kindness of heart. . . . If Salaman had been 'keeping' Varda, there would have been nothing much to it, but (so far as anything sexual can be certain in this world) she never became his mistress" (*Infants,* 96–97).

13.   *À la Vache enragé* seems to be based on the famous Boeuf sur le Toit in Paris where Cole Porter is said to have composed "Let's Do It."

14.   Powell has commented on the Berlin cinema world of Eric von Stroheim as if personally acquainted with it (*Punch,* 20 January 1954, 114–15; see *Messengers,* 154).

15.   Count Gaston de la Tour d'Espagne, at the emotional focus of the novel (174), recites Gérard de Nerval's sonnet about the knight returning from a mission to find his land in ruins, a sonnet that had earlier struck a responsive chord in Cecil Gray as well as T. S. Eliot. Count Robin de la Condamine (who acted on the London stage under the name of Robert Farquharson) is a possible model here. See James Laver, *Museum Piece* (London: Deutsch, 1963), 119–20.

16.   Robert Browning's poem "Waring" seems to have led Powell rather than his character Alec Pimley (who is not much of a reader of poetry) to the alias T. T. Waring. Pimley does share the melancholy of E. M. Forster: "A hundred years ago Browning's Waring could give all civilization the slip and vanish from the midst of his friends into the unknown." But our era is more brutal, Forster complains. "Waring, today, couldn't slip off in his little boat" ("Ivory Tower," *Atlantic Monthly,* January 1939, 54).

Chapter Three

1. *Spectator,* 30 June 1939, 1134, and 8 March 1946, 247–48.
2. *Punch,* 1 June 1955, 688.
3. See Powell's long article on Amiel in *Cornhill* 161 (December 1945) 481–88, and 162 (April 1946) 78–81. When Alexander Dru died, Powell supplemented the obituary in the *Times* with a letter adding to the list of his accomplishments.
4. Marvin Mudrick, "Man Alive," *Hudson Review* 17 (Spring 1964) 119. Almost all critics of The Music of Time have erred about character motivations—for example, James Hall's supposition that Jean Templer left her husband because she preferred the "artistic temperament" of Jenkins (*The Tragic Comedians* [Bloomington: Indiana University Press, 1963], 142), when her motives later seem to have been quite ruthlessly sensual. The motive behind Powell's new style has been missed, and we are not used to a central, intelligent narrator who is repeatedly in error, much as we realize that we ourselves are repeatedly in error in our assessment of others. Powell is doing something new, and the style is a necessary part of it.
5. *Punch,* 22 January 1958, 160. See also *The Memoirs of Lord Chandos* (London: Bodley Head, 1963), passim.
6. *Sunday Times,* 28 April 1963, 8.
7. *Times Literary Supplement,* 29 June 1962, 476.
8. *Daily Telegraph,* October 7, 1960, 18.
9. John Russell, *A Portrait of Logan Pearsall Smith* (London: Dropmore, 1950), 13. See also Robert Gathorne-Hardy, *Recollections of Logan Pearsall Smith: The Story of a Friendship* (London: Constable, 1949), and Cyril Connolly, "Logan Pearsall Smith," *Atlantic Monthly,* June 1964, 129–30.
10. *Time and Tide,* 2 July 1960, 764–65, and 9 July 1960, 808–9. *New Review* also published a character index by James Tucker, enlarged some years later in his book on Powell. Both of these have been supplanted by Hilary Spurling's *Handbook to Anthony Powell's Music of Time* (London: Heinemann, 1977).
11. Henry James had visited Osterly, the great country house of the Earls of Jersey. In *Within the Family Circle,* Violet Powell writes that his "long story *The Lesson of the Master* opens with an account of a Sunday under the cedar trees on the lawn at Osterly. But when he sent a copy of the story to his hostess [the Countess of Jersey, Violet Powell's grandmother], admitting his debt for the background, he denied that he had made use of what he called 'the human furniture.'" Violet Powell adds: "Making every allowance for a novelist's right to compound one character from different aspects of many, observed and transformed by creative processes, I have never been convinced that there was not an element of self-protection in James' disclaimer. The hostess of Summersoft (Osterly) expressed [sentiments] not alien to my grandmother" (20–21).
12. If Lady Warminster in some respects resembles the present Countess of Longford, in other respects she resembles Lady Burghclere, the

mother of the Honorable Evelyn Heygate, to whom Powell dedicated his third novel. See Lady Burghclere's obituary, *Times,* 3 October 1933, 7, and *Messengers,* 65–69.

13. The connection of Orwell with Erridge is also made by Bernard Crick in his biography *George Orwell: A Life* (London: Secker and Warburg, 1980), 296n.

14. Somerset Maugham (who had publicly expressed scorn for writers whose knowledge of the aristocracy came mostly from "the illustrated papers") once at luncheon with Powell remarked, "It's amusing in Trollope's novels how the Duke will address his son by his courtesy title." When Powell remembered "at least half-a-dozen boys at school" who were so addressed, and was thoughtless enough to say so, Maugham abruptly ended the conversation (*Faces,* 44–45).

15. One model for General Conyers is surely the friend of Powell's father, Captain, later Major General, J. F. C. 'Boney' Fuller. Fuller, rather than Montgomery, was probably the British general most respected by American staff officers in World War II. As military philosopher and theorist, he had prophesied the panzer blitzkrieg that stunned the world in 1940. Like General Conyers, he had a modest interest in the occult (*Infants,* 49).

16. *Punch,* 19 September 1956, 346.

17. Evelyn Waugh, *Spectator,* 24 June 1962, 864.

18. James Laver reports that when his book on Nostradamus was published, he received a letter from Aleister Crowley, beginning, "Do what thou wilt shall be the whole of the Law. . . ." The letter invited him for a visit at his hotel in Hastings in 1947, and Laver recorded the visit (226–31). So similar is the description, from heroin to Tarot cards, that Powell almost certainly based his account of Dr. Trelawney on someone's visit to Crowley there.

19. In the legend of Gyges, the chief officer of King Candaules is coerced by the king against his sense of right and wrong to view the full beauty of his queen ("Wouldst thou have me behold my mistress when she is naked? Bethinks thou that a woman, with her clothes, puts off her bashfulness?") and is detected by the queen as he slips out. "Instantly divining what had happened, she neither screamed as her shame impelled her, nor even appeared to have noticed." But determined on vengeance, the next morning she summons Gyges and offers him the choice of his own death or the murder of the husband who betrayed her. "Gyges was afterwards confirmed in the possession of the throne by an answer of the Delphic oracle" (Herodotus [London: Dent, 1910], 1.6–10). Powell says, in the preface to his wife's *The Album of Anthony Powell's "Dance to the Music of Time"* (London: Thames and Hudson, 1987): "I had always found the relationship of Candaules and Gyges of peculiar fascination. At one moment I planned to attempt a play on the subject, finally deciding somehow to insert the story into a novel. Part of its interest consisted in supposing that . . . it had never been used by any of the old masters. "After I had introduced the incident into Dance I found that [the subject had been used by] several French

painters . . . even our own Etty, and that I must have seen the picture by Jordaens reproduced here, when I went round the Gallery in Stockholm not so very many years ago. Somehow it had completely passed from memory." But the Jordaens painting depicts the queen as "a strapping Netherlands vrow, a Flanders mare," and "is in every respect the antithesis of what the Tiepolo would have been" (8). Hence Powell's pleasure in imagining how Tiepolo would have depicted the scene.

20.   Delavacquerie may owe something to V. S. Naipaul, who also came from the furthest Antilles (Trinidad) to Oxford on a scholarship, wrote marvelously funny novels (novels without a touch of farce), married an English-woman, and became a friend of Powell. See *The Strangers All Are Gone* (London: Heinemann, 1982), 163–66.

Chapter Four

1.   *The Garden God,* in *Two Plays* (Boston: Little, Brown, 1972), 26.

2.   *The Rest I'll Whistle,* in *Two Plays,* 109–10.

3.   David Pryce-Jones, *Cyril Connolly: Journal and Memoir* (New York: Ticknor and Fields, 1984), 111.

4.   Joseph Conrad, *Chance* (New York: Norton, 1968), 7–8.

5.   In 1968 Powell's son Tristram married the painter Virginia Lucas, granddaughter of Field Marshal Lord Grenfell (*Strangers,* 166).

6.   Powell, like Evelyn Waugh at this point in life, saw his future as that of painter or illustrator. Drawings of his were published before any fiction, in the *Eton Candle* and later in the Oxford magazine the *Cherwell.* Plate 12 of *Infants of the Spring* reproduces a quite respectable drawing Powell made at 16: "Colonel Caesar Cannonbrains of the Black Hussars: drawing by AP in The Eton Candle, 1922."

7.   *Messengers,* 139. Students of London may note that Powell in *Messengers* identifies several places of social assembly in his novels. The Cavendish figures to some degree in *Agents and Patients* (54); Foppa's (in several volumes of The Music of Time) is identified with Castano's Restaurant in Greek Street, Soho; the opening scene of *Agents and Patients* with Legrain's nearby; and Casanova's Chinese Restaurant "to some small extent" with Maxim's Chinese Restaurant on the same Soho street (*Messengers,* 167–71).

8.   *O, How the Wheel Becomes It!* (London: Heinemann, 1983).

9.   *The Fisher King* (London: Heinemann, 1986), 21.

10.   Beals' career parallels that of Ian Fleming, who in the 1950s left his career in the City after successfully adding sexual frankness to a genre hitherto devoted to spying, in the now-famous series of novels featuring James Bond. Powell seems not to have known Fleming personally, though Waugh and other friends knew him well, his wife, Ann, perhaps better.

Selected Bibliography

PRIMARY WORKS

The Comic Novels

Afternoon Men. London: Duckworth, 1931. New York: Holt, 1932. London: Heinemann, 1952. Boston: Little, Brown, 1964. Also issued in paperback by Little Brown, 1964. London: Mandarin Paperback, 1992

Venusberg. London: Duckworth, 1932. First published in the United States in 1952. New York: Periscope-Holliday, with "Agents and Patients," under the title *Two Novels.* Reissued separately, London: Heinemann, 1955. London: Mandann Paperback, 1992

From a View to a Death. London: Duckworth, 1933. New York: Vanguard, 1934, under the title *Mr. Zouch, Superman.* London: John Lehmann, 1948. London: Heinemann, 1954. London: Mandann Paperback, 1992

Agents and Patients. London: Duckworth, 1936. New York: Periscope-Holliday, 1952, under the title *Two Novels.* With dustjacket illustrations by Osbert Lancaster. Reissued separately, London: Heinemann, 1955. See *Strangers,* 91–93.

What's Become of Waring. London: Cassell, 1939. London: Heinemann, 1953. Boston: Little, Brown, 1963. London: Mandann Paperback, 1992

The Music of Time Sequence

The University of Chicago Press is in the process of publishing all 12 books, in 4 volumes, as *A Dance to the Music of Time: First Movement.* The publication date is scheduled for 1995.

A Question of Upbringing. London: Heinemann, 1951. New York: Scribners, 1951. New York: Berkley Medallion Paperback, 1965. Collected ed., Boston: Little, Brown, 1962: *A Question of Upbringing, A Buyer's Market,* and *The Acceptance World* issued under the title *A Dance to the Music of Time: First Movement.* Reissued in paperback as *A Dance to the Music of Time. 1 Spring.* New York: Popular Library, 1976.

A Buyer's Market. London: Heinemann, 1952. New York: Scribners, 1953. New York: Berkley Medallion Paperback, 1965.

The Acceptance World. London: Heinemann, 1955; New York: Farrar, Straus, & Cudahy, 1956. Farrar Straus also issued a paperback edition that, Powell says, by "now must have become quite a bibliographic rarity." *Strangers,* 90–94. New York: Meridian Paperback, 1960. New York: Berkley Medallion Paperback, 1965.

At Lady Molly's. London: Heinemann, 1957. Boston: Little, Brown, 1958 and 1964. *At Lady Molly's, Casanova's Chinese Restaurant,* and *The Kindly Ones* reissued collectively under the title *A Dance to the Music of Time: Second Movement.*

Casanova's Chinese Restaurant. London: Heinemann, 1960; Boston: Little, Brown, 1960.

The Kindly Ones. London: Heinemann, 1962; Boston: Little, Brown, 1962. New York: Berkley Medallion Paperback, 1965. London: Fontana Paperback, 1971.

The Valley of Bones. London: Heinemann, 1964. Boston: Little, Brown, 1964. New York: Berkley Medallion Paperback, 1966. Collected ed., Boston: Little, Brown, 1971: *The Valley of Bones, The Soldier's Art,* and *The Military Philosophers* reissued as *A Dance to the Music of Time: Third Movement.*

The Soldier's Art. London: Heinemann, 1966. Boston: Little, Brown, 1967.

The Military Philosophers. London: Heinemann, 1968. Boston: Little, Brown, 1968.

Books Do Furnish a Room. London: Heinemann, 1971. Boston: Little, Brown, 1971. Collected with *Temporary Kings* and *Hearing Secret Harmonies* and published as *A Dance to the Music of Time: Fourth Movement.*

Temporary Kings. London: Heinemann, 1973. Boston: Little, Brown, 1973.

Hearing Secret Harmonies. London: Heinemann, 1975. Boston: Little Brown, 1975. London: Mandarin Paperback, 1991.

Other Books

Caledonia: A Fragment. London, 1934. Frontispiece designed by Edward Burra. Comic poem on Scotland. "Printed in a limited edition of 100 copies by Desmond Ryan in 1934 as a wedding present for the author."

John Aubrey and His Friends. London: Eyre and Spottiswoode, 1948; New York: Scribners, 1948. Rev. ed., London: Heinemann, 1963; New York: Barnes and Noble, 1963. 2d rev. ed., London, 1988.

The Garden God and *The Rest I'll Whistle.* Two plays, with four set designs by Osbert Lancaster. London: Heinemann, 1971. Entitled *Two Plays.* Boston: Little, Brown, 1971.

Infants of the Spring. Vol. 1 of The Memoirs of Anthony Powell. London: Heinemann, 1976. New York: Holt, Rinehart & Winston, 1977.

Messengers of Day. Vol. 2 of The Memoirs of Anthony Powell. London: Heinemann, 1978. New York: Holt, Rinehart & Winston, 1978.

Faces in My Time. Vol. 3 of The Memoirs of Anthony Powell. London: Heinemann, 1979. New York: Holt, Rinehart & Winston, 1981.

The Strangers All Are Gone. Vol. 4 of The Memoirs of Anthony Powell. London: Heinemann, 1982. New York: Holt, Rinehart & Winston, 1983.

O, How the Wheel Becomes It! London: Heinemann. 1983. New York: Holt, Rinehart and Winston, 1983. New York: New American Library/Plume Paperback, 1985.

To Keep the Ball Rolling. London: Penguin, 1983. A paperback abridgement of the four volumes of memoirs.

The Fisher King. London: Heinemann, 1986. New York: Norton, 1986. Norton paperback ed., 1987. London: Mandarin Paperback, 1991.

Miscellaneous Verdicts: Writings on Writers 1946–1989. London: Heinemann, 1990. Chicago: University of Chicago Press, 1992. Book reviews, essays, and brief memoirs from the *Daily Telegraph,* the *Times Literary Supplement,* the *Balliol Register,* etc.

Under Review: Further Writing on Writers 1946–1989. London: Heinemann, 1991. Chicago: University of Chicago Press, 1994. Reviews and essays mostly from the *Daily Telegraph, Apollo, Punch,* the *Spectator,* and the *Times Literary Supplement.*

A Reference for Mellors. London: Moorhouse & Sorensen, 1994. Separate publication of the Laurentian story first published in the *New Savoy,* I.1 (1946) 111–20 and reprinted in *Winter Tales 12,* below.

Journals 1982–1986. London: Heinemann, 1995.

Parts of Books

Barnard Letters, 1778–1824. London: Duckworth, 1928. Powell edited this selection from the letters of Sir Andrew Francis Barnard (1773–1855), Thomas Barnard, Bishop of Limerick (1728–1806), and Lady Anne Barnard Lindsay (1750–1825). Introduction, 9–16.

The Old School: Essays by Divers Hands. Edited by Graham Greene. London: Jonathan Cape, 1934. Contains Powell's memoir of Eton, "The Wat'ry Glade," 147–62. Reissued (in paperback) by the Oxford University Press, 1984.

Novels of High Society from the Victorian Age. London: Pilot Press, 1947. Powell selected the novels—*Henrietta Temple* by Benjamin Disraeli; *Guy Livingstone* by G. A. Lawrence; and *Moths* by Ouida (Marie Louise de la Ramée)—and wrote the introduction, vii–xv.

John Aubrey: Brief Lives and Other Selected Writings. Edited by Anthony Powell. London: Cresset Library, 1949; New York: Scribners, 1949. Introduction and notes by Powell.

Raffles: The Amateur Cracksman, by E. W. Hornung. Reissued London: Eyre and Spottiswoode, 1950. Powell's introduction is reprinted in his collection *Under Review,* 1991.

The Pick of Punch: An Annual Selection. Edited by Nicholas Bentley. London: Deutsch, 1957; New York: Dutton, 1957. Contains Powell's skit, "Leaves from Notable New Diaries—Kingsley Amis."

The Complete Ronald Firbank. London: Duckworth, 1961; New York: New Directions, 1961. Preface by Powell.

The Compleat Imbiber. Edited by Cyril Ray. London: Vista Books, 1963. Contains Powell's memoir of Rosa Lewis and the Cavendish Hotel.

The Compleat Imbiber 7: An Entertainment. Edited by Cyril Ray. London: Studio Vista, 1964. New York: Paul S. Eriksson, 1964. Contains Powell's essay "Not Well Ordered until 1670: John Aubrey and Some Seventeenth Century Drinking," 65–67.

Burke's Genealogical and Heraldic History of the Landed Gentry. London: Burke's Peerage, 1965. Powell contributed one of the three introductions, "Reflections on the Landed Gentry."

Winter Tales 12. Edited by A. D. Maclean. London: Macmillan, 1966. Contains "A Reference to Mellors." See above.

Authors Take Sides on Vietnam. Edited by Cecil Woolf and John Bagguley. London: Peter Owen, 1967. New York: Simon and Schuster, 1967. Contains Powell's response to a questionnaire.

Constant Lambert: His Life, His Music, and His Friends. By Richard Shead. London: Simon Publications, 1973. With a memoir by Anthony Powell.

Maurice Bowra: A Celebration. Edited by Hugh Lloyd-Jones. London: Duckworth, 1974. Contains Powell's memoir, "The Bowra World and Bowra Lore."

The Orchid Trilogy. By Jocelyn Brooke. London, 1981. Three volumes of fictionalized reminiscences brought together and introduced by Powell, focusing on Brooke's merits as an original writer.

The Adventures of Mr. Verdant Green, An Oxford Undergraduate. By Cuthbert Bede. The reissue of a novel (first published in three parts, 1853–57) with an introduction by Powell. Oxford University Press, 1982. Introduction reprinted in *Under Review,* 1991.

Oxford, China, and Italy: Writings in Honour of Sir Harold Acton. Edited by Edward Chaney and Neil Ritchie. London: Thames and Hudson, 1984. Contains Powell's "brief life" of Acton in the style of John Aubrey.

The Album of Anthony Powell's "Dance to the Music of Time." By Violet Powell. London: Thames and Hudson, 1987. Preface by Anthony Powell.

Kingsley Amis: In Life and Letters. Edited by Dale Salwak. New York: St Martin's Press, 1991. Contains "Amis Country," by Anthony Powell.

A leve med Proust og andre essays. Edited by Gordon Holmebakk. Oslo: Gyldendal, 1992. Contains Powell's essay on Marcel Proust in Norse translation, "Til bords."

Periodical Publications

Articles, sketches, poems, stories, and reviews by Powell have appeared in the London *Daily Telegraph* (1936–38, 1958–93), the *Spectator* (1937–39, 1946, 1990–92), and *Punch* (1953–58). As early as 1924 he was contributing reviews, most only initialed A. D. P., to the *Cherwell* and other Oxford student journals. In 1936 Graham Greene, the literary editor of *Night and Day,* invited Powell to join that newly founded London journal, but he seems to have contributed only some letters from Hollywood. In 1947 Powell joined the staff of the *Times Literary Supplement* and contributed a number of anonymous reviews; he was writing reviews for *TLS* (now signed) as late as 1992. Powell also set several competitions in *Time and Tide* during 1940–41.

SECONDARY WORKS

Allen, Walter. *Tradition and Dream: The English and American Novel from the Twenties to Our Time.* London: Dent, 1964. One of the first popular surveys to treat Powell as a major novelist.

Amis, Kingsley. "Powell: The Dancing Years," *Sunday Times* (London), (15 December 1985) 40. An interview.

———. *Memoirs.* London: Hutchinson, 1991. New York: Summit Books, 1991. Contains a brilliant chapter on Amis's acquaintance with Powell (and cogent remarks passim). Indexed.

Bader, Rudolf. *Anthony Powell's "Music of Time" as a Cyclic Novel of Generation.* Schweizer Anglistische Arbeiten (Swiss Works in English) 101. Bern: Francke Verlag, 1980. With notes and bibliography. A major scholarly work, using the English texts.

Bergonzi, Bernard. *Anthony Powell* London: Longmans, Green, 1962. Writers and Their Work pamphlet 144. Rev. and enl. ed., 1971. Brief but intelligent survey of Powell's novels.

Boston, Richard. "A Talk with Anthony Powell." *New York Times Book Review,* 9 March 1969, 2, 36. On his home life and methods of composition.

Carpenter, Humphrey. *The Brideshead Generation: Evelyn Waugh and His Friends.* Boston: Houghton Mifflin, 1990. From the birth of the Eton Society of Arts to Waugh's death, the best survey to date; scholarly, judicious, well written.

Clements, Keith. *Henry Lamb: The Artist and His Friends.* Bristol: Redcliffe, 1985. Biography of Powell's brother-in-law.

Cockburn, Claud. *The View from the West.* London: MacGibbon and Kee, 1961. On Powell as literary editor of *Punch.*

Craig, David. *The Novels of Anthony Powell.* London: Macmillan, 1976. Reissued 1979. Bibliography. Index.

Crick, Bernard. *George Orwell: A Life.* London: Secker & Warburg, 1980. Good on Powell's relationships with Orwell. Indexed. See Shelden.

Daintry, Adrian. *I Must Say.* London: Chatto and Windus, 1963. Judicious, well-written autobiography of a painter who knew Powell in school and in the art worlds of London and Paris.

Davin, D. M. *Snow upon Fire: A Dance to the Music of Time.* W. D. Thomas Memorial Lecture. University College Swansea, 1977.

Davis, Douglas M. "An Interview with Anthony Powell, Frome, England, June, 1962." *College English* 24 (April 1963): 533–36. Some personal details not elsewhere revealed.

Ellis, G. U. *Twilight on Parnassus.* London: Michael Joseph, 1939. First book to recognize Powell as a novelist of genius.

"From a Chase to a Death." *Times Literary Supplement,* 16 February 1951, 100. Good essay on the novels before *A Question of Upbringing.*

Frost, Laurie Adams. *Reminiscent Scrutinies: Memory in Anthony Powell's A Dance to the Music of Time.* Troy, N.Y.: Whitston Publishing Co., 1990. Bibliography. Index.

Glazebrook, Mark. "The Art of Horace Isbister, E. Bosworth Deacon, and Ralph Barnby." *London Magazine* 7 (November 1967): 76–82. Relates the painters in The Music of Time to painters Walter Sickert, Augustus John, and others.

Green, Martin. *Children of the Sun: A Narrative of "Decadence" in England after 1918.* New York: Basic Books, 1976. Index. More social criticism than literary, in the puritan tradition of F. R. Leavis. At bottom a condemnation of the privileged class in England, using novels and memoirs by Anthony Powell, Harold Acton, Cyril Connolly, Evelyn Waugh, Henry Green, and others as ammunition and leveling all with humorless disdain.

Gutwillig, Robert. "A Walk around London with Anthony Powell." *New York Times Book Review,* 30 September 1962, 5, 30. Witty interview focused on the London of Powell's novels.

Hall, James. "The Uses of Polite Surprise: Anthony Powell." *Essays in Criticism* 12 (April 1962): 167–83. On Powell's techniques in The Music of Time.
———. *The Tragic Comedians: Seven Modern British Novelists.* Bloomington: Indiana University Press, 1963. Contains a study of the first four volumes of The Music of Time.

Howarth, Herbert. "Discords in the Music of Time," *Commentary* 53 (January 1972): 70–75. Indignant critique of Powell for not satirizing adequately the society he depicts.

Joyau, Isabelle. *Investigating Powell's A Dance to the Music of Time.* New York: St. Martin's Press, 1994. Bibliography. Index.

Kermode, Frank. *Puzzles and Epiphanies: Essays and Reviews 1958–1961.* London: Routledge and Kegan Paul, 1962. Contains Kermode's review of *Casanova's Chinese Restaurant.*

Lee, James War. "The Novels of Anthony Powell." *Dissertation Abstracts* 25 (March 1965): 5281–82. Summary of an Auburn University doctoral thesis.

Lewis, Wyndham. "Satire in the Twenties." *Times Literary Supplement,* 27 September 1947, 493, and 4 October 1947, 507. Letters objecting to Powell's article on his comic novels.

Lilley, George P. *Anthony Powell, a Bibliography.* Winchester, U.K.: St. Paul's Bibliographies, 1993. Winchester Bibliographies of 20th Century Writers. New Castle, Del.: Oak Knoll Books, 1993.

Longford, Elizabeth. *The Pebbled Shore: The Memoirs of EL.* New York: Knopf, 1986. On Powell's visit to Ireland, where he became better acquainted with her sister-in-law, Lady Violet Pakenham.

McCall, Raymond G. "Anthony Powell's Gallery." *College English* 27 (December 1965): 227–32. On the painter's eye of the narrator in The Music of Time.

McKewan, Neil. *Anthony Powell.* Modern Novelists Series. London: Macmillan, 1991. New York: St Martin's Press, 1991. A concise and judicious introduction. See also McKewan's discussion of *A Dance to the Music of Time* in his survey *The Survival of the Novel: British Fiction in the Later Twentieth Century.* New York: Barnes and Noble, 1981.

McSweeney, Kerry. "The End of *A Dance to the Music of Time.*" *South Atlantic Quarterly* 76 (Winter 1977): 44–57. Good correlation of *Hearing Secret Harmonies* with the earlier volumes.

Meixner, Susan Turnquist. "Partisan Politics and the Sequence Novels of Evelyn Waugh, C. P. Snow, and Anthony Powell." *Dissertation Abstracts* 41 (1979): 262. Summary of a University of Kansas doctoral thesis.

Mizener, Arthur. "A Dance to the Music of Time: The Novels of Anthony Powell." *Kenyon Review* 22 (Winter 1960): 79–92. First major article about Powell in the United States.

———. *The Sense of Life in the Modern Novel.* Boston: Houghton, Mifflin, 1964. Sympathetic evaluation of Powell's contribution to the novel.

Morris, Robert K. "The Early Novels of Anthony Powell: A Thematic Study." *Dissertation Abstracts* 25 (January 1965): 4152–53. Summary of a University of Wisconsin doctoral thesis.

———. *The Novels of Anthony Powell.* Pittsburgh: University of Pittsburgh Press, 1968. Survey of Powell's novels through *The Soldier's Art.*

Motion, Andrew. *The Lamberts, George, Constant, and Kit.* New York: Farrar Straus Giroux, 1987. History of three generations of a gifted family, focusing medially on Powell's friend Constant.

Powell, Lady Violet. *Five Out of Six.* London: Heinemann, 1960. Memoirs of youth, by Powell's wife.

———. *Within the Family Circle.* London: Heinemann, 1976. Memoirs of the Pakenham family and of her marriage.

———. *The Album of Anthony Powell's "Dance to the Music of Time."* Preface by Anthony Powell. Introduction by John Bayley. London: Thames and Hudson, 1987. 224 illustrations, 152 pages. Key passages from The Music of Time introduced and bridged with italicized notes by the author's wife, who has selected visualizations of place and period to clarify atmosphere and background.

Pritchett, V. S. *The Working Novelist.* London: Chatto and Windus, 1965. On the "bored barbarians" of Powell's later novels.

Pryce-Jones, David. *Cyril Connolly: Journal and Memoir.* New York: Ticknor & Fields, 1984. Profile of an Eton classmate who became one center of Bohemian London in the 1930s and 1940s.

Ruoff, Gene W. "Social Mobility and the Artist in *Manhattan Transfer* and *The Music of Time.*" *Wisconsin Studies in Contemporary Literature* 5 (Winter–Spring, 1964): 64–76.

Russell, John. "Quintet from the '30s: Anthony Powell." *Kenyon Review* 27 (Autumn 1965): 698–726. On the early novels.

———. *Anthony Powell: A Quintet, Sextet, and War.* Bloomington: Indiana University Press, 1970. Good in-depth study of Powell.

Selig, Robert L. *Time and Anthony Powell: A Critical Study.* Rutherford, N.J.: Fairleigh Dickinson University Press, 1991. Bibliography. Index.

Shead, Richard. *Constant Lambert: His Life, His Music, and His Friends.* London: Simon Publications, 1973. See "Books with Sections" by Powell.

Shelden, Michael. *Orwell: the Authorized Biography.* New York: HarperCollins, 1991. Traces the growth of Powell's friendship with Orwell, 1936–50.

Spurling, Hilary. *Handbook to Anthony Powell's Music of Time.* Preface by Anthony Powell. London: Heinemann Educational Books, 1977. Published in the United States as *Invitation to the Dance: A Guide to Anthony Powell's "A Dance to the Music of Time."* Boston: Little, Brown, 1977. Essays and synopses, with indexes of characters, books cited, paintings, and places. Excellent.

Tucker, James. *The Novels of Anthony Powell.* London: Macmillan, 1976. New York: Columbia University Press, 1976. The first major book on Powell to deal with all 12 volumes of The Music of Time (which Tucker unhappily—but typically—refers to as ADTTMOT).

Zigebell, James J. "Anthony Powell's Music of Time: Chronicle of a Declining Establishment." *Twentieth-Century Literature* 12 (October 1966): 138–46. On the "breakdown" of society.

See also publications of the Anthony Powell Society, *Anthony Powell Communications.* Edited by Nancy Cutbirth. Western Michigan University, 1968–.

Index

Acton, Harold, 10, 18, 146, 148, 180; *Memoirs of an Aesthete*, 12, 14
Adams, Charles, 122
Adams, Henry, 122
Aesthetes, 11–14, 17, 21, 148
Airlie, Earl of, 80
Amiel, Henri Frédéric, 71–72
Amis, Kingsley, 154, 158, 167, 180
Anglesea, Marquis of (usually Anglesey, Earl of), 8
Arabian Nights, The, 166
Aragno, Riccardo, 136
Archipenko, Aleksandr Porfirievich, 37
Ariosto, Ludovico, 31; *Orlando Furioso*, 129–30, 134
Asquith Family, 153
Asquith, Margot, 75
Aubrey, John, 13, 20, 67–70, 144
Aveling, Edward, 159

B.B.C., 53
Baedeker, 47, 138
Bakst, Lèon, 6
Baldwin II, 7
Balliol College, Oxford, 13, 15, 147, 149
Balston, Thomas, 16, 146, 150
Balzac, Honoré de, 108
Baring Brothers, 80
Barnardo, Dr. T. J., 27
Barrie, Sir James, *The Admirable Crichton*, 96
Bashkirtseff, Marie, 53
Baudelaire, Charles, 19
Beardsley, Aubrey, 6, 17
Bede, Cuthbert, 180
Beerbohm, Max, 12, 46, 167
Bell, Kenneth, 147–48
Berenson, Bernard, 14
Bernini, Giovanni, statue *Truth Revealed by Time*, 98, 134
Betjeman, John, 15, 148
Blair, Eric. *See* Orwell, George
Blake, William, 145
Bloomsbury, 16–18

Bodleian Library, Oxford, 69, 169
Bowen, Elizabeth, 152
Bowra, Sir Maurice, 148–49, 180
Bradley, General Omar, 4
Brooke, Jocelyn, 153, 180
Browning, Robert, 32, 107–9, 125, 151, 155, 173n16
Buckley, Denys, 147
Burke's Landed Gentry, 1, 169n2, 179
Burton, Richard, 66, 121
Burton, Robert, *The Anatomy of Melancholy*, 31, 120–21
Bushell, Tony, 15
Byron, George Gordon, Lord, 106, 165; *Manfred*, 142
Byron, Robert, 10, 148–49

Calder-Marshall, Arthur, 102
Carter, John, 29
Casanova, Giovanni, 154
Charles I, 9
Charles II, 7, 52
Chateaubriand, François René, 5
Chaucer, Geoffrey, 106
Chekhov, Anton, 36
Child-Villiers, Arthur, 80
Churchill, Winston, 113
Cockburn, Claud, 14, 181
Coincidence, 9–10, 23, 65, 75–6, 90, 96, 99, 103, 106–9, 113, 119, 130, 134, 146
Coleridge, S. T., 165
Connolly, Cyril, 10, 12–13, 143, 145, 147, 149, 156
Conquest, Robert, 154
Conrad, Joseph, *Chance*, 143–44; *Victory*, 154
Corvo, Baron (Frederick Rolfe), 64
Coward, Noel, 61, 83
Cozzens, J. G., 3
Crane, Stephen, 7
Cresset Press, 69
Crowley, Aleister, 18, 101
Cummings, E. E., 70

Curzon, Lord, 147–48
Cyrano de Bergerac, 129

Daintry, Adrian, 23, 181
Daniel, Samuel, 9
Davidson, John "Earl Lavendar," 167
Debrett's Peerage, 6
Deeping, Warwick, 150
Delius, Frederick, 22
Descartes, René, 115
DeVries, Peter de, 117
Diaghilev, Sergei Pavlovich, 19
Dickens, Charles, 9, 20
Donne, John, 1
Doughty, Charles, 66
Douglas, Norman, 18
Dowson, Ernest, 35
Doyle, Sir Arthur Conan, *The Priory School Adventure*, 159
Drayton, Sir Harold, 80
Dru, Alexander, 71, 150, 152, 173n3
Duckworth, Gerald, 16, 150
Duggan, Alfred, 110, 148
Duggan, Hubert, 148–49
Dunsany, Lord, 25
Dymoke Family, 7–9
Dynevor, Lord, 25

Edward VI, 92
Edward VIII, 23, 92, 99
Eliot, T. S., 57, 70; *The Waste Land*, 33, 46, 105, 161, 173n15
Eliot, George, 65
Epicurus, 115
Epstein, Jacob, 18
Eton College, 6, 10, 146–48; Eton Society of Arts, 11, 148; *The Eton Candle*, 16, 146–47
Eugenius Philalethes, 128
Eyre & Spottiswoode, 68

Farquharson, Robert, 173n15
Fielding, Henry, *Tom Jones*, 79
Firbank, Ronald, 29, 36, 60, 70, 179
Fitzgerald, F. Scott, 25, 152
Flaherty, Robert, 58
Flaubert, Gustav, 49, 53

Fleming, Ian, 176n10
Foch, Marshall, 98
Forster, E. M., 173
Freud, Sigmund, 98
Fry, Roger, 18, 59

Gardner, the Hon. Evelyn (married successively to Evelyn Waugh, John Heygate and Ronald Nightingale), 27, 150, 174n12
Gaselee, Stephen, 18
Gassendi, Pierre, 45, 115
Genealogy, 2, 5, 93, 145
George III, 55
George IV, 8, 146
Gilbert, Sir William Schwenck, 22
Gissing, George, 157
Gladstone, W. E., 3, 10, 50
Goethe, Johann Wolfgang von, *Faust*, 142
Golden Bough, The, 123, 161
Goodheart, A. M., 10
Gosse, Edmund, 18
Graef, Roger, 136
Graham, Sheilah, 26
Gray, Cecil, 21, 99
Gray, Thomas, 146, 148, 155
Green, Henry, 9–10, 15, 25, 146–47, 149; *Blindness*, 11, *Pack My Bag*, 11
Greene, Graham, 13, 68, 152; *The Name of Action*, 45; *Night and Day*, 180; *The Old School*, 12; *The Oxford Outlook*, 15
Grenfell, Joyce, 26
Gurdjieff, Georgi, 102

Hamnett, Nina, 23–24, 172n7
Hardy, Thomas, *A Question of Upbringing* (film), 123
Hart-Davis, Rupert, 154
Hayward, John, 69, 152
Heidegger, Martin, 159
Hemingway, Ernest, 3, 25, 37–38, 70, 152, 156
Henry II, 140
Herbert, George, 1
Herbert, Laura, 150
Herbert, Lady Margaret, 16

Heseltine, Philip, 19–21, 99
Heygate, John, 14, 27, 150–51
Hitler, Adolf, 102
Hollis, Christopher, 15
Holmes, Sherlock. *See* Doyle, Sir Arthur
  Conan
Homer, *The Iliad*, 137
Horner Family, 153
Howard, Brian, 11
Hugo, Victor, *Les Miserables*, 76
Hulme, T. E., 17
Huxley, Aldous, 11, 21, 35, 48, 66, 102
Hypocrites Club, 14, 18, 148–49

Irving, Washington, *The Legend of Sleepy
  Hollow*, 79
Isherwood, Christopher, 62

James, Henry, 34, 39, 45, 92, 174n11
James II, 8
Jersey, Countess of, 25, 174n11
John, Augustus, 122, 149, 181
Jonson, Ben, 58
Jowett, Benjamin, 13
Joyce, James, 19, 74, 137, 139

Kalla, Colonel, 153
Ketton-Cremer, Wyndham, 148
Kierkegaard, Søren, 152
King's Champion, 7–9, 145–46
Kipling, Rudyard, 22
Knox, Monsignor Ronald, 153–54
Kolkhorst, George, 148
Kronacker, Major, 153

Laclos, Choderlos de, *Les Liaisons dan-
  gereuses*, 86
Lamb, Henry, 25, 149
Lambert, Constant, 17, 19–21, 71, 173,
  180, 183
Lampedusa, Giuseppe di, *The Leopard*, 6
Laver, James, 173n15, 175n18
Lawrence, D. H., 21, 53; *Lady Chatterley's
  Lover*, 54, 121, 154
Leverson, Ada, 17
Lewis, Wyndham, 19, 34, 70, 182
Lewis, Rosa, 23, 92, 150

Lincoln, Earl of, 9
Lindsay, A. D., 13
Longford, Lt. Col. the Earl of, 171
Longford, Countess of (Elisabeth
  Harman, Mrs Frank Pakenham)
  174n12, 182
Loveday, Raoul, 18
Lyautey, Marshall, 115

Machen, Arthur, 101
Maclaren-Ross, Julian, 153
Maclean, Donald, 23
Mansfield, Katherine, 171n52
Marmion, Robert, 7; Marmion
  (Marmyun) Estate, 146; Marmion
  Family, 145
Martyr Champion, 8–9
Marx, Karl, 159
Matisse, Henri, 87
Maugham, Somerset, 19–20, 29, 174n14
May, Betty, *Tiger Woman: My Story*, 18
Melville, Herman, *Moby Dick*, 140
Messel, Oliver, 11
Michelangelo, 155
Millard, Christopher, 84
Mitford, Nancy, 25
Modigliani, Amedeo, 119, 134
Molière (Jean Baptiste Poquelin), 165
Montgomery, Field Marshall, 113
Morrell, Lady Ottoline, 92, 149, 172n8
Mozart, Wolfgang Amadeus, 165;
  Abduction from the Seraglio, 124–25
Muggeridge, Malcolm, 68, 152, 154
Myth: of Candaules and Gyges, 124–26,
  175n19; of Don Juan, 165; of the
  Eumenides (or Furies), 102, 104, 120;
  of The Fisher King, 161–5; the
  Nibelungs, 113; Orestes, 104; of
  Priapus, 137–39; Roland, 129;
  Siegfried, 113; Sisyphus, 30;
  Tannhäuser, 47–8, 114
Myths, comic, 77–79

Naipaul, V. S., 154, 175n20
Nerval, Gérard de, 173n15
Nietzsche, Friedrich Wilhelm, 21–22, 40,
  48, 66, 151, 157

Nightingale, the Hon Mrs., 27. *See* Gardner, Evelyn

Ogilvy, Angus, 80
Ormond, Duke of, 8
Orwell, George, 94, 96, 147, 174n13, 181, 183
Oxford University Press, 68
Oxford Broom, 14

Pakenham, Lady Violet. *See* Powell, Lady Violet
Pakenham, Lady Mary, 25, 27
Pakenham, Frank (later Earl of Longford), 10
Parody-raissoneur, 42–44, 47, 72
Patton, General George, 4
Peacock, Thomas Love, 157
Pepys, Samuel, 7, 92, 157
Phipps, Tommy, 26
Planchette, 89, 134
Plato, 95
Poe, Edgar Allan, 122
Popular Songs, 95, 97, 121, 125
Porter, Cole, 173n13
Poussin, Nicolas, painting *A Dance to the Music of Time*, 22–24, 74, 129
Powell, Anthony Dymoke: and attitude toward Jews, 172; and experience at Eton, 10–13, 146–47; and experience at Oxford, 13–15, 147–49; father's family, 3–6, 145–46; and marriage to Lady Violet Pakenham, 24–25, 152–53; military service of, 67–71, 152–53; mother's family, 6–9; as painter, 176n6; as playwright, 136–42; as publisher's assistant, 15–25, 150; schooling of, 146; as scriptwriter, 25–27

Works
   The Acceptance World, 84–91
   Afternoon Men (novel), 18, 20–23, 29–44, 153
   Afternoon Men (play), 136–37
   Agents and Patients, 24, 57–64, 150–51
   At Lady Molly's, 91–97
   The Barnard Letters, 69

Books Do Furnish a Room, 116–21
A Buyer's Market, 79–84
Casanova's Chinese Restaurant, 97–99
Faces in My Time, 151–53
The Fisher King, 161–67
From a View to a Death, 16, 23–24, 48–57, 61
The Garden God, 137–39
Hearing Secret Harmonies, 127–35
Infants of the Spring, 144–49
Journals 1982–1986, 179
John Aubrey and His Friends, 67–69
The Kindly Ones, 100–104
Messengers of Day, 149–50
The Military Philosophers, 112–16
Miscellaneous Verdicts, 167
Mr. Zouch, Superman, 22
Novels of High Society, 69
A Question of Upbringing, 67–79
O, How the Wheel Becomes It! 155–61
A Reference for Mellors, 179
The Rest I'll Whistle, 139–42
The Soldier's Art, 107–12
The Strangers All Are Gone, 153–55
Temporary Kings, 121–27, 162
To Keep the Ball Rolling, 143
Under Review, 167
The Valley of Bones, 104–7
Venusberg, 4, 27, 45–48
What's Become of Waring? 16, 18, 64–66
Powell, John, 27
Powell, Tristram, 153, 171n52, 176n5
Powell, Lady Violet (née Pakenham), 25, 74, 151–52, 174n11, 175n19, 183
Princess Alexandra of Kent, 80
Proust, Marcel, 60, 67, 70, 78, 143
Pryce-Jones, Alan, 15
Prynne, William, 8

Quennell, Peter, 14, 173n12

Rimbaud, Arthur, 21
Ratigan, Terence, 152
Rhys ap Gruffydd, 145
Rimbaud, Arthur, 21
Robinson, Heath, 35

Rossetti, Dante Gabriel, 68
Russell, Bertrand, 17, 34–35
Salisbury, Lord, 80
Scheherazade, 166
Scott, Sir Walter, 162; *Marmion*, 145–46
Shakespeare, William, 9, 46, 51, 128, 154; *Hamlet*, 144–46, 155–56; *King Lear*, 107, 139–40, 151
Sickert, Walter, 18, 134, 181
Simpson, Wallis, 99
Sitwell, Sir Osbert, 11, 13, 17, 149
Sitwell, Edith, 17
Sitwell, Sacheverell, 17
Smith, Logan Pearsall, 174n9
Spencer, John, 147, 170n24
Spender, Stephen, 62
Starkie, Enid, 19
Stendhal (Marie Henri Beyle), 64, 81
Stephen, Sir Leslie, 16
Stevens, Wallace, 155
Stirner, Max, 117
Strindberg, August, 134
Stroheim, Erik von, 173n14
Sullivan, Sir Arthur, 3
Swinburne, Algernon, 21, 158
Symons, A. J. A., *The Quest for Corvo*, 64
Synnott, Pierse, 148–49

Alma-Tadema, Sir Lawrence, 84
Thackeray, W. M., 106
Thomas, Dylan, 152
Tiepolo, Giovanni Battista, 124, 175n19
Tolstoi, Count Lev Nikolaevich, 118
Traherne, Thomas, 1
Trollope, Anthony, 20, 108, 174n14
Tschaikovsky, Peter Ilich, 166

Urquhart, F. F. (Sligger), 148

Valéry, Paul, 72
Van Gogh, Vincent, 59
Vasari, Giorgio, 155
Vaughan, Henry, 1, 128, 140–41
Vaughan, Thomas, 128
Vorhees, Richard, 35

Walpole, Horace, 148
Walter, A. R., 16
Warlock, Peter. *See* Philip Heseltine
Warner Bros., 25–26
Waugh, Evelyn, 15, 17, 25, 29, 71, 102, 147–49, 154, 172n9; *Brideshead Revisited*, 14; *Decline and Fall*, 15, 18, 45; *A Little Learning*, 93, 110; *Scoop*, 46; *Vile Bodies*, 18
Welch Regiment, 4, 152
Wellington, Duke of, 9
Wellington, Gerry, 152
Wells, H. G., 157
Wells-Dymoke, Maud Mary, 7
Wesley, John, 58
Wheeler, Sir Mortimer, 154
Wilde, Oscar, 12, 17, 29
William the Conqueror, 7
Wise, T. J., 84
Wood, Anthony à, 20
Woolf, Virginia, 16, 74

Yeats, W. B., 74, 101, 108

Yorke, Henry. *See* Henry Green

Zaharoff, Sir Basil, 81

The Author

Neil Brennan was a student of chemical engineering at Rice University in Texas before World War II. During the war he was a tank platoon leader in Europe, where he was awarded the Silver Star and the Distinguished Service Cross. At the University of Chicago he was cowinner of the Ann Watkins Fiction Fellowship for 1948 and received an M.A. in English in 1949. After spending a year at the Sorbonne he taught at Auburn University, the University of Illinois (where he completed work for a doctorate in 1959 with a thesis on the modern British comic novel), Cornell University, and Villanova University. He retired in 1987.

With the late Alan Redway in England he began preparing a bibliography of Graham Green in 1952. A partial version was published in *Graham Greene: Some Critical Considerations* in 1963. The first edition of his study *Anthony Powell* appeared in 1974. Reviews and articles of his have appeared in *Accent, Commonweal, Epoch,* and other journals. His most recent publication—a review—of Martin Stannard's biography of Evelyn Waugh—appeared in the winter 1993 issue of *Four Quarters.*